EFFECTIVE CLINICAL PRACTICE IN THE TREATMENT OF EATING DISORDERS

EFFECTIVE CLINICAL PRACTICE IN THE TREATMENT OF EATING DISORDERS

The Heart of the Matter

Edited by

Margo Maine • William N. Davis • Jane Shure

Routledge
Taylor & Francis Group
New York   London

Routledge
Taylor & Francis Group
270 Madison Avenue
New York, NY 10016

Routledge
Taylor & Francis Group
2 Park Square
Milton Park, Abingdon
Oxon OX14 4RN

© 2009 by Taylor & Francis Group, LLC
Routledge is an imprint of Taylor & Francis Group, an Informa business

Printed in the United States of America on acid-free paper
10 9 8 7 6 5 4 3 2

International Standard Book Number-13: 978-0-415-96461-6 (Hardcover)

Library of Congress Cataloging-in-Publication Data

Effective clinical practice in the treatment of eating disorders : the heart of the matter / edited by Margo Maine, William N. Davis, Jane Shure.
    p. ; cm.
  Includes bibliographical references and index.
  ISBN 978-0-415-96461-6 (hardbound : alk. paper)
  1. Eating disorders--Treatment. I. Maine, Margo. II. Davis, William N. III. Shure, Jane.
  [DNLM: 1. Eating Disorders--therapy. 2. Mind-Body Relations (Metaphysics) 3. Psychotherapeutic Processes. 4. Psychotherapy--methods. WM 175 E27 2008]

  RC552.E18E345 2008
  616.85'2606--dc22   2008021058

Visit the Taylor & Francis Web site at
http://www.taylorandfrancis.com

and the Routledge Web site at
http://www.routledge.com

Dedication

—

To George, for his remarkable love, laughter, and partnership

Margo Maine

To Kristy and to my wife Sara, who showed me a different awareness

William Davis

To Bob, for his unwavering love, support, and patience

Jane Shure

Contents

Section One: Effective Clinical Practices: Approaches

Section Two: Effective Clinical Practice: Methods

Section Three: Effective Clinical Practices: Special Themes

Foreword

In November 1991, the Renfrew Center Foundation convened its first National Conference in Philadelphia. Many of the attendees were new to the field and had been treating eating disorders for only a few years. Although some worked in treatment programs, the majority were clinicians in private practice. Everyone felt challenged by their patients' complicated medical, psychological, and social issues. The conference attendees not only were seeking knowledge and skills but also were looking for a place to openly share ideas and find support as they struggled to do this highly specialized, intensive, and demanding clinical work. Among the dilemmas was how to most effectively address life-threatening symptoms and how to respond to the growing realization that the culture was playing a large part in the increased incidence of eating disorders. Informed by the work of Carol Gilligan and the Stone Center, there was a great deal of discussion about the possibility women might have different therapeutic needs than men and that eating disorders in particular might require a different type of treatment.

At the time of this first conference, the Renfrew Center had been open for 5 years, providing specialized eating disorder treatment for women in a residential setting. In contrast to most psychotherapy, which was based on a male model of development, and most treatment programs, which utilized a medical model for the delivery of care, Renfrew was experimenting with many types of group therapy and the healing power of community. Gradually, these relational approaches cultivated in our clinical work with women became the foundation for our educational efforts.

Since 1994, the spirit and focus of the conference has purposefully encompassed and reflected the feminist values of collaboration, connection, and mutually respectful relationships. Over time, the meetings have fostered a strong sense of companionship and camaraderie among the many women and men who return to Philadelphia every November. In addition, each year clinicians new to the conference or to the field are welcomed into a community of eating disorder professionals. What began, and still remains, as an important training conference has extended its scope and its influence to become a venue for sharing and rejuvenating among therapists committed to understanding eating disorders through the lens of gender. The focus remains on improving the lives of women suffering with these disorders.

All of the writers in this impressive and groundbreaking anthology, *Effective Clinical Practice in the Treatment of Eating Disorders: The Heart of the Matter,* have been pioneers in rethinking and reshaping clinical theory and practice. They have shared their work, often taking risks, as they have disclosed stories revealing the integration of their professional work and personal growth, encouraging their audiences to develop new skills, insights, and a deeper appreciation of their patients' lives and needs. As a result, each author has enhanced our understanding of eating disorders and the importance of the therapeutic relationship. Their expertise and dedication to the field have been invaluable. Indeed, many of the authors have become mentors and role models for the next generation of therapists. The publication of *Effective Clinical Practice in the Treatment of Eating Disorders: The Heart of the Matter* will allow many other trainees and clinicians to benefit from their accumulated wisdom. As the Renfrew Center Foundation Conference chair for almost 20 years, I have had the good fortune and the privilege to know and collaborate with all of the contributors. Our associations as both friends and colleagues have grown ever more richly intertwined over the last two decades. This book further deepens our connections and affirms the authors' seminal contributions to the well-being and recovery of all those suffering from eating disorders.

Judi Goldstein
Renfrew Center Foundation

Senior Editor

Margo Maine, PhD, FAED, clinical psychologist and cofounder of the Maine and Weinstein Specialty Group, has specialized in eating disorders for nearly 30 years. She is author of *The Body Myth: The Pressure on Adult Women to Be Perfect* (with Joe Kelly, Wiley, 2005); *Father Hunger: Fathers, Daughters and the Pursuit of Thinness* (Gurze, 2004); and *Body Wars: Making Peace With Women's Bodies* (Gurze, 2000), and she is a senior editor of *Eating Disorders: The Journal of Treatment and Prevention* and board member of the Eating Disorders Coalition for Research, Policy, and Action and of Dads and Daughters. A founding member and fellow of the Academy for Eating Disorders, a member of the Founder's Council and past president of the National Eating Disorders Association, Dr. Maine is the 2007 recipient of the Lori Irving Award for Excellence in Eating Disorders Awareness and Prevention given by the National Eating Disorders Association.

Editors

William N. Davis, PhD, FAED, maintains a private practice specializing in the treatment of eating disorders in New York City and Media, Pennsylvania. As the former clinical director of the Renfrew Center of Philadelphia and director of the Renfrew Center of New York City, he helped to originate Renfrew's Meal Time Support Therapy and made significant contributions to the center's distinctive feminist-relational treatment model. Dr. Davis presents frequently on topics related to eating disorders and is the coeditor of *The Drinking Man, The Bulimic College Student,* and the Renfrew Center's CD *Healing Through Relationship: Fostering Body-Mind Integration* and is former editor of the *Renfrew Perspective,* an educational newsletter for professionals. A member of the eating disorders field for 30 years, he is the founder of the Center for the Study of Anorexia and Bulimia and a founder of the National Eating Disorders Association and the Academy for Eating Disorders.

Jane Shure, PhD, LCSW, a psychotherapist for over 30 years known for her work with trauma, shame, and eating disorders, is cofounder and coauthor of the *Inside/Outside Self-Discovery Program for the Middle School Years: Strategies to Promote Emotional Well-Being, Fortify Resilience, and Strengthen Relationships* (Toucaned, 2008), coauthor of "The Body as a Shame Container," in the Renfrew Center's *Healing Through Relationship: Fostering Body-Mind Integration* CD, and cocreator of www.SelfMatters. org, dedicated to strengthening self-esteem. Named a Top Doc for Women by *Philadelphia Magazine*, Dr. Shure writes for the *Huffington Post*, leads personal growth workshops at the Kripalu Center for Yoga and Health and Transformations Holistic Learning Center, has taught Family Therapy with Eating Disorder Families for the Family Institute of Philadelphia's training program, and serves on the board of A Chance to Heal Foundation, where she spearheads ParentTalk, educational programs designed to prevent eating disorders.

Authors

Marion Bilich, PhD, is a psychologist in private practice on Long Island. She is the author of *Weight Loss From the Inside Out: Help for the Compulsive Eater* and coauthor of *Shared Grace: Therapists and Clergy Working Together* as well as many professional clinical articles and chapters. She also responds to "Ask the Psychologist" on the *American Baby* magazine Web site. Her own site, www.marionbilich.com, focuses on how to access one's own inner wisdom using energy psychology and imagery techniques.

Andrea Bloomgarden, PhD, a clinical psychologist, was the director of outpatient services at the Renfrew Center, Philadelphia, from 1994 to 2002 and a clinical assistant professor at the Philadelphia College of Osteopathic Medicine (PCOM) from 2002 to 2005. Dr. Bloomgarden has presented and published on numerous topics, including, but not limited to, eating disorders, therapist self-disclosure, dialectical behavior therapy, eye movement desensitization and reprocessing (EMDR), and multicultural awareness. She maintains a private practice in Center City, Philadelphia. Her Web site is www.centerforacceptanceandchange.com.

Douglas Bunnell, PhD, FAED, a clinical psychologist, is vice president and director of outpatient clinical services for the Renfrew Center and oversees the clinical programming for Renfrew's nonresidential treatment centers. Dr. Bunnell is the current editor of *The Renfrew Perspective*, an educational newsletter for professionals, is a charter member and Fellow of the Academy for Eating Disorders, has served as the president of the National Eating Disorders Association, and remains active in eating disorder advocacy and awareness. Dr. Bunnell maintains a private practice in Wilton, Connecticut, specializing in the treatment of people and families with eating disorders.

Deb Burgard, PhD, specializes in the treatment of eating disorders and body image. She created the BodyPositive.com Web site and is one of the founding proponents of the Health at Every Size model. Her published work includes the book, *Great Shape: The First Fitness Guide for Large Women*, and chapters in *Feminist Perspectives on Eating Disorders* and *The Fat Studies Reader*. Dr. Burgard is also guest editor for the body image issue of the *Journal of Lesbian Studies* and coleads the Sustainable Health Practices Registry, an online project investigating how people create ongoing practices that support their health.

Carolyn Costin, MA, MEd, LMFT, recovered herself from anorexia, has specialized in the treatment of eating disorders for 30 years. Carolyn is founder and director of the Eating Disorder Center of California and Monte Nido and Affiliates, which now has three unique residential centers in natural, home-like settings. Carolyn is a sought-after speaker at national conferences and is known for engaging her audiences and giving hands-on skills. Carolyn's books, *The Eating Disorder Source Book* (2007), *100 Questions and Answers About Eating Disorders* (2007), and *Your Dieting Daughter* (1997), have helped professionals and the lay public in understanding, treating, and preventing eating disorders.

Steven Wiley Emmett, PhD, MDiv, is a pastoral psychologist and ordained Unitarian-Universalist minister. He conceived of and cofounded the Renfrew Center, the nation's first free-standing residential eating disorders treatment facility. He is chairperson of Dads and Daughters, a nonprofit organization dedicated to promoting the power and potential of young females, and serves on the editorial board of *Eating Disorders: The Journal of Treatment and Prevention*. Rev. Dr. Emmett, a former Peace Corps volunteer, writes and lectures frequently about the intriguing interactions among mind, body, and spirit.

Judi Goldstein, MSS, LSW, is vice president of the Renfrew Center Foundation and has been responsible for the development of its annual conference. She has been with the Renfrew Center since it first opened in 1985, formerly served as director of admissions and as vice president of professional relations and education and is a founder of the National Eating Disorders Association.

Beth Hartman McGilley, PhD, FAED, is a psychologist in private practice, specializing in the treatment of eating and related disorders, body image, sports psychology, trauma, and grief. A fellow of the Academy for Eating Disorders, Dr. McGilley has practiced for nearly 25 years, writing, lecturing, supervising, and directing an inpatient eating disorders program, and providing individual, family, and group therapy. Dr. McGilley has addressed national and international audiences regarding eating disorders and body image concerns and has published in both academic journals and the popular media. She is currently writing her first book.

Adrienne Ressler, MA, LMSW, CEDS, is the national training director for the Renfrew Center Foundation. She is on the board and is a fellow of the International Association of Eating Disorder Professionals. Adrienne's work has been published in the *International Journal of Fertility* and *Women's Medicine and Pulse*, the official publication of the International Spa Association. She is coauthor of the chapter "Reframing Body Image Identity in the Treatment of Eating Disorders" in *Healing Through Relationship: Fostering Body-Mind Integration* CD. Adrienne serves as body image curriculum designer for the Peeke Week Women's Retreats at Red Mountain Resort and Spa in Utah.

Judith Ruskay Rabinor, PhD, director of the American Eating Disorders Center of Long Island, is the author of *A Starving Madness: Tales of Hunger, Hope and Healing in Psychotherapy* (Gurze Books, 2002). Faculty and supervisor at the Center for the Study of Anorexia and Bulimia in New York City, she is an adjunct at Long Island University and a consultant to the Renfrew Center Foundation and the FEGS Eating Disorders Prevention Project, NoBody's Perfect. She has written extensively on eating and body image disorders, lectures and conducts professional training nationwide, and has a private practice in Manhattan and on Long Island, New York.

Robin Sesan, PhD, received her doctorate in psychology from Michigan State University in 1983. She is the founder and director of the Brandywine Center in Wilmington, Delaware, a group private practice specializing in the treatment of women and women's issues. She is an adjunct faculty member at the University of Delaware, where she teaches seminars on eating disorders and provides training for predoctoral psychology interns. Dr. Sesan has published articles on the treatment of eating disorders and presents regionally and nationally on topics related to women's mental health. Her Web site is www.brandywinecenter.com.

Anita Sinicrope Maier, MSW, LSW, is a psychotherapist in private practice in Pittsburgh, Pennsylvania, specializing in eating disorders, abuse, and family work. In 1984, after her daughter's recovery from an atypical eating disorder, she founded the Pennsylvania Educational Network for Eating Disorders (PENED), a nonprofit organization. In 1987, she was a founder of the National Eating Disorders Association. She is a writer, educator, advocate, and media spokesperson for both the professional and general population. Ms. Maier received the Jefferson Award for Public

Service and the Lifetime Achievement Award from the Eating Disorders Coalition for Research, Policy, and Action.

Beth Weinstock, PhD, is a psychologist with over 30 years of clinical practice. She was one of the original consultants at the Renfrew Center when it opened in 1985 and has taught at universities on both coasts. She is currently on the faculty of the Kripalu Center for Yoga and Health and Transformations Learning Center. Dr. Weinstock founded Women's LeadershipWorks, a nonprofit organization for leadership development, writes for the *Huffington Post*, coauthored "The Body as a Shame Container" in the Renfrew Center's *Healing Through Relationship: Fostering Body-Mind Integration* CD, and cocreated www.SelfMatters.org, a Web site dedicated to strengthening self-esteem.

Cynthia Whitehead-LaBoo, PhD, is the associate director of clinical services at the Emory University Student Counseling Center and coordinator of the Emory University Eating Disorders Program. She is a member of the Eating Disorders Information Network (EDIN) and the Atlanta Eating Disorders Coalition. In addition, she has presented at national conferences each year on various topics related to eating disorders, body image, and psychotherapy with African American women and has delivered keynote presentations on multicultural aspects of eating disorders and body image.

Barbara Wingate, MD, MSW, ABHM, has a long history of working with women with eating disorders and other complex medical psychiatric cases. A past medical director of the Renfrew Center (1991–1993) and consulting-liaison psychiatrist at the Hospital of the University of Pennsylvania (1993–1998), Dr. Wingate has been a member of the adjunct faculty at the University of Pennsylvania Medical School since 1998. In her private practice, she has pursued an interest in holistic integrative health. She was certified in Kundalini yoga and meditation in 2003 and became a diplomate of the American Board of Holistic Health in 2005.

Stephen Zimmer, LCSW, began to treat teenagers suffering with anorexia in 1978. Surprised at the lack of resources, he established the first eating disorder support group in New York City and soon after was named the first director of group treatment at the Center for the Study of Anorexia and Bulimia, the metropolitan area's largest outpatient treatment center. In 1995 Mr. Zimmer collaborated with the Renfrew Centers to start the Renfrew Center of New York City, where he served as clinical director until 2000. Mr. Zimmer maintains a private practice in Manhattan.

Acknowledgments

We want to acknowledge our appreciation and thanks to all who have inspired, taught, mentored, supported, and challenged us to think outside the box and listen to our inner wisdom as guide in forging relationships that empower others in their journey to a healthier self.

Special thanks to Beth Weinstock for her contributions in helping us conceptualize the focus for this book and assisting in the proposal writing that made this volume a reality.

While it is true that it takes a village to raise a child, it also takes a village to raise a competent and well-grounded therapist. The Renfrew Center Foundation's annual conference has allowed us that village. Thanks to all who have touched us professionally, personally, and politically, helping to open our hearts and strengthen our courage to take risks, speak our minds, and trust our guts.

With great respect, we thank our patients for all that they have taught us, for their willingness to trust us and reveal their vulnerability and pain, and for the joy in witnessing their spirits come alive through the process of recovery.

We especially want to thank George Zimmar and the Routledge Mental Health Division of Taylor & Francis for believing in this book and helping to make it available to the next generation of clinicians.

We are grateful to our parents, who nurtured a sense of compassion for others and supported the validity of our own voices.

Last, we are forever grateful to our spouses (George, Sara, and Bob) and our many loyal friends for their steadfast support, interest, and encouragement that has helped to sustain us throughout the writing process.

Introduction

Eating disorders, including anorexia nervosa, bulimia nervosa, binge eating disorder, and eating disorder not otherwise specified (EDNOS), are extremely serious psychiatric conditions. Anorexia has the highest mortality rate of any mental health diagnosis, and every eating disorder signifies a host of psychological and medical problems that can be exceptionally costly, not only economically, but also in terms of physical, emotional, spiritual, and social suffering. Furthermore, eating disorders can be extremely difficult to treat successfully. Too frequently, the price and the torment exacted by eating disorders goes on, engulfing lives and crippling future potential. Thus far, empirical research has provided little in the way of treatment techniques that resolve the psychological issues underlying the beginnings of these disorders and permanently reduce symptoms. In fact, a recent report issued by the U.S. Department of Health and Human Services lamented the lack of reliable, clinically relevant empirical findings and emphasized the importance of more qualitative studies to broaden the base of available treatment information and expertise.

The original idea for this book emerged during a conversation about the many years of effort, energy, and determination each of us had put into the treatment of eating disorders. We realized that, together, we have amassed more than 90 years of clinical experience, and if we were to add up the additional years of experience gathered by our senior colleagues in the field, the accumulated time working with eating disorders would easily total many centuries. This led us to imagine an edited book offering expert commentary from a wide variety of authors on essential components of successful eating disorder treatment. In addition to the chapters authored by ourselves, we asked 13 colleagues to take part in the project and directed them to write about an area or aspect of treatment that was of particular importance to them and would be instructive to others in the field. The result, in the pages to follow, is a series of qualitative studies, each of which offers a clinical perspective on the question of how to treat eating disorders.

Effective Clinical Practice in the Treatment of Eating Disorders: The Heart of the Matter reflects the individual therapeutic skills and collective wisdom of very experienced clinicians, all of whom are pioneers in the field. It demonstrates the complexity and power of the therapeutic process; in particular, it articulates and explores essential information, significant issues, and unresolved questions about eating disorder treatment. In short, it addresses the "heart of the matter," the interventions and interactions that constitute life-saving treatment for these devastating conditions.

Based on innumerable therapeutic challenges, conundrums, breakthroughs, and triumphs, this book seeks to make a unique contribution to the field. Its primary purpose is to pass on a collective expertise, derived in vivo from actual clinical work, and thereby benefit less-experienced therapists encountering the complexities and complications of eating disorder treatment.

Most of the contributors to this book began their clinical training during the 1960s and 1970s, when psychoanalytically inspired, psychodynamic psychotherapy was the dominant treatment. Although framed from different perspectives and articulated in different language, all the chapters share one underlying commonality. Following the fruits and the struggles of their own clinical experiences, the authors eschew the traditional treatment model in favor of an approach that makes use of the impact and the influence of interpersonal connection and collaboration and envisions the therapeutic relationship as the heart of effective clinical practice.

In part, this may be due to the nature of the disorders. People suffering from anorexia, bulimia, EDNOS, and binge eating disorder are unusually attached to their symptoms, even if repelled by them at the same time. Consequently, therapists must find approaches or methods that can overcome recalcitrant symptoms and speak to the "hearts" of those who are disordered. It is significant and instructive that the eating disorder pioneers featured in this book have come to believe that collaborative therapeutic relationships hold the key to recovery.

In addition, and perhaps even more important, the common thread running through *Effective Clinical Practice in the Treatment of Eating Disorders: The Heart of the Matter* derives from the nature of those who have suffered and are still suffering with eating disorders. During the last several decades, and perhaps since eating disorders were first reported, there is no question but that they occur much more frequently in women than in men. In spite of some speculation to the contrary, it is still true that about 90% of those treated for anorexia, bulimia, and EDNOS are female. The contributors to this book therefore are writing about the therapeutic wisdom they have accumulated while treating *women* with eating disorders. They are emphasizing the importance of interpersonal connection in the therapeutic relationship because experience has taught them that this is what is most likely to move women toward recovery.

Worth noting here is the fact that during the last several decades, as eating disorder clinicians have labored to find effective approaches to treatment, feminist scholarship about the psychological development of women and psychotherapy for women began to underscore the crucial importance of relationships. Relationships, especially those that are mutually rewarding or enhancing, were identified and described as that aspect of human experience that gives meaning and fulfillment to women in particular and perhaps to people in general. From this perspective, a primary goal of psychotherapy is to promote psychological growth by increasing the depth and complexity of interpersonal connection rather than by fostering individuation and interpersonal separation.

Hearing and reading about feminist scholarship on relationships was a revelation to the three of us and to many of our contributing authors. Given the emphasis on therapeutic neutrality and distance in traditional professional training, it was extremely validating, even relieving, to discover that contemporary theory and research on women mirrored the direction we were taking clinically based on intuition and an inductive examination of what seemed to be effective in treatment. By the same token, and perhaps just as important, the clinical wisdom illustrated in this book offers qualitative evidence in support of feminist convictions about the crucial significance of relationships among women.

Effective Clinical Practice in the Treatment of Eating Disorders: The Heart of the Matter is divided into three separate sections. The first, "Effective Clinical Practice: Approaches," offers different approaches to eating disorder treatment. These chapters are more broadly based than others and, either directly or indirectly, offer a conceptual framework for implementation of treatment. The first chapter, "Beyond the Medical Model: A Feminist Frame," is particularly significant since it speaks directly to the common issue that underlies most of the contributions to the book. In the second section, "Effective Clinical Practice: Methods," each chapter describes a particular kind of treatment method or type of treatment, including works on individual therapy, family therapy, group therapy, countertransference, guided imagery, and mind-body therapy. The final section of the book, "Effective Clinical Practice: Special Themes," contains contributions that are even more focused and emphasize how to work with a particular treatment issue or dilemma. These include descriptions of clinical work with shame, sexuality, self-harm, body image, and difference as well as the challenge of treating patients at markedly different points in the course of their illness. The final chapter in this section explores the complicated notion of forgiveness, guiding clinicians to consider ways in which the practice of forgiveness may be an empowering element in helping women open up to life.

For both novice and seasoned therapists, this book provides a wellspring of clinical acumen and reflection on the creative use of collaboration and connection during the treatment of eating disorders to dispel the mystery of the therapeutic process and maximize successful treatment outcomes. We hope that it will empower therapists to actively engage with women in this complicated struggle against forces that cause the mind-body system to function like an autoimmune disease, turning otherwise life-sustaining resources against the self. Equipped with the clinical knowledge gleaned from years of lessons learned, we hope to guide clinicians in their efforts to foster recovery and healing in women suffering from an eating disorder and to contribute to a strengthening of women, providing them with greater resilience and sense of health and well-being.

Effective Clinical Practices: Approaches

chapter one

Beyond the Medical Model
A Feminist Frame for Eating Disorders

Margo Maine

Introduction

Being born female is the single-best predictor of risk for developing an eating disorder (Striegel-Moore & Bulik, 2007). Although eating disorders are not the only gendered psychiatric condition, the degree of gender disparity is much greater than in other diagnoses. Anorexia nervosa and bulimia nervosa are 10 times more common in females than males, and binge-eating disorder is 3 times more common (Treasure, 2007). The increased incidence of eating disorders since the late 1970s suggests that something is happening in the lives of contemporary women to place them at such risk. To understand and effectively treat these conditions, we must use a paradigm that helps to answer the questions: Why women? Why now? The objective, linear medical model falls short, while the feminist framework appropriately conceptualizes eating disorders as solutions to the dilemmas of powerlessness and oppression that women experience.

In their evidence-based review of women's mental health, the World Health Organization (WHO, 2000) concluded that gender is the strongest determinant of mental health, social position, and status as well as the strongest determinant of exposure to events and conditions endangering mental health and stability. Furthermore, WHO noted a positive relationship between the frequency and severity of social stressors and the frequency and severity of mental health problems in women. While overall rates of psychiatric illness are gender neutral, women suffer much higher rates of unipolar depression, anxiety, and somatic complaints, in addition to eating disorders, and are more likely to have persistent, debilitating depression and comorbid conditions. Gender-biased risk factors include emotional or physical victimization; socioeconomic stress due to gender inequities in pay; and multiple roles, including the responsibility for considerable caregiving, family responsibilities, and unpaid work.

Historically, the medical model has been the prominent paradigm in the treatment of eating disorders. Of all psychiatric illnesses, they are the most lethal, with the highest morbidity and mortality rate (Sullivan, 2002). While all dimensions of eating disorders need attention, often the associated medical conditions are seen as the most important, and treatment focuses more on the body than on the person. This chapter examines the limitations of the medical model when addressing clinical eating disorders and the advantages of a feminist framework for both conceptualization and treatment. The medical model sees the individual woman as sick or defective, and its intent is to subdue her disease. The feminist framework literally frames the woman's eating disorder and behavior in the context of her entire sociocultural experience, viewing the contradictions and pressures in the lives of contemporary women as the underlying problem.

Words About Words

I use the broad terms *medical model* and *feminist frame* deliberately. The medical model views the individual's condition as a puzzle to be solved rather than a joint pursuit of her health. While the science of the medical model may objectify people, reducing them to physical problems, the art of providing medical care occurs when caregivers pay attention to the individual as a whole person: mind, body, and spirit. No matter how problem oriented and technical medicine may be, some professionals will always find a way to practice the art of medicine. Ironically, in the less "scientific" areas of medicine such as psychiatry, many professionals still stick to the medical model and objectify those they are intending to help.

I use the term *feminist frame*, rather than *feminist therapy*, because tenets of feminism can be incorporated into many different therapy techniques. Specifically, feminism believes that the issues bringing women to therapy are often related to powerlessness, low self-esteem, the idealization of masculine qualities, and the devaluation of feminine ones (Katzman, Nasser, & Noordenbos, 2007). Even objective, packaged approaches such as cognitive-behavioral therapy (CBT) can be applied within a feminist frame when they are based on respecting and empowering women to regain control of their lives.

Despite my preference for the feminist frame over the medical model, I use the word *patient*, not *client*. To some, *patient* represents the medical model in which the patient is more the object and less the subject of care; yet, to me the word is one of great honor and partnership. In contrast, the word *client* sounds more like a contractual arrangement, for legal or financial advice, perhaps important but not as critical to the person's spiritual or physical survival. The word patient has a very personal meaning to me as well. I was very close to my dad, a dentist, a model of caring and commitment that I internalized. The word patient was one I understood and honored early on. Later, I trained and worked in hospitals, further cementing the word patient for me.

Finally, there is the F-word. In 1994, Fallon, Katzman, and Wooley published a seminal work, *Feminist Perspectives on Eating Disorders*, reflecting that feminist perspectives have long informed clinicians working with eating disorders, yet theirs was among the first and very few books devoted to this topic. Unfortunately, that truth still holds today. Feminist research tends to be ignored by mainstream science and to be marginalized in a few journals, such as *Psychology of Women Quarterly*. The index of the *International Journal of Eating Disorders* (2001–2006) includes no articles mentioning feminism in the title. *Eating Disorders: The Journal of Treatment and Prevention*, of which I am a senior editor, published seven articles with feminism in the title in its entire first 14 years of publication. In fact, there are no references to feminism in the index of most major textbooks on eating disorders.

While feminism seems to be at the core of clinical work for many programs and professionals dealing with eating disorders, it still is marginalized in the literature and research. The field of eating disorders is polarized between the biogenetic biases of the medical model and the feminist, sociocultural view. It is time to acknowledge the essential value of the feminist framework in eating disorders treatment.

The Medical Model and Theories on Women's Mental Health

History elucidates the tensions between the medical model and the feminist frame in the treatment of women's mental health. Modern medicine replaced spiritual and emotional explanations for human conditions with strictly physical and mechanical ones. As Bordo (1993) stated, the intent of modern science is to make the body a transparent object for medical professionals and technologies but to keep it opaque to its owner.

In ancient days, hysteria was seen as a disease caused by the "wandering womb," whose movement throughout the body created various symptoms. Treatment included fumigation of the vagina so that it would stay in its place. Such emphasis on biology continued into the 19th century, with "uterine irritation" as the cause of any emotional distress in women. Gradually, the woman's nervous system was seen as the culprit; women were seen as more delicate and sensitive than men, destined to have more nervous disease. Today, medicine has traded the womb for hormones: Endocrinological disorders, such as premenstrual syndrome, are thought to make women less reliable, accident prone, and even potentially violent. Modern biological theories on depression also suggest that the reproductive system places women at greater risk for depression (Malson & Nasser, 2007).

Both medical practice and the legal system reflect the powerful impact of beliefs regarding women's mental health and resources. Until the late 1800s, women were not allowed in public schools as education was believed to have negative consequences on mental and reproductive health (Malson & Nasser, 2007). In the United States, women were not given the right to vote until 1920 and are still underrepresented in elective office. Even in advanced Western culture, consequences of antiquated theories of women's mental health are far reaching.

Gradually, mental health approaches have considered women's lives instead of their bodies as the sole cause explaining their problems; for example, social theories of depression demonstrate that women's depression is often the result of adverse life experiences (Malson & Nasser, 2007).

Through the work of the Stone Center at Wellesley College, the Women's Therapy Centre Institute in New York City, and others, feminist treatment models evolved for depression, anxiety, trauma, eating disorders, and other problems. These focus on the unique aspects of women's lives, especially the social burdens and injustices that they face. They explore the many contradictions and limitations associated with the culturally prescribed role for women and demonstrate how the idealization of masculine qualities and devaluation of the feminine contribute to women's mental health problems.

Despite these trends, the medical model still has great influence on conceptualizations regarding psychiatric conditions. Since the publication of the human genome sequence in 2003, psychiatric research has been mesmerized by the gene; still, it is unlikely that a gene for eating disorders will be found. Genes do not code behavior or disease, they code RNA and DNA, the building blocks of cells, creating variations associated with risk. Regardless of revolutionary advances, we are far from knowing how genomic variations alter protein development in the cell and affect the functional circuits of neurons. In fact, leaders at the National Institute of Mental Health envision behavior as "the most challenging level of analysis" and "the least technical and most skilled level of study" (Chavez & Insel, 2007, p. 164). Thus, the feminist frame has great relevance for understanding and treating conditions such as eating disorders.

The History of Eating Disorders

Early references to eating disorders are found in the psychiatric literature starting in the late 17th century, describing them as a "nervous disease,"

a form of hysteria, requiring somatic treatment and nutritional rehabilitation (Striegel-Moore & Bulik, 2007). During this first century of recorded
history of eating disorders, treatments were extremely biological, including the use of nasogastric tubes or hyperalimentation, medications, and
electroconvulsive therapy (Sesan, 1994). In the 1930s, Freud's influence
emerged. Conceptualizing eating disorders as neurotic conflicts about
sexuality, including fears of oral impregnation, he envisioned developing
a "properly maternal form of femininity" as the goal of treatment (Gremillion, 2003, p. 2). By the 1960s, concerns about the chronicity of anorexia
nervosa prompted the use of behavioral therapies incorporating forced
feeding, positive reinforcement of weight gain, and negative reinforcement for weight loss.

With the influence of Hilde Bruch's writing, treatment became more
psychiatric, integrating medical and psychological components. Although
Bruch (1974) warned that coerced weight gain usually did not last and, in
fact, could make the matter worse, much of the inpatient treatment in this
era was based on behavior modification, with restricted activities and the
use of nutritional supplements and forced feeding to restore weight. Supportive counseling was given to the patient and family, especially around
the issues of relapse after lengthy inpatient treatment (Sesan, 1994). In general, patients were not allowed to discuss weight or food issues in psychotherapy as such discussions were thought to lead to power struggles, and
family meetings avoided examination of deeper dynamics (Werne, 1996).

Historically, the clinical literature has focused much more on anorexia
nervosa than on the other disorders. In fact, the diagnosis of bulimia
nervosa, seen initially as a variant of anorexia, was first recognized in
1979, attributed to Russell. However, based on her work with college-aged
women, Marlene Boskind-Lodahl had actually described it a few years
earlier (1976) as bulimarexia and explained it as the result of multiple
sociocultural issues affecting women.

Despite published insights of clinicians like Boskind-Lodahl, most
early theories regarding eating disorders made little reference to gender
as a contributor. Bruch's etiological formulations focus on developmental
and family issues and perceptual or cognitive tendencies. For example,
while the mother-daughter relationship is seen as critical, it is isolated
from the mother's role in the greater culture and even from her role as
coparent. Fathers are essentially ignored, as are power dynamics in the
family or culture. These theories recognize the tyranny of slenderness
and unreasonable cultural ideals for beauty as major contributions but
fail to conceptualize their devastating impact on women's power, safety,
or status. The emphasis is on how these affect the self-perception and self-
esteem of women and girls but not how they also affect men and contribute to great power imbalances.

A feminist framework for understanding eating disorders emerged in the 1980s, largely from feminist therapists and writers who were not part of the dominant medical establishment. Susie Orbach (1986) and Kim Chernin (1981, 1985) began to articulate how cultural, economic, historical, familial, and psychological issues intersect to create the gendered realities underlying eating disorders. While acknowledging that mothers sometimes pass on gendered cultural expectations, negatively influencing daughters, Orbach and Chernin stressed that these mothers are also products of an unhealthy culture. It is not dieting or the pursuit of thinness per se, but how these behaviors and attitudes reflect cultural values and keep women "in their place" of disempowerment; thus, the real problem is the "cultural construction of femininity" (Bordo, 1993, p. 47). This view challenged the frame that even the most sophisticated clinicians held at the time.

During the 1980s, specialized residential and hospital-based care began to integrate behavior management with other modalities of treatment and to acknowledge sociocultural issues such as the pressure to be thin, the focus on body image, and other "women's issues." Still, much emphasis was on weight gain and CBT was the most frequent intervention. Bruch (1974) cautioned about the overuse of techniques such as CBT, and Wooley (as cited in Sesan, 1994) warned that CBT could teach women to suppress their emotions rather than explore the underlying reasons for their distress.

More recently, due to the evolution of "managed care" and concerns about cost containment, outpatient treatment programs and partial hospital programs have become more prevalent. When approved by third-party payers, inpatient treatment tends to be brief, and the number of outpatient sessions approved can also be limited. Since the late 1990s, disorder treatment has also seen rapid expansion of the use of psychotropic medications, with little research support, and the promotion of CBT as the standard treatment, although less than 50% of cases respond favorably (Wilson, Grillo, & Vitousek, 2007). While tried-and-true interventions, such as family therapy, are still part of most comprehensive treatment approaches to eating disorders, more programmed and less-individualized techniques, such as the Maudsley method, are increasingly utilized. Another trend driven by cost containment is the use of manualized care, by which the tenets of CBT are provided in self-directed psychoeducational books or Internet programs. While feminist principles can be integrated into these approaches, both the healing aspect of a therapeutic relationship and the examination of the gender-based dilemmas experienced by women with eating disorders may be lost.

Therapeutic Relationships: Psychoanalytic Theories and Beyond

Psychoanalysis, a formative force in the developing theories on mental health and treatment, upholds the medical model rather than embracing a feminist frame. In psychoanalysis, the analyst's neutrality, or blank face, is central. Analysts do not take sides with the patient's struggles or attempt to meet the patient's needs. They are to be impartial, to interpret the patient's transference but not to acknowledge or discuss their own contributions. Despite these very firm edicts, Freud believed that patients needed to fall in love with him to benefit from the treatment process. He practiced a much more personally involved treatment than his writing suggests, sometimes lending money or taking patients on vacation with his family (Lott, 1999). While his writing reflects the rigidity of the medical model, his actions did not, although they were far from feminist.

Winnicott and object relations theorists provided corrective influences in the evolution of therapeutic relationships. For example, Winnicott generalized his concept of a good-enough mother to treatment: The therapist is to hold the patient symbolically the way a mom holds a baby, helping to organize and contain emotional states; make sense of confusion; and provide reliability, consistency, calmness, and empathy (Lott, 1999). Thus, the therapist was active, involved, empathic, and tried to understand and meet the patient's needs.

Over time, "unconditional positive regard," a concept developed by Carl Rogers, challenged the tenets of the psychoanalytic relationship. In the 1960s and 1970s, humanistic psychology defined authenticity, empathy, and the importance of being genuine as key ingredients to psychotherapy. In this approach, therapists learned that they can be warm and involved emotionally while still maintaining the necessary protective frame around the relationship (Lott, 1999).

The relational model, based on the Stone Center's work on gender, stresses that the therapeutic relationship is the "heart" of relational therapy requiring authenticity, connection, mutuality, trust, and empathy (Jordan, 1997; Jordan, Kaplan, Miller, Stiver, & Surrey, 1991). Relational treatment focuses on the disconnections and disruptions in relationships that contribute to the development of eating disorder symptoms and contextualizes these problems by acknowledging the many forces that disconnect women from their own emotional, psychological, and physical needs (Tantillo, 2000). The woman's relationship with food and her body mirror other disconnections in her life; food and body will no longer be the focus of relational energy once she has other satisfying connections.

Validating the importance of the therapeutic relationship, the American Psychiatric Association's Practice Guidelines (2006) stress that treatment of eating disorders requires a therapeutic alliance based on empathy, support, validation, and concern for the patient. Paul Hamburg (1996) described "a judicious mixture of empathy, interpretation, support, and behavioral intervention" (p. 80) as essential to eating disorders treatment. Describing a long-term case that the medical model would label as incurable or chronic, he showed that seriously ill patients can make significant progress in the midst of a relationship of empathy and connectedness.

Cutting-edge brain research actually upholds the tenets of the relational model (Banks & Jordan, 2007). SPECT (single-photon emission computed tomography) show how the brain functions in real situations. The same centers are activated whether a pain is physical or social; in other words, psychic pain is as real as physical. Furthermore, the human brain is "hardwired to connect," with our neurons firing as mirrors in response to the firing of another's neurons, and with isolation actually causing parts of our brain to atrophy. Science now validates the relational emphasis on attunement and mutuality as SPECT findings show that our brains reregulate just as a result of sitting and talking to each other. Whether therapist or patient, we are transformed as we engage in the process of treatment.

The Culture of Treatment

An ethnographic study of a specialized inpatient program (Gremillion, 2003) showed just how difficult it is to treat eating disorders. Treatment programs can easily reinforce battles for control, especially if the meaning of the symptoms and the patient's need for control are not examined and respected. Even in very specialized and sensitive treatment programs, powerful assumptions reign. For example, separation and individuation from families are seen as essential to recovery, and the role of culture and socialization may not be explored at any depth. Ironically, sometimes women are placed on bed rest, isolated from the community and their families, when they most need connection. Treatment may intend to address underlying issues but may actually silence women by demanding compliance and accommodation with rigid treatment protocols (Sesan, 1994).

The treatment culture can re-create the conflicts patients already have by overvaluing self-control and encouraging the patient to craft the ideal presentation of self in a perfectly fit body. Even with other forms of therapy integrated into the program, the behavioral emphasis on weight and symptom management creates a constant surveillance of the body and its processes. With weights precise to decimal points and calorie counts and physical activity constantly monitored, many patients learn how to be more controlled or learn new symptoms. The unspoken power differentials in treatment programs also can speak volumes. Frequently, important treatment decisions are made in a hierarchy that reflects issues of professional status, seniority, gender, ethnicity, and class that are never examined yet have tremendous implications to women trying to reassert power and control in their lives (Gremillion, 2003).

Only recently has the mental health field begun to value the patient's voice or beliefs in the treatment process. For my dissertation (Maine, 1985), I interviewed women who had recovered from eating disorders. Only 3 of the 25 women felt their treatment was essential to their recovery, saying they felt support, caring, and validation; were relieved that they could talk without being punished; and feared that they would have died or killed themselves without the help. Four felt treatment made them worse, contributing to bingeing to get out of treatment, ignoring their painful relationship to food or their bodies, and creating a greater sense of power-lessness. For most, treatment was a neutral experience, and relationships and experiences outside of treatment were more helpful than treatment itself. Their words of wisdom continue to inform me.

A research study (Lott, 1999), involving 274 women in outpatient ther-apy for various problems, validated the importance of the therapeutic relationship, with love, attachment, and dependence profoundly helpful. According to these women, feeling "gotten," seen as who they really are, and feeling fully understood are the ingredients of successful treatment experiences. In shorter or more technique-oriented treatments, women were less likely to report a positive treatment impact.

A Feminist Framework: How It Works

First and foremost in the feminist frame, the power differential between the treater and the treated must be minimal, making collaboration and psychoeducation central (Sesan, 1994). The feminist frame acknowledges that the treater has implicit power, so there is always potential for abuse. In contrast, the medical model is essentially a male hierarchy in which the mode is "power over" versus "power with." As Bergman and Sur-rey (1997) pointed out, men react to uncertainty, conflicts, or threats with attempts to gain and impose control or gain power over, while women prefer to gather more information and include more voices in the solution to problems, thereby sharing power with.

According to Wooley (1994), the medical model insists on a boundary with a profound difference between the clinician and the patient, a bound-ary that men can maintain much easier than women. Furthermore, due to the common ground of their gender and shared experiences, women often speak more openly with female therapists. In response, women therapists may find it easy to be authentically present, reducing the power differen-tial. Male clinicians, grounded in feminist theory, however, can also work within the feminist framework, especially if they continually assess how their therapeutic style or interventions might reflect power imbalances. Male or female, clinicians need to acknowledge the ongoing impact of power differentials when working with female patients and should seek training in the feminist, relational model to develop the necessary collaborative stance to empower women toward recovery.

The feminist framework recognizes that many women have been victimized or traumatized and conceptualizes sexism and oppression as primary contributions to the problems that bring women into treatment. Within this model, an eating disorder is seen as a solution to a woman's dilemma; for her to recover, the dilemma must be understood and addressed. The focus must surpass symptom change and explore the gender-prescribed roles in contemporary culture; instead of idealizing the masculine and devaluing the feminine, the feminist framework helps women to identify and value their strengths. The need women have for emotional connection and interdependence is seen then as a strength, not a weakness (Katzman et al., 2007; Sesan, 1994). These basic tenets have many implications for treatment. For example, in light of women's relational needs and resources, treatment settings should encourage connection, utilize group therapies, and incorporate families, friends, and other natural support systems in the healing process. And, in light of the social and systemic contributions to eating disorders, involvement in social action may be important to the recovery process. In other words, healing does not only occur in a treatment setting or within the confines of a professional relationship.

A Feminist Therapist: How I Work

Working within the medical model, especially in high-profile hospitals, enables clinicians to see themselves as experts. Training also teaches us to feel so, and I certainly did. Early in my career, I worked in a children's hospital where, with the support of administrators and colleagues, I developed a comprehensive, interdisciplinary eating disorder program; later, I ran similar programs in psychiatric hospitals. Despite immersion in the medical model and in the paternalistic and disempowering milieu of hospitals, my actual work with patients became increasingly influenced by feminist principles.

The ironic truth is that now, the longer I am in the field, the more I learn; the more patients I treat, the less I feel I know. While well informed by my experiences and knowledge base, now more than ever I approach each person, situation, and treatment hour with a "beginner's mind," a Buddhist concept reflecting the importance of "open, unencumbered inquiry" in meditation and in life: "In the beginner's mind there are many possibilities, but in the expert's mind there are few" (Kabat-Zin, 2005, p. 85).

Still, many patients see me as the expert, the author, and the answer to all their questions. I often find myself saying, "I'm an expert in eating disorders and that will really help, but you are the expert about you [your daughter]. With these two experts combined, we can really make a difference. Alone, neither of us can do much."

From the start, with a new patient or family, I try to equalize our importance by showing respect for their knowledge and contributions to our work together. I want to know what they have already tried and what they have found helpful and not helpful. By the end of the first meeting, I discuss my thoughts about their treatment needs, how I might help, and how we will assess progress together to determine if we are doing enough or whether the need is other interventions or a higher level of care. I teach them that eating disorders are biopsychosocial phenomena and help them to access medical and nutritional assessment and follow-up. By collaborating with other providers, I demonstrate that we all need others. In other words, I may be the eating disorder expert, but I am not afraid to admit that I need help as well.

Psychoeducation about the mental, emotional, spiritual, and medical effects of starvation and other eating disorder symptoms is essential in the feminist framework. It gives the patient information to guide her decisions about behavior change, making her a more effective collaborator in her care. The goal is to share power with rather than yield power over. Included in psychoeducation is an emphasis on the process of recovery and the need to challenge distorted and self-defeating thoughts and to set gradual goals. I stress that recovery is not a black-and-white, still-frame photo but a colorful moving picture, with many different emotions, and a tape that has to be replayed to be remembered and eventually mastered.

I try to avoid power plays or ambushes: I want my patients to feel empowered and informed of their options. If it seems a patient is not making progress or is getting to a risky point in her medical or psychological status, I talk about this and offer alternative interventions, such as more frequent treatment, more involvement of family members, or a higher level of care. I try not to threaten but to explain what the risks are if we do not make a proactive plan. I have found that the respect and empathy that clients experience in a feminist therapeutic relationship, as well as the ongoing discussion of progress and treatment goals, often helps them to be more open and accepting when a higher level of care, or other major treatment change, is needed.

The most important thing I do is to inquire, listen, and help my patient to tell the story of her life, her pain, her disappointments, her doubts, and her fears. I witness her life without judgment and with much empathy. I allow her to cry without shame, and gradually, I help her to laugh genuinely. In an atmosphere of acceptance and trust, we begin to explore the many issues underlying her eating disorder; the more she understands, the easier it is to let go of the symptoms. This takes time and patience. I show tremendous respect for her eating disorder and express understanding for how it has functioned in her life. I always convey hope that change is possible, and that it is probably happening right now, but we just cannot see it. I often share the story of being on a boat in Alaska, when a glacier calved; there was a powerful, deep sound, a little vapor escaping, but the ice formation did not look any different. Like the glacier, we are often changing in deep and powerful ways underneath but cannot see this with our naked eye.

The feminist frame also demands that therapists constantly explore their own values, biases, and tendencies to support the status quo. Sometimes, we need to shake up a system, whether it is an individual, a family, a couple, or even a treatment team, hospital administration, or insurance company; sometimes it is ourselves. We have to say unpopular things at times and take risks outside our comfort zone.

In contrast to the expert position I had in the medical model, the feminist frame is a great equalizer; for example, I do not expect a patient to do something I do not do. If I expect them to work on their spiritual development, their self-awareness, their relationships, and their limit setting, then the same applies to me. This need for self-awareness, for being in a parallel process of personal growth, is great much of the time, but it is also challenging and exhausting. In other words, as Gandhi taught us: "You must be the change you wish to see."

Final Thoughts: The Path of Least Resistance or a Path of Mutual Growth?

As convinced as I am of the value of the feminist frame, I sometimes find myself slipping back into the medical model; after years immersed in it, that path of least resistance is very familiar. Here are my warning signs:

- Thinking more about her symptoms than about what underlies them.
- Seeing her as "borderline" or chronic.
- Conceptualizing lack of symptom change as resistance or manipulation or "treatment failure."
- Focusing on her history of past unsuccessful treatment or on behaviors that I dislike.
- Experiencing difficulty feeling empathic.
- Acting like the expert.

When any of these occur, I am having difficulty being fully present; this is always about me, although there may be particular similarities in the clinical situations that evoke this. So, this is the time to figure out what unresolved issues I am avoiding by hiding behind the expert façade. I may be feeling powerless or incompetent in response to the veracity of her symptoms. I may be trying to avoid feeling the pain or despair of her life. I may not want to recognize the common ground of our experiences. I may be tired or overwhelmed. Whatever it may be, my job is to understand and address the issue so that I can be fully present to my patients and regard them with the respect they deserve.

When I was immersed in the medical model, I felt very much the expert, a gratifying and comfortable role. Now, with the advantage of decades of experience, I recognize that the more human and available I am, the more my patients can trust me and open themselves up to the rigors of self-discovery and personal transformation. Early clinical training routinely urges the clinician to separate herself from the client and to create a boundary that may be necessary at that early stage of the therapist's development. The medical model magnifies that separation, while the feminist frame teaches clinicians how to be fully present and available, putting ourselves back into the therapeutic equation.

Therein lies a significant distinction between the feminist frame and the medical model: The feminist frame is one of mutual growth within connection, while the medical model allows me to hide behind the cloak of my expertise and knowledge, sometimes a more comfortable place to be but far less satisfying in the end and far less helpful to the women I treat.

References

American Psychiatric Association. (2006). *Practice guideline for the treatment of eating disorders* (3rd ed.). Arlington, VA: Author.

Banks, A., & Jordan, J. V. (2007). The human brain: Hardwired for connections. *Research and Action Report. Wellesley Centers for Women, 28*(2).

Bergman, S. J., & Surrey, J. L. (1997). The woman-man relationship: Impasses and possibilities. In J. V. Jordan (Ed.), *Women's growth in diversity: More writings from the Stone Center* (pp. 260–87). New York: Guilford Press.

Bordo, S. (1993). *Unbearable weight: Feminism, Western culture, and the body.* Berkeley: University of California Press.

Boskind-Lodahl, M. (1976). Cinderella's step-sisters: A feminist analysis of anorexia and bulimia. *Signs: A Journal of Women, Culture, and Society, 2,* 342–356.

Bruch, H. (1974). The perils of behavior modification in the treatment of anorexia nervosa. *Journal of the American Medical Association, 230,* 1419–1422.

Chavez, M., & Insel, T. R. (2007) Eating disorders: National Institute of Mental Health's perspective. *American Psychologist, 62*(3), 159–166.

Chernin, K. (1981). *The obsession: Reflections on the tyranny of slenderness.* New York: Harper & Row.

Chernin, K. (1985). *The hungry self: Women, eating, and identity.* New York: Harper & Row.

Fallon, P., Katzman, M. A., & Wooley, S. C. (1994). *Feminist perspectives on eating disorders.* New York: Guilford Press.

Gremillion, H. (2003). *Feeding anorexia: Gender and power at a treatment center.* Durham, NC: Duke University Press.

Hamburg, P. (1996). How long is long-term therapy for anorexia nervosa? In J. Werne & I. D. Yalom (Eds.), *Treating eating disorders* (pp. 71–99). San Francisco: Jossey-Bass.

Jordan, J. V. (1997). Relational development: Therapeutic implications of empathy and shame. In J. V. Jordan (Ed.), *Women's growth in diversity* (pp. 138–161). New York: Guilford Press.

Jordan, J. V., Kaplan, A. G., Miller, J. B., Stiver, I. P., & Surrey, J. L. (1991). *Women's growth in connection.* New York: Guilford Press.

Kabat-Zin, J. (2005). *Coming to our senses: Healing ourselves and the world through mindfulness.* New York: Hyperion.

Katzman, M. A., Nasser, M., & Noordenbos, G. (2007). Feminist therapies. In M. Nasser, K. Baistow, & J. Treasure (Eds.), *The female body in mind: The interface between the female body and mental health* (pp. 205–213). London: Routledge.

Lott, D. A. (1999). *In session: The bond between women and their therapists.* New York: Owl Books.

Maine, M. D. (1985). An existential exploration of the forces contributing to sustaining and ameliorating anorexia nervosa: The recovered patient's view. *Dissertation Abstracts International, 46*(6-B), 2071 (1986-52919-001).

Malson, H., & Nasser, M. (2007). At risk by reason of gender. In M. Nasser, K. Baistow, & J. Treasure (Eds.), *The female body in mind: The interface between the female body and mental health* (pp. 3–16). London: Routledge.

Orbach, S. (1986). *Hunger strike: The anorectic's struggle as a metaphor for our age.* New York: Norton.

Sesan, R. (1994). Feminist treatment of eating disorders: An oxymoron? In P. Fallon, M. A. Katzman, & S. C. Wooley (Eds.), *Feminist perspectives on eating disorders* (pp. 251–271). New York: Guilford Press.

Striegel-Moore, R. H., & Bulik, C.M. (2007). Risk factors for eating disorders. *American Psychologist, 62(3),* 181–198.

Sullivan, P. (2002). Course and outcome of anorexia nervosa and bulimia nervosa. In C. G. Fairburn & K. D. Brownell (Eds.), *Eating disorders and obesity* (2nd ed., pp. 226–232). New York: Guilford Press.

Tantillo, M. (2000). Short-term relational group therapy for women with bulimia nervosa. *Eating Disorders: The Journal of Treatment and Prevention, 8,* 99–121.

Treasure, J. (2007). The trauma of self-starvation: Eating disorders and body image. In M. Nasser, K. Baistow, & J. Treasure (Eds.), *The female body in mind: The interface between the female body and mental health* (pp. 57–71). London: Routledge.

Werne, J. (1996). Introduction. In J. Werne & I. D. Yalom (Eds.), *Treating eating disorders* (pp. xiii–xxxix). San Francisco: Jossey-Bass.

Wilson, G. T., Grillo, C. M., & Vitousek, K. M. (2007). Psychological treatment of eating disorders. *American Psychologist, 62(3),* 199–216.

Wooley, S. (1994). The female therapist as outlaw. In P. Fallon, M. A. Katzman, & S. Wooley (Eds.), *Feminist perspectives on eating disorders* (pp. 324–325). New York: Guilford Press.

World Health Organization. (2000). *Women's mental health: An evidence based review.* Geneva, Switzerland: Mental Health Determinants and Populations, Department of Mental Health and Substance Dependence, World Health Organization.

chapter two

Wholeness and Holiness
A Psychospiritual Perspective

Steven Emmett

Introduction

Eighteen-year-old Sarah shuffles into my office with an air of helplessness surrounding her 72-pound frame. With dead eyes and monotonic speech reflecting a self devoid of spirit, she sacrifices her body and being in the name of some ill-conceived "perfection" and desire to maintain control over her empty life.

At 47, Mary has been seeking a sense of serenity and security for nearly three decades, compulsively bingeing and purging in an unsuccessful attempt to ward off toxic feelings linked to her painful past and, via manipulation of her body, find some shallow measure of acceptance. Despite all the sacrifice of time, money, and energy and no matter how dedicated to distracting herself with an obsessional awareness of caloric intake and nutritional food values, she remains adrift, filled with self-loathing and shame.

Tim, nearly 140 pounds overweight, has relied on food to deal with myriad emotional issues confronting him throughout his life, be it anger, stress, loneliness, or boredom. His binges have resulted in a serious sacrifice of health and self-respect, leading to a hopeless spiral of meaningless gorging.

Poet W. B. Yeats observed that, "Too long a sacrifice makes a stone of the heart" (2000, p. 73). Such are the stone-hearted lives of eating-disordered individuals like Sarah, Mary, and Tim, who poignantly sacrifice themselves in a vain attempt to evade core personal truths about their existence.

My exposure to the intriguing connection between eating disorders and psychospiritual dysfunction came during an intake with the first eating-disordered person I had ever encountered. "I absolutely worship my bulimia," Janna said in passing, and at that very moment, I glimpsed the all-consuming emotional straitjacket of alienation, shame, powerlessness, and despair inherent in eating disorders. Sufferers are harshly self-critical, cut off from compassionate feelings for both themselves and their fellow human beings, while their ability to be vulnerable and truthful is often seriously compromised. Eating disorders thus are stark manifestations of spiritual disharmony. A psychospiritual perspective keeps this disharmony in the forefront of the individual's awareness and addresses the fundamental existential struggle to reclaim the self and restore a healing sense of wholeness and holiness.

Psychospiritual therapy engages people at the most personal depths of their being. Ultimately, these core aspects of our authentic selves are the most universal and thus the truest form of religious expression. The heart of this therapy involves not "fixing" a problem by simple removal but rather honoring the symptoms and, patiently and respectfully, learning from what they tell us. These natural forces are seen not merely as challenges to be eliminated or endured but as radical opportunities for growth, intimacy, and transformation. In the pursuit of wholeness via holiness, the therapist and client can step back together and, in a "fellowship of suffering," peer into the individual's soulful struggles as they begin the arduous journey of self-discovery through self-reflection. Thus, a psychospiritual lens slowly evolves through which clients can better evaluate their anger, fears, hopes, and motivations. This holistic approach requires a vigilant assessment of how the manner in which one thinks, feels, and acts is anchored in the person's relationship to life's ultimate concerns. Emphasis is placed on understanding rather than blaming, and symptoms are continually filtered through a prism linked to the individual's core values. Such an approach sharpens and deepens the focus of the therapeutic work, enabling individuals to comprehend the meaning and impact of their eating dysfunction in a far more complete manner, while it exposes them to the myriad healing influences offered by a spiritual orientation.

The significant healing influence of spirituality in the therapeutic process is perhaps the most underresearched, underestimated, and underutilized agent of change in modern-day mental health practice. The most challenging task facing a therapist influenced by this approach is to create a psychospiritually centered holding environment in which a sort of psychospiritual CPR (cardiopulmonary resuscitation) on the deadened heart of the sufferer can be caringly and faithfully performed. Spiritual reawakening can function as a formidable healing force in recovery for the emergent sense of empowerment, inspiration, gratitude, comfort, and belonging wrought by this soul-stirring process serves as an ideal antidote to the feelings of helplessness, unworthiness, ineffectuality, discouragement, and anhedonia inherent in eating disorders.

For those of us who have spent years battling these stubborn scourges, it feels as if we have been trapped within a dizzying morality play. Dramatic dualities inform every aspect of the illness, from good/bad body to good/bad food, pervading the eating-disordered individual's entrenched dysfunctional thinking. While utilization of cognitive-behavioral, family systems, psychodynamic, feminist, and biogenetic theories is necessary when understanding and treating eating disorders, it is not sufficient. Illnesses that seduce the soul and commandeer one's entire identity demand a therapeutic approach that engages clients at the core of their being. Faith, forgiveness, trust, hope, love, intuition, will, wonder, prayer, imagination, compassion, and courage are the essential existential tools required when confronting such all-encompassing conditions

We are defined, ultimately, by what we believe and trust. Psychospiritual psychotherapy is committed to tapping into this energy, helping people to relinquish their self-limiting idolatrous beliefs and, via courageous risk and mindful reflection, discover a path leading to healthier forms of self-expression and self-control. Ignoring the power of the sacred in the psychotherapeutic process is akin to spelunking without a flashlight. An enduring recovery must include reclamation of one's spiritual identity if it is to survive the dark nights of the soul that life inevitably spawns.

Step 1: The Requisite "Leap of Faith"

From the shallowness of celebrity worship to our rampant and frenzied consumerism, there is ubiquitous evidence of the futile drive to fill our spiritually bankrupt lives. Over 150 years ago, the Danish philosopher Soren Kierkegaard described this societal tendency as "tranquilization by the trivial" (1989, p. 41), a delightfully apt description of today's world as well. The psychospiritual approach seeks to reverse the repressive, bankrupting processes of eating disorders by challenging individuals to be propelled by the profound, by taking a Kierkegaärdian "leap of faith" into a far more vital form of existence. This phrase brings to mind a compelling Zen Buddhist story with a theme that contains a foundational aspect of this perspective.

In this tale of initiation, a young monk is given a *koan*, an incredibly cryptic puzzle (e.g., "What is the sound of one hand clapping?") and asked to solve it. The student then spends months and months meditating on the koan, utilizing every ounce of his rational ability attempting to answer the impossibly difficult question. Eventually, in utter frustration on not discovering a solution, the initiate returns to his teacher and confesses his failure. At this moment, the story likens the demoralized young monk to someone desperately holding on to a branch above a gaping abyss. As he acknowledges his helplessness and illusion of self-reliance, he lets go of the branch and plunges into the chasm, experiencing what Zen Buddhists call "the great death." But happily, the morality tale does not end here. At the exact moment the despairing aspirant relinquishes all hope of finding the elusive answer on his own, it magically surfaces in his consciousness, and as he floats serenely back to Earth, the young student is graced with what Zen masters describe as "the great joy." A true psychospiritual therapy serves to facilitate this letting go while creating a supportive, nurturing environment in which individuals may reclaim their formerly "tranquil-ized" selves.

This perspective celebrates the liberating symbolism of the hand that lets go and is open, for it is only then able to receive, and requires a will-ingness to relinquish the illusion that we are "in control," to face the real-ity of our inherent vulnerability. It is grounded in a fundamental belief in the influence of the intertwined threads of faith and identity. Faith is understood as a primary motivating power in the evolution of the self and as a central aspect of one's being. As an active ordering process, it func-tions more as a verb than a noun. One lives it rather than passively pos-sesses it. One's "faithing" gives a form and coherence to existence while generating a sense of purposeful relatedness to our surrounding environ-ment. Faith plays a key role in how we understand our place in the world by shaping our responses to the myriad terrifying foundation-shaking events that unpredictably bombard our fragile lives. Without the commit-ment undergirding our faithful relationships in life, human beings could not long maintain a reliably stable selfhood.

Psychospiritual Literacy

An integral component of my work with people like Janna involves facili-tation of psychospiritual literacy: the ability to derive meaning, purpose, and genuine contentment beyond the constraints of an emotionally, cog-nitively, and behaviorally constrictive lifestyle. This literacy develops, in part, as one gradually acknowledges the fear and pain motivating the idol-atrous worship underlying the eating disorder, the horrible toll it takes on the self and relations with others, and the vast spiritual emptiness that it generates. "Being on the same page" requires a mutual understanding of not only terminology but also a shared awareness of what the illness does to a person's entire being.

An eating disorder restricts one's capacity to think and conceptual-ize beyond a self-contained, self-controlled sphere. Repeatedly delving beneath the quotidian dynamics of the eating disorder by linking the obsessive thought patterns and compulsive spirit-deadening behaviors to the despair lurking below the surface is a constant feature of the treat-ment. I regularly encourage clients to ponder questions that create a con-frontation with their desperately disconnected selves, challenge them to sort out what the eating disorder worship means (and does) to them sym-bolically and literally, and urge them to imagine a higher power calling them to a life centered around self-respect and loving service to others.

For example, I suggest that patients ask of themselves: What would it mean to live in harmony with Mother Nature? How am I demonstrating spiritual irresponsibility? When, why, and how did my reverence for the superficial aspects of existence develop? Merely asking these questions instills a more contemplative attitude, and it is this introspective stance that inspires interpretation of the illness as a disease of the spirit as well as the mind and body. The key is to develop a common language that may be utilized to create clear communication and a robust rapport. A specific religious doctrine or dogma is never imposed. Rather, clients are free to discover in what ways their particular understanding of the sacred may enter into their own thirsting soul.

The following vignette demonstrates the teaching of psychospiritual literacy.

Sally would cautiously step on her scale 10 to 12 times daily. Trepidation inevitably accompanied the ordeal. We explored the enervating process, and over time, she began to understand how this had become a completely ritualized aspect of her daily existence. We discussed how much noxious influence the repetitive action exerted, its negative spiritual implications, and the extent to which her fragile sense of self-esteem, purpose, and control was linked to this religiously observed practice. At no time did I make a judgment or interpretation vis-à-vis the activity. The sole goal of any therapeutic intervention at this point is to simply create sufficient detachment to enable the individual to see the compulsive behavior as a self-constructed religion involving the worship of a "small g" god. This psychospiritual reframing is applied to the entire range of eating disordered thought and behavior. One's particular religious preference has no bearing on the relabeling task for agnostics and atheists are just as susceptible to being dominated by the same unyielding anxieties, self-loathing, and demanding false idols.

When to introduce the psychospiritual dimension is often a matter of intuition. Save for when a spiritually explicit issue is raised directly, it helps to apply the approach when a person is expressing utter despair regarding the futility of living with her disease, when she seriously questions the purpose and value of her entire existence, is grasping for something offering genuine direction and support, or acknowledges her desperate isolation and disengagement from anything providing solace and intimacy. These gut-wrenching moments of heightened vulnerability can break down defenses, leading to insight-producing breakthroughs.

As a centuries-old vehicle offering comfort, forgiveness, and loving connection, spiritually based interventions are the most effective way to draw out toxic secrets and elicit a willingness to risk. When a person is struggling to make some sense of her life, valiantly attempting to forge new meanings and to discover alternative ways to cope with debilitating insecurities, exploration of faith, hope, and the healing influence of the sacred is most compelling. Alcoholics Anonymous characterizes these crisis/opportunity occasions as "hitting bottom," when a person is most apt to "let go and let God" and is most amenable to adopting a psycho-spiritual perspective.

Introducing Spirituality

My clients' awareness of my training as a minister allows an easy intro-duction of spiritual topics, but formal religious education is not a prereq-uisite for engaging in holistic psychotherapy. Most of my peers have no ministerial training, yet those with many years of experience increasingly incorporate theistic elements into their practice. The recent publication, *Spiritual Approaches in the Treatment of Women With Eating Disorders* (Rich-ards, Hardman, & Berrett, 2007), is a comprehensive overview and much-needed resource for clinicians working in the field of eating disorders. I encourage both my clients and my colleagues to carefully consider the religious underpinnings of each and every aspect of their lives as a means to deepen and enrich the quality of their daily existence.

Conducting an initial spirituality evaluation is essential. Data includ-ing one's religious upbringing, nature of the relationship (if any) to a higher power, possible traumatizing experiences associated with religious observance, and an enumeration of organizing core values can be most helpful in determining an individual's spiritual orientation. If there is no discernible place for the holy in a person's life, it is noted as an important marker deserving further exploration. Antipathy toward the sacred side of existence can be just as revealing as a devout posture. Examining the contributing factors leading to the formation of one's guiding principles and ultimate concerns is imperative when developing a profound under-standing of how someone views herself and her place in the world. At this juncture, it is crucial to communicate that terms such as religious, faith, God, or prayer are altogether unique to each person, and that no way is better than another. The person is simply invited to participate in a search for the sacred to discover in what ways it may contribute to per-sonal enlightenment and healing.

A spiritual perspective triggers the penetrating questions that are all too often neglected in secular therapies: What do I most deeply value and cherish? Where do I derive ultimate meaning, hope, and direction? To whom or what could I surrender myself in total trust? For what or whom would I be willing to sacrifice my life? These topics mobilize the spiritual dimension of both therapist and client, enriching their mutual awareness of the depth of the problems explored. This psychospiritual archeology exposes what one truly worships in life. Understanding the function of how and why people ground their lives in the idiosyncratic ways in which they do can be an extremely instructive undertaking because what one most deeply values is a direct reflection of who they truly are and of what has most profoundly shaped them as human beings.

Spirituality 101: "You Must Study"

Years ago, as a graduate student in Boston, I had the great fortune of riding alone in an elevator (for all of 30 seconds) with holocaust survivor Elie Wiesel, who had just delivered a riveting lecture on the topic "God and Silence." I was struggling at the time with a personal spiritual conundrum: reconciling my inherited Jewish and Christian faiths. I asked the esteemed Nobel Prize winner what I might do to resolve this dilemma. He thought for a moment and then quietly replied, "You must study."

I cherish the memory of this chance encounter and apply it every time I exhort clients to study their own existential circumstances. Psychospiritual bibliotherapy is a unique aspect in this search for a divine connection. Ever mindful of the "many paths, one Creator" credo, I encourage investigation of a variety of sacred writings. Biblical entreaties to "lose the self to find the self" and paradoxes, such as "when I am weakest then I am strongest," are explored along with texts from Native American, Hindu, and Zen sources and the more recent works on mindfulness such as Jon Kabat-Zinn's *Wherever You Go, There You Are* (2005).

Early in therapy, I am primarily concerned with providing exposure to the potentially healing sacred aspects of existence. A close examination of the history of humanity's inherent hunger for salvation and eternal search for wholeness promotes a richer appreciation of the universality of the need to create meaning via the forging of a broad matrix of beliefs, symbols, and rituals. Many of my clients have never been introduced to these holy elements, much less utilized them. Thus, the first designated goal is simply to learn what, for example, prayer involves. Dossey's classic *Healing Words* (1993) is a useful resource for the uninitiated at this early psychoeducational stage of treatment. The few books examining the intriguing interface between pathological eating and spirituality provide a corroboration of the fact that, at their core, eating disorders represent sicknesses of the soul (see the recommended readings at the end of the chapter).

Psychospiritual Restructuring

Whereas psychospiritual literacy promotes development of a new (or renewed) language and learning, psychospiritual restructuring entails a shift in one's fundamental orientation to the world, one's primal understanding of place and purpose in the universe. It redirects one's heart, mind, and spirit vis-à-vis relationship to oneself, others, and the divine. Such a radical existential reconfiguration induces dramatic changes in how one thinks and acts as it stimulates the reawakening of a spiritual identity, humanity's most potent healing force. A tragic consequence of an eating disorder is its anesthetization of a person's ability to feel and respond to their heart's deepest longings.

The all-consuming nature of the illness sweeps away any willingness to place faith in, and derive sustenance from, honest loving relationships with family, friends, and a higher power. Psychospiritual recalibration challenges irrational beliefs and destructive activities ignited by this numbing flight from the self, while it encourages a reconnection with what is most important in life: the capacity to live an authentic life rooted in timeless values, empowering the spirit and nurturing the soul.

My in-depth work with Laura highlights various dimensions of this psychospiritual restructuring. She entered treatment with virtually no identity apart from the rigid dictates of a harsh eating disorder-dominated conscience. Isolated and riddled with shame, she evinced little capacity to access the spiritual sphere of her being. At 34, Laura was thrice married and divorced and, because of myriad medical misfortunes, had been forced to transfer the care of her two teenaged children to relatives. She manifested an inability to savor even the most rudimentary pleasures of life, and her emaciated body seemed to symbolically reflect the absence of a fulfilling purpose around which she might organize a meaningful, nourishing existence. Her journal poignantly captured this spiritual void:

> I am nothing without my anorexia. It is the be-all
> and end-all of my entire life. It rules me and I must
> obey … nothing else at this point matters. I am
> trapped, empty, and alone—but at least I'm safe.

This expression of ambivalence toward the eating disorder, and the dual isolation and security it creates, leads to deeper emotional paralysis and increasingly entrenched risk-avoidant behavior. The guiding goal of my psychospiritual restructuring therapy with Laura was to help facilitate the rebirth of the sacred core of her being, triggering both an acknowledgment and an affirmation of her inherent worth as a child of creation. The heart of our spiritual journey together entailed confronting her soulless belief system and behavior, gradually replacing it with a life rooted in faith, hope, and honesty. Self-limiting placation of demons and worship of false gods in the church of anorexia were slowly substituted with a devotion to enduring life-enhancing values bringing integrity, compassion, and intimacy. Like so many eating-disordered clients, Laura had a poorly developed sense of the transcendent, as reflected in her few specific allusions to an eternal power:

> I must be a huge disappointment to God. ... I've
> lost my relationship with Him. ... I've never come
> close to taking advantage of the life He gave me. ...
> Where is God? I need God's help.

She would periodically allude to this disconnection in therapy. It was always linked to the notion that, owing to her self-destructiveness, she was undeserving of support from a loving Deity.

Laura's trust in a just and caring world had been shattered time and again in childhood. Significant authority figures broke promises and abandoned her emotionally, leaving her fearful and suspicious, unable to believe in anything beyond that over which she exerted total control. Cultivating a fortifying faith is another ongoing priority in psychospiritual therapy. It slowly forms as a predictably loving and trusting bond is established between client and therapist.

As therapy progressed, Laura finally experienced consistent unconditional caring. I answered her queries about my own beliefs openly. Like a toddler clinging tenaciously to her tattered security blanket, she carried with her my unflagging faith in her ability to engage in this radical process of self-discovery and liberation. We scrutinized the terrible toll her loss of belief had exacted on her relationship with others and with a higher power. Finally, she was encouraged at every step along the therapeutic path to take small leaps of faith, risk new trusting behaviors, and in so doing, break free of the solipsistic straitjacket her spiritual self-betrayal had engendered.

Authenticity

Eating-disordered individuals have essentially substituted their illness for an authentic identity. The meticulous attention to mind-numbing rituals and reverence paid to the deified numbers of pounds, calories, or grams of fat form an impenetrable barrier to self-awareness. This faulty religion functions as a mesmerizing distraction from the fears, hurt, anger, and confusion plaguing people paralyzed by eating disorders. The associated magical thinking seduces the soul by creating a predictable black-and-white world in which the person blindly assumes a detached, invulnerable, god-like posture, alternately worshipping and dreading the rigid dictates of draconian self-devised rules, impervious to the challenging vagaries associated with real life. Such a controlled "tunnel vision" existence isolates the individual from intimate connection with fellow human beings and from the comfort of a higher power as it diminishes resiliency and the capacity to both give and receive love.

Reclaiming one's basic sense of spiritual worthiness and reconnecting to the healing force flowing from faith in the unconditional caring of others and God are foundational elements in the recovery of an authentic identity. Laura was living out the "eating disorder lie," the misguided belief that all of her basic human needs for comfort, security, self-esteem, and purposeful selfhood would be met by strictly following the constricted laws of her eating-disordered world. The task of the therapist is to help clients confront the isolating consequences of this turtle-like existence. Creating an existential dissonance expands their previously shrunken hearts, awakening their minds to the possibility of a life in which the grace and guidance of a higher power, and the comforting presence of a concerned community, supplies an enduring hope and direction that is secure and meaningful.

In exposing the falsity and hurt pervading this way of life, therapeutic restructuring explores spiritual concepts, including forgiveness, grace, love, suffering, service to others, the faith to be vulnerable, and openness to the positive influence of a higher power. Sensitive dismantling of the eating-disordered identity, and the misguided belief that it will offer lasting safety and comfort, is inhibited by the entrenched habits bolstering the sickness. I have found, much like a mountain climber laboriously carving out precious foot- and handholds, that painstaking attention to dislodging, step by glacially slow step, the various aspects of the habit-dominated lives of my clients is key to their eventually creating a better existence. Once the strength and will are summoned to relinquish just one of the long-held habits, like falling dominoes, a momentum builds that often leads to bigger risks and increased freedom. Discovering that they are acceptable and worthwhile despite their human imperfections, that they are loved "warts and all," that they possess a uniqueness imparted just by being who they naturally are apart from their eating disorder is enlivening.

Exploration of soul-soothing alternatives to bingeing, purging, and starvation, such as prayer, listening to sacred music, spiritual journaling, meditation, and quiet communion with nature, engenders a connection to a whole and holier self. Reliance on our divinely inspired imagination to envision an illness-free existence is a part of this radical act of re-creation. Continually asking, What would God (or, for nonbelievers, Mother Nature) intend for me to do (or be or feel) in this situation? involves imagining a life steered and supported by a benevolent sacred force and is often the first vital step in charting a path toward recovery.

The Psychospiritual Therapeutic Relationship

At the outset of therapy, I invite thoughtful scrutiny of my background and emphasize my many years of experience working in the eating disorders field. Inspiring an attitude of confidence in both the therapist and the therapy is key to establishing a belief in the efficacy of treatment as well as building a rapport rooted in respect and optimism. This facilitates intimate confiding, a principal aspect of psychospiritual therapy, for confessions of the soul abide at the heart of self-awareness and self-forgiveness. Even with the most disheartened individuals, I am guided by hopeful expectations for I have had the great privilege of witnessing unexpected leaps of growth time and again. Clients must know of my faith and be similarly infused with such an indomitable hope. However, this must always be balanced with humility and an acknowledgment that therapists cannot do the willing for their clients. Ultimately, it is they who are responsible for their own growth. We walk a tenuous tightrope between elicitation of admiration and idealization. The former breeds creative connection, the latter paralyzing dependency.

Just like those who come to us, when faced with unfathomable mysteries or crushing hurt, we are often tempted to turn away. In the role of helper, there is ample room to evade and safely engage in professional posturing. But, the mask of the "healer" conceals the essential attributes of one's humanity so crucial in establishing a healing foundation of empathy and trust. Articulating one's own despair and utilizing this as the starting point of service to another, drawing on one's own angst as a source of healing, has led to the image of "wounded healers": those who relinquish their impartial persona as psychotherapists, enter the more personal realm of fellow seekers, no longer objective, distanced observers, but vulnerable human beings who place their humanity at the disposal of their clients. This is consistent with the psychospiritual perspective, which holds that:

> Sufferings can only be dealt with creatively when they are understood as integral to the human condition … shared pain is no longer paralyzing but mobilizing when understood as a way to liberation. When we become aware that we do not have to escape our pains, but that we can mobilize them into a common search for life, those very pains are transformed from expressions of despair into signs of hope. (Nouwen, 1979, p. 93)

While there is a healing power in mutual confessions of hurt and confusion as the artificial barrier between a supposed omnipotent therapist and self-abnegating client is breached, it is a risky process, for the therapist must:

> allow others to enter his life, come close to him and ask him how their lives connect with his. ... Nobody can predict where this will lead us ... he takes a risk not knowing how they will affect his life. But it is exactly in common searches and shared risks that new ideas are born, that new visions reveal themselves and that new roads become visible. (Nouwen, 1979, p. 100)

For those of us schooled in the classic psychodynamic doctrine of maintaining an objective, detached stance, this collegial approach requires a radical transcendence of our training and movement into an unfamiliar therapeutic sphere of well-timed, wisely considered openness. It is in this courageous willingness to open oneself to life's mysteries and the possibility of change and in the ongoing shared pursuit of sustaining meaning and purpose in the face of suffering and a seemingly indifferent world that the wounded healer is transformed from a reflective mirror into a translucent window. Only in this genuine manner may the client glimpse something of his or her own struggle refracted through the interior odyssey of the therapist, who serves as a healing model of how to best utilize the spiritual resources of the soul. In bearing witness to our own unshakable faith in the enduring values of existence, in resolutely affirming its inherent worth, we nurture our clients' ability to risk exploring their own divine nature, so that they may begin the liberating pilgrimage away from a life rooted in shameful self-disgust, futile self-manipulation, and phobic fears into a world inspired by loving connection to self, family, community, and the eternal.

Many years ago, on my return from a stint with the Peace Corps in Micronesia, I suffered what was then euphemistically called "reentry culture shock." I wandered for many months in a psychospiritual wilderness; my former confident, resilient, and extroverted self vanished, replaced by a person emotionally more dead than alive, helplessly wracked with doubts and paralyzing insecurities. The devastating anxiety and depression I experienced triggered a journey that continues to this day. Just as necessity is the mother of invention, so does desperation give birth to vulnerability, insight, and receptivity to self-truth.

There is a timelessness to such a profoundly life-altering event that keeps it very much present, and if intuition spurs me, I share this experience with clients. This self-revelation unfailingly enlivens the therapeutic encounter and can be of enormous help in aiding an individual to get "unstuck." An aura of intimacy enters into the exchange as the distance wrought by client idealization is diminished. Such exposure also serves as a way to undermine their fears of judgment and the suffocating shame that strangles their lives. In this way, I model the manner in which a breakdown can lead to a breakthrough, inspiring a faith that "the quickest way out is through" and challenge them to believe that they are strong enough to be vulnerable. Most important, this open communication lets my clients know that I possess a strong sense of the hurt and fear they are feeling, having been there myself. One of the great paradoxes in life is how tragedy and pain can bring profound awareness and, over time, be transformed into treasured wisdom. (Parenthetically, it is this combined motivating/enlightening aspect of psychic pain that impels me to resist the standard practice of automatically suggesting drug interventions. Acute symptoms of emotional distress can be invaluably instructive in that they reflect authentic expressions of the soul and must be respected rather than immediately tranquilized.)

Traditionalists would certainly view this intimate sharing as grossly heretical, heightening the risk of introducing complicated countertransferences and dangerously undermining the therapist's authority. While ever mindful of the importance of maintaining appropriate boundaries and the necessity of offering timely transference interpretations, psychospiritual therapy remains firmly committed to the notion that only a nurturing relationship of deep respect and honesty, caring and concern, authentic empathy, and mutual openness can foster the faith required to take growth-producing risks of the magnitude suggested here. Moore captured the essence of this profound engagement when he wrote:

> Taking an interest in the soul is a way of loving it. The ultimate cure, as many ancient and modern psychologies of depth have asserted, comes from love and not logic. Understanding doesn't take us very far in this work, but love, expressed in patient and careful attention, draws the soul in from its dispersion in problems and fascinations. It has often been noted that most, if not all, problems brought to therapists are issues of love. It makes sense then that the cure is also love. (1992, p. 14)

Psychospiritual Psychotherapy: Sowing the Seeds

When asked what sort of work I do, I usually mention the nurturing of people's essential sacred nature. I often employ the image of sowing seeds of faith, hope, and love, which serve as activating soul-ripening catalysts. Such a perspective allows the individual to see the world with new eyes, process their problems in novel ways, and begin to explore more constructive tools to combat boredom, undercut debilitating shame, soothe the self, and regulate tension while finding more creative paths of self-expression and self-control.

A psychospiritually oriented therapy is as much about teaching and inspiration as it is about cognitive restructuring and interpretation. A majority of my younger clients have either never been raised religiously or have rebelled, viewing God as obsolete at best or nonexistent at worst. I respect this rebellion as an important piece of the searching client's quest for autonomy and empowerment. Thus, when we are examining their desire to set an ideal body weight goal falling significantly below a healthy range, I reflect on the dynamics of set point and what Mother Nature might intend for them to be. The key is to develop a common language to create clear communication and a robust rapport. A specific religious doctrine or dogma is never imposed; rather, the individual is free to discover in what ways the sacred may enter into her own thirsting soul. Therapy introduces not only the fundamentals of prayer, meditation, and guided imagery but also offers critical psychospiritual literacy (much as we teach media literacy to offset the corrosive impact of advertising) so that clients might develop an objective observing ego that can detect the insidious influence of an idolatrous action or a projection of hurt and rage onto an unseen Creator. Finally, the psychospiritual perspective strives to open windows onto what may inspire the person to take risks, explore new directions, and adopt the faith to shed their fraudulent selves as they absorb the promising curative possibilities of affiliation with the holy.

The healing forces of hope and belief are often untapped by traditional therapies. Psychospiritual psychotherapy continually draws on these powerful agents of change, nurturing their growth through creative imagination and faith development. At the heart of the "miraculous" recoveries I have had the privilege of witnessing is a harnessing of hope and belief in their better soulful selves. The reversal of decades-long eating disorder pathology could never have been accomplished without an evolving sense of unconditional love and worth rooted in connection to a higher power and incorporation of others' abiding faith in their natural God-given abilities to heal.

Much has been made recently of genetically mediated contributions to understanding the etiology of eating disorders and the undeniable environmental effect on their course and outcome, all neatly captured in the popular maxim "genetics loads the gun, environment pulls the trigger." Seeing firsthand the mysterious healing workings of the spirit in the desperate lives of so many who were deemed beyond help enables me to confidently add to this phrase "and spirituality deflects the bullet."

References

Dossey, L. (1993). *Healing words*. San Francisco: Harper Collins.

Kabat-Zinn, J. (2005). *Wherever you go, there you are: Mindfulness meditation in everyday life*. New York: Hyperion.

Kierkegaard, S. (1989). *The sickness unto death*. New York: Penguin Books.

Moore, T. (1992). *Care of the soul*. New York: Harper Perennial.

Nouwen, H. J. M. (1979). *The wounded healer*. New York: Image Books.

Richards, P., Hardman, R., & Berrett, M. (2007). *Spiritual approaches in the treatment of women with eating disorders*. Washington, DC: American Psychological Association.

Yeats, W. B. (2000). *Poetry, drama and prose: Authoritative texts, contexts, criticism*. New York: Norton.

Recommended Reading

Bell, R. M. (1985). *Holy anorexia*. Chicago: University of Chicago Press.

Bynum, C. (1987). *Holy feast and holy fast. The religious significance of food to medieval women*. Berkeley: University of California Press.

Lelwica, M. M. (1999). *Starving for salvation: The spiritual dimensions of eating problems among American girls and women*. New York: Oxford University Press.

chapter three

Individual Psychotherapy for Anorexia Nervosa and Bulimia
Making A Difference

William N. Davis

Introduction

Since the 1980s, a vast and still-growing treatment and information industry has emerged within the field of eating disorders. Yet, as more and more treatment is offered to more and more people, it is still unclear why someone recovers, or does not, and what is necessary or sufficient to facilitate recovery. The Agency for Healthcare Research and Quality of the United States Department of Health and Human Services (2006) issued a comprehensive report reviewing all published research on the effectiveness of treatment for eating disorders. Despite the scope of the effort, findings were relatively sparse, especially with regard to anorexia nervosa. The report noted that the literature on the treatment of eating disorders is inconsistent in quality and emphasized the urgent need for further studies to investigate novel forms of therapy, optimal duration of intervention, and approaches for those who do not respond to medication or manual-based techniques. In addition, the report mentioned the importance of qualitative studies on eating disorders treatment given the lack of reliable, clinically relevant findings in the empirical literature.

Significantly, the most common treatment modality for eating disorders is probably outpatient individual psychotherapy; yet, this particular form of intervention is rarely studied and seldom described in the professional literature. This means that the most popular, most frequently utilized treatment for these very serious conditions is also the least understood and least articulated. Witton, Leichner, Sandhu-Sahota, and Filippelli (2007) constructed the Research Directions Survey to determine patient and parent priorities for future research. Both groups ranked individual psychotherapy as most important. In other words, the consumers of therapeutic services for eating disorders are, understandably, most interested in furthering knowledge about the type of eating disorders treatment with which they are most familiar and on which they are most dependent.

This chapter offers information about individual psychotherapy for eating disorders, especially anorexia and bulimia, to clinicians and students interested in these challenging conditions. It is based primarily on my treatment experiences since 1976 and represents the kind of accumulated wisdom that accrues over the passage of time and innumerable therapeutic surprises, crises, triumphs, frustrations, disappointments, and satisfactions. Each of the following sections describes an ingredient of individual psychotherapy that appears to support the treatment process and contributes to recovery. The separate discussions are not intended to represent a comprehensive appraisal of all those aspects of psychotherapy that can be beneficial; altogether, they do not comprise an overview of individual psychotherapy for eating disorders. Instead, they articulate specific therapeutic positions, themes, or emphases that, in my practice at least, seem to really make a difference.

Context

To provide a context for subsequent opinions, conclusions, and recommendations, this initial section presents a brief summary of my current thoughts about the definition, etiology, and treatment of eating disorders (e.g., Davis, 2005).

Eating disorders are best understood as psychological disorders because, in every case, food and eating are symbolized or given meaning beyond ordinary nourishment and consumption and because, as food and eating is symbolized, a variety of medical, psychological, and social problems are created. The defining characteristic of anorexia nervosa and many suffering from bulimia nervosa and eating disorders not otherwise specified (EDNOS) is a dread of fatness and a concomitant pursuit of thinness.

Women with eating disorders are suffering from conditions with origins that always have both psychological and sociocultural components. Often, the influence of these components is grounded in and exacerbated by various genetic or physiological predispositions. The onset of an eating disorder is driven by emotional difficulties that precede the expression of symptoms; frequently, onset is shaped and intensified by contemporary cultural messages that unrealistically glorify the virtues of thinness and dieting, objectify the female body, and create confusion about a woman's identity and role in the world.

The development and course of anorexia and bulimia represent a maladaptive effort to be self-constructive or self-protective rather than an expression of self-destructiveness. Most often, an eating disorder begins with what appears to be an ordinary diet. In fact, it contains, and conceals, what Sullivan (1953) called a "happy solution" to problems of living that seem otherwise insoluble (Bruch, 1973). In other words, an eating disorder diet serves as a way to avoid situations, real or imagined, that feel too frightening to face and attempt to resolve. Since the diet is more about creating a psychological diversion than losing pounds, there is no meaningful target weight. On the contrary, the diet must sustain itself or it loses its value.

Often encouraged by well meaning but otherwise uninformed family members and friends, an eating disorder diet assumes a powerful presence. As it is rewarded and "works" to solve problems, it becomes increasingly entrenched, and then its function, its capacity to distract or avoid, starts to generalize to other problems. Over time, it is not uncommon for purging behaviors to evolve to compensate for "slips," such as impulsive food binges or a lackadaisical exercise day.

The experience of an eating disorder changes dramatically during its course. It is psychologically accurate and therapeutically useful to conceptualize these changes in relational terms. At first, an eating disorder is experienced as a valued "friend," a secret companion that "helps" to intensify the diet. Little by little, as an eating disorder becomes more established, it begins to feel burdensome, like a "stern taskmaster" that requires increasing compliance with its rules and regulations. When an eating disorder is extremely severe, the internal experience is like being dominated by an abusive tyrant who demands constant attention to its dictates and harshly punishes "transgressions" with ever more stringent commands. At this point, someone's "relationship" with her eating disorder is often the single most significant relationship in her life.

As an eating disorder evolves, it tends to become "functionally autonomous" (Allport, 1961). In other words, eating disorder symptoms gradually lose their connection to the problems and vulnerabilities that stimulated their onset and begin to take on a life of their own, like ingrained habits with their own rhythms of expression. Consequently, most eating disorders are best understood as two different disorders. The initial or "primary" disorder results from the dynamic interaction between problems too frightening to face and the search for an absorbing diversion. The "secondary" disorder evolves due to generalization and reinforcement. It emerges gradually, causing symptomatic behaviors to become increasingly preoccupying. Effective individual psychotherapy requires therapeutic interventions that address disordered eating behaviors (the secondary disorder) and those that deal with significant psychodynamic issues (the primary disorder). Thus, treatment requires a dual focus, simultaneously addressing eating disorder symptoms and psychological reactions to emotional vulnerabilities.

(The goals of treatment are to help patients resolve the symptoms of their eating disorder, come to terms with the underlying emotional problems that led to their initial development, and develop the self-esteem and skills necessary to move ahead with meaningful living. To achieve these goals, it is crucial to create a therapeutic environment that is safe, reliable, and consistently caring. The actual content of treatment will vary from person to person, but the process of individual psychotherapy is most beneficial when it is active, personal, egalitarian, and collaborative. While eating disorder treatment can include psychodynamic, cognitive-behavioral, psychoeducational, and supportive interventions, the quality of the treatment relationship is the single most important element in recovery.)

Approach Eating Disorders as Ordinary Problems

When an eating disorder is described and thought about as an ordinary problem that needs to be resolved, just like any other problem that must be dealt with, it tends to "free" those who are associated with its development and ongoing course. This therapeutic approach parallels traditional medicine, in which an illness or injury is identified and diagnosed and then a treatment plan is devised to cure the illness or remediate the injury (Lock, LeGrange, Agras, & Dare, 2001). Throughout the medical treatment, all eyes are on fixing the problem regardless of how or why it occurred. These are secondary concerns, relevant to be sure, but primarily in relation to the prevention of future illness or injury. During eating disorder treatment, this kind of thinking contributes to healing because it encourages open, consistent, and nonjudgmental collaboration.

In contrast, it is all too common for eating disorders to be viewed primarily as a sign of serious, damaging emotional conflicts. This perspective, often shared by therapists, patients, and family members, can easily break down into a nontherapeutic morass of blame and defensiveness. Especially in psychodynamic psychotherapy and at the outset of treatment, the best-intended (even accurate) interpretations can precipitate intense feelings of guilt or resentment in both patients and parents, leading to a pretense of compliance or fierce resistance. Rushing in to identify, or imply, that the central issue (i.e., the "source" of the problem) is a neglectful mother, an enmeshed family, an abusive father, or a sexually confused and immature patient can be absolutely counterproductive to recovery.

All this is not to say emotional issues are irrelevant. On the contrary, they are extremely important, especially during the development and treatment of the primary disorder. However, it is just as important to realize that when therapists, either correctly or incorrectly, describe an eating disorder as something that has been brought about by certain conflicts or unresolved issues they risk undermining patient (and family) collaboration. The therapeutic skill here, most often demonstrated in the context of a hard-won and firmly established therapeutic relationship, is to explore origins gently without emphasizing or attributing blame.

Eating disorders are also frequently experienced, by both patients and families, as failures or deficiencies. This moral perspective implies that the development of an eating disorder is a "bad" thing, and that it is "wrong," perhaps even "dirty" or "yucky" to be diagnosed with such a condition. As a result, to have an eating disorder feels like having a stigma, creating a pervasive sense of secrecy and shame. This attitude is anathema to successful treatment because it undermines open, collaborative communication and encourages deceit and manipulation. Therapeutic neutrality is not helpful in the context of a moral perspective. Therapists need to challenge the idea that an eating disorder signifies something shameful and, when necessary, to do this over and over. Again, promoting the idea that eating disorders are "regular" problems, albeit serious ones that must be fixed, but after all, nothing that has to have extra meaning or "baggage," can be a useful therapeutic intervention, particularly at the beginning of treatment.

Work Hard to Engage the Patient

When someone suffering from anorexia or bulimia enters individual psychotherapy, she is almost always going to feel some trepidation. However much pain and torment the person is undergoing, due to purging or the need to follow rigid, unnatural guidelines regarding food and eating, she is also "hearing" inner voices that warn her not to trust therapy and the therapist. This is because patients with eating disorders usually know they have problems with food, weight, and dieting, and that an important goal of therapy is to overcome these problems. Inevitably, then, therapists are associated with eating more, eating without purging, weight gain, fears about fatness, and loss of control. Consequently, unlike other psychotherapy patients, a patient with an eating disorder is rarely motivated to cooperate with the therapist. In fact, therapists are viewed as threats, intent on stripping away the safe haven an eating disorder has provided. This is true even when the disorder has become very severe, resulting in an overwhelming preoccupation with symptoms. Attitudes and beliefs about therapy and therapists, or the "resistance," form the crux of the therapeutic problem and the key to recovery.

During initial sessions, therapists should anticipate being experienced as the "enemy." Individual psychotherapy will flounder, perhaps even fail right away, if the therapist assumes a traditional stance of passive, neutral

inquiry. The challenge for therapists is not to gather appropriate information or instigate meaningful exploration but to find a way to get beyond
the powerful resistance enveloping patients with eating disorders.

Imagine a filter or a thick mist surrounding the consciousness, attention, and interest of a patient with an eating disorder. The mist separates
the patient from the office environment and keeps her in connection with
vivid, persistent thoughts about her nightly meal or her daily exercise
regime. Then, think of a therapist waiting quietly to hear the patient's
response to an inquiry about family relationships; asking how she understands the coincidence of her freshman year in college and the onset of
dieting; or not saying anything at all, waiting for the patient to bring up
something. This is no contest. Even if the patient has an interest in participating in the session, this approach is not likely to succeed.

At the beginning of treatment, the therapist needs to grab the patient's
attention, to wrench her away from her relationship with eating disorder
symptoms and toward the other person in the room. Remaining aware of
appropriate boundaries, therapists can do this by acting in nontraditional
ways and by communicating their knowledge about eating disorders. Acting in a nontraditional manner gets the patient thinking and wondering
about you, so that she starts to experience the therapist's presence. The
actual content is not so much the point as is the cadence, the spontaneity, the
"non-plannedness" of the therapist's behavior. So, for example, in my first
session with Laura, I suddenly began to tell her in an earnest voice about my
interest in an upcoming sports event; during the third session with Diana, I
made a point of noticing her earrings and complimenting her jewelry-mak-
ing skills; and at the end of Jane's initial session, I told her it would be smart
for her to pay more attention to me than to her eating disorder.

The goal of demonstrating that you know about your patient's "problem" is twofold. First, it enables the patient to imagine that there is someone
out there who understands, so perhaps she is not as alone as she sometimes
feels. Second, it represents a threat of sorts. If the therapist really gets it,
then it is possible the therapist is going to know what is really going on with
symptoms and might even know how to interfere with them or take them
away. Feeling understood engenders both a promise of support and a sense
of foreboding. Either way, the patient is more likely to be aware of her therapist and therefore less enveloped by the shroud of her eating disorder.

Take Symptoms Seriously

When Alice first entered treatment with a 7-year history of bulimia, I told
her I imagined that she was grappling with her symptoms every day,
and that it was likely she thought about them constantly, perhaps more
than anything else. I said that this is what happens to almost everybody

who struggles with an eating disorder. At the same time, I let her know I wanted to hear all about her own particular experiences because each person develops a deeply personal relationship with symptoms.

In fact, eating disorder symptoms, the actual behaviors, as well as the ideas, beliefs, and emotions that surround them, come to dominate the patient's lived experience. At first, there is a playfulness, a kind of delicious secrecy about one's connection with eating disorders. Given enough time, however, this very same friendship turns into a sort of tormented slavery, in which patients feel trapped in a kind of hopeless, anguished depression, unable to imagine ever living a normal life.

As much as treatment must push through the fog of the eating disorder experience, it must also respect its existence. Therefore, with any patient, it is important to acknowledge symptoms, including the aching distress they may create. Especially at the beginning of treatment, it is not therapeutic to regard symptoms as phenomena to simply be "understood" and "interpreted." This is like taking a vital piece of internal experience and ignoring its impact, imposing one construction of reality on top of another, or calling the sky red instead of blue.

Eating disorder treatment moves forward when therapists meet patients on their own terms and respect their conscious, ongoing, often relentless preoccupations with body parts, fatness, fears of eating, purging rituals, and the like. Focusing on symptoms has several important therapeutic consequences. First, it helps the patient reveal herself, making the mostly secret relationship she has nurtured and then endured less "tight" or symbiotic. Also, an emphasis on the actual nature of symptomatic behaviors helps patients to feel less ashamed. Therapists who gloss over the details to "understand" the dynamic underpinnings of eating-disordered attitudes and behaviors risk communicating that symptoms themselves are not only rather unimportant but also quite dark and ugly. On the other hand, therapists who send the message, "I'm interested in what you're thinking, what you're doing, and how you're doing it," provide the opportunity to redefine symptoms as aspects of behavior that can be described and explored just like anything else. Finally, paying close attention to symptoms gives therapist and patient a chance to assess an eating disorder. This best measure of how someone is doing lies in knowing the ongoing strength and rigidity of symptomatic behaviors and the best way of assessing this is to know the specific details of the patient's experience.

Much of the time, working with symptoms is slow, not a particularly glamorous therapeutic activity. This aspect of treatment is about getting to know and then challenge the secondary disorder, usually over and over again. Cognitive behavioral techniques, such as reframing and self-monitoring are appropriate, as is support and some gentle "nudging." Sometimes, the goal is to create distance between patients and their eating disorder, to externalize it and raise awareness about the harm that symptoms can do, in contrast to the potential benefits of more adaptive behavior. At other times, therapists will have to work toward helping patients "own" their symptoms, to acknowledge that they are deeply involved in their symptomatic attitudes and behaviors, as opposed to being passive victims of them, so they can begin to accept responsibility for them and take charge of initiating changes.

Use Interpretations Sparingly and Without High Expectations

In the field of psychotherapy, especially dynamic psychotherapy, interpretations are regarded as the crux of treatment because they are thought to be responsible for insights, which in turn provide the raw material for psychological change. Among therapists, the time-honored assumption is that dynamic, meaningful, and functional connections exist between conscious experiences or behaviors and other experiences or behaviors that are unconscious or out of awareness. In general, interpretations are most likely to "work" when patients are psychologically minded and motivated to make use of what their therapists have to offer.

During eating disorder treatment, interpretations should be used cautiously, with careful consideration of the patient's relationship with her eating disorder and her commitment to change. When an eating disorder is deeply entrenched, a heavy dose of interpretations is more likely to create therapist frustration than patient insight. This is because patients with eating disorders often do not want to collaborate with their therapists or even to consider what they are being offered. Or, they do not have the capacity, the psychological space, to hear an interpretation amid the ongoing din of symptomatic thoughts and feelings.

When interpretations are understood to be the major "tool" of psychotherapy and they have no discernible impact, therapists are at risk for strong countertransference reactions. These include intense anxiety and inadequacy, which can set off counterproductive feelings of neediness, frustration, helplessness, and futility, leading sometimes to premature termination. In effect, therapists who rely on interpretations need to prepare themselves to be "rejected" by their patients with eating disorders.

The work I did with one of my first such patients aptly illustrates the problems that can accompany too many interpretations. During our first several sessions, Valerie revealed that she was bulimic. Since she expressed a great deal of shame about purging, we agreed to focus on reducing the number of times she vomited. Somewhat to my surprise, she was able to do this, but at the same time she began to restrict her food intake. Soon, she was visibly thinner. I was sure I understood what was happening and made numerous interpretations about her extremely conflicted transference, some that addressed her idealization of me and others that emphasized her hostile, envious feelings toward me. I offered these interpretations, convinced they would have a positive impact on her condition.

On the contrary, Valerie continued to lose weight. Typically, she acknowledged what I had to say but did not seem able to use it. There was something "wrong" or disconnected in our relationship. I began to feel terrible, resentful of Valerie for not getting any better and desperate to find some inkling of understanding that would finally have an impact. However, nothing I had to offer made any difference, and finally Valerie was hospitalized due to her low weight. We never resumed our work together.

Clearly, Valerie was not ready to consider the interpretations I used to construct an understanding of her psychology. However truthful or realistic they may have been, they were, at the least, premature and too heavily freighted with my belief that they would be instrumental to her progress. Just as traditional inquiry is sometimes not powerful enough to engage patients with an eating disorder, so also are traditional psychodynamic interpretations not strong enough to have an effect on an eating-disordered psyche. Regardless of the quality of the interpretations, no matter how "on target" and well timed, there may not be an "aha." They simply will not register.

Even worse, resistant patients with eating disorders may appear to take an interest in their therapists' offerings to keep treatment away from the issues that really matter: thoughts, feelings, and behaviors related to food, weight, and dieting. This explains why so many patients in their second or third treatment experience claim to understand their eating disorder and yet have not made any real behavioral changes. In short, therapists are well served to keep their insights close to the vest until their patients are not struggling as much with the preoccupations of the secondary disorder.

Look for Opportunities to Provide Psychoeducation

In contrast to the psychological and psychodynamic insight offered by interpretations, psychoeducation provides a more mundane kind of understanding, and yet it can play a crucial part in effective psychotherapy. Psychoeducating means teaching by giving patients information that is psychologically relevant and important. Sometimes this is hard, factual information, and sometimes it is really more like informed opinion.

As mentioned, patients with an eating disorder need to know that their therapist knows about their problems. When a therapist provides accurate information about anorexia or bulimia, it feels reassuring and contributes to a feeling of safety in the therapeutic relationship. In contrast, when a therapist asks a patient to explain the ins and outs of her eating disorder, it can create fearful, lost, or contemptuous feelings toward the therapist and the therapy. Furthermore, in spite of being enmeshed with symptoms, many patients do not have very much real knowledge about their condition. They may not know, for example, that as many as 80% of patients with an eating disorder recover over the course of 10 years (Strober, Freeman, & Morrell, 1997); that, in general, it takes about 3,500 calories in excess of normal maintenance over the course of 1 week to gain 1 pound (Ravussin & Bogardus, 1992); or that there is increasing evidence that genetics may play an important part in a predisposition to anorexia (Johnson, 2005). This information helps because it demystifies an eating disorder, placing it in a broader context that invites more rational, realistic thinking. In turn, patients are more likely to question their relationship with their eating disorder and think about it in a less-secretive or magical manner.

Finally, and extremely important, patients with an eating disorder are usually quite good at taking care of others and quite incompetent about taking care of themselves. When it comes to their own needs, they are likely to be silent and either unwilling or too frightened to be openly curious and ask pertinent questions. As a result, these patients often look and act as if they know more than they do, causing them to feel like imposters and intensifying feelings of inadequacy and insecurity. A therapist who provides actual information about actual issues in a patient's actual life helps the patient gather important facts that can boost self-confidence and, over time, encourage her to risk asking for herself. Moreover, this kind of personally relevant psychoeducation highlights the importance of a real relationship in the real world, as opposed to an internal relationship with eating disorder symptoms.

Opportunities to offer psychoeducation abound during individual psychotherapy. These are a few examples: role-playing a job interview and going over how to improve credibility; editing an essay for a college application; discussing how to drive a stick shift car; suggesting how to deal with a loving but overly intrusive mom; demonstrating how to express anger; practicing how to ask a roommate if she wants to go out or share an apartment next year; and so on.

In general, issues about being female, dating, and sexuality are perhaps the most meaningful psychoeducational topics for patients with eating disorders. Arguably, this area of living is central to the development of every young woman, and some believe it is critical in the etiology of most eating disorders (e.g. Crisp, 1995). Nonetheless, entire psychotherapies and residential treatments for eating disorders can take place without much attention to sex, body parts, and bodily sensations, makeup, how to dress seductively or demurely, saying no at the right time, feeling okay about saying yes, or figuring out how and when to discuss intimacy and love (S. Zimmer, personal communication, October 11, 2007). This is like coaching a football quarterback but neglecting to mention much about passing, or tutoring a would-be college student for the Scholastic Aptitude Tests and ignoring the subject of math. Psychotherapy for eating disorders must include discussions of the multiple ways in which sexuality can and should be a concern for eating disorder patients. Therapists need to help patients to express their thoughts, feelings, and questions about sexuality; to discover what they need to know; and to support them as they begin to navigate what is often new and uncertain territory.

Indeed, especially in the treatment of adolescent and young adult females, when attempting to offer psychoeducational information about sexuality, therapists must recognize that this entire area can be charged with a fear of the unknown and tainted by a multitude of negative, humiliating associations. Male therapists, in particular, need to proceed gently and with ongoing attention to appropriate boundaries, and they must remain ever sensitive to the culturally derived impact of their gender, resisting occasions to act in a way that reinforces a "power over" or exploitive relationship. On the other hand, female therapists need to be alert for how their own conflicts may interfere with a capacity to approach the topic of sexuality, resulting in a minimum of discussion or inhibiting patients from exploring their own sexual curiosity and desire.

Be Very Aware of the Process of Therapy

The way an eating disorders therapist approaches treatment and relates to patients, that is, the ongoing "process" of psychotherapy, is crucial to successful outcome. Indeed, it is not too much to say that this is a necessary, if not sufficient, condition for effective treatment.

A traditional psychiatric approach to individual therapy, characterized in the extreme by a white-coated doctor who behaves as a distant, aloof "expert" cautiously assessing and separately concluding how best to direct the process, is counterproductive. It strengthens resistance and undermines treatment because it creates an impersonal, hierarchal therapeutic relationship.

At the beginning of treatment, many people diagnosed with eating disorders, including some with several courses of previous therapy, may not be very knowledgeable about what's going to happen during their sessions. Typically, therefore, in addition to the general threat therapists may represent, patients are uneasy about "how it will go." In these circumstances, it is very important to allay anxiety about the unknown. By engendering a formal, impersonal, and rather cold therapist-patient interaction, the traditional approach achieves just the opposite.

Furthermore, as a result of its separated or disconnected and "expert" nature, the traditional approach tends to produce a sense of being imposed on, as if the therapist is going to "act on" the patient. Although patients with an eating disorder almost always know, deep down, that they are stuck in a serious dilemma, one that sometimes seems almost impossible to endure, they are highly unlikely to accept help when it feels controlling. Indeed, this prospect raises the horrendous specter of becoming helpless and powerless, of unstoppable weight gain and deep humiliation.

The most effective way to approach and conduct eating disorder therapy is to maintain an open, friendly, warm, and personal stance with patients. This helps to establish and promote the sense that therapy is a collaborative venture, a joint effort to share thoughts and feelings, experiences, and expertise to find ways and means to resolve the problem.

At the outset of therapy this kind of therapeutic stance means taking time to explain candidly the course and goals of treatment. In the first or second session, I always find a way to describe what I am going to try to accomplish during therapy, such as to reduce or eliminate eating disorder symptoms and to make it possible to get back to living in a hopeful and meaningful way. Also, I often explain that I am going to try to make this happen by building a strong connection with my patient, one that will turn out to be more important and valuable than the one she has had with the eating disorder.

To be open, friendly, warm, and personal means to convey a genuine interest in a kindly, gentle way. It means being calm and focused as well as patient and determined. More often than not, it also means revealing your actual feelings about a patient's general situation, or about a specific circumstance the patient reports, in an unconcealed manner. The point is to be a person, albeit one with particular expertise, with another person, one struggling with some problems, sharing and working together to find solutions.

In regard to being open, frequently it is helpful to invite questions from patients. To ask what a patient might want to know about you at the beginning of treatment, or about your reaction to such and such event during any particular later session, is to encourage the patient's awareness of your presence, stimulate curiosity, and demonstrate your willingness to be a "real " person with her.

Self-disclosure, whether in response to a patient's question or freely offered, is not necessarily a problem or psychologically damaging unless it is obviously so. Granted, and for good reason, appropriate professional and personal boundaries must be respected and maintained during all individual psychotherapy. Therapists who abuse patients, whether verbally or otherwise, or who use self-disclosures in the service of their own narcissistic or self-destructive needs are absolutely wrong.

However, it is also true that self-disclosure can contribute to the effectiveness of eating disorder treatment when it is woven into the ongoing fabric of the therapeutic relationship. It can help to deepen the importance of the therapeutic relationship, model normative behaviors, demonstrate that it is possible to be comfortable with authenticity, provide needed reassurance and reality testing, and affirm that all people are more simply human than otherwise (Sullivan, 1953).

Rely on the Impact of the Treatment Relationship

Ultimately, the influence of the therapeutic relationship is most responsible for real change in both the primary and secondary eating disorder. The reason to work hard at engaging patients, take symptoms seriously, use interpretations sparingly, offer significant psychoeducational information, and conduct therapy in a caring, personal manner is to construct a therapeutic relationship that is more compelling than the relationship a patient has with the eating disorder.

When a therapist is persistently kind and caring, takes a patient's inner experiences seriously, and does not attempt to force psychological explanations regarding what someone feels or does, a kind of haven is created, one that is not increasingly harsh, demanding, and exhausting as is the case with an eating disorder. On the contrary, it is calming and soothing, a place where it is possible to feel safe, rather than threatened and badgered.

Furthermore, when a therapist offers advice and information regarding real-life skills that have a noticeably positive effect on a patient's life, the realistic "value" of treatment is heightened. This value added is in contrast to the difficulties, conflicts, and bleakness that, over time, are all that an eating disorder has to offer.

In short, when a therapist demonstrates that a therapeutic connection is more attractive, psychologically and practically, than an eating disorder connection, patients are more willing to give up their resistance to treatment (Levenkron, 1982). Once the resistance is relinquished, they are much more likely to cooperate with their therapists in a collaborative effort to reduce symptoms and, similarly, much more likely to participate in a joint effort to understand the origins of their disorder. Overcoming the resistance by steadfastly emphasizing the value of the therapeutic relationship is the key to effective psychotherapy for eating disorders.

Conclusion

The treatment of eating disorders is a difficult, yet extremely rewarding venture. Individual psychotherapists who treat anorexia nervosa, bulimia nervosa, and EDNOS with prominent anorexic or bulimic features need to remain focused on actually making a difference as treatment proceeds. Based on my clinical experience, this chapter attempts to specify and elucidate several of the therapeutic stances, themes, and emphases that make a genuine contribution to healing and eventual recovery.

References

Allport, G. W. (1961). *Pattern and growth in personality.* New York: Holt, Rinehart and Winston.

Bruch, H. (1973). *Eating disorders: Obesity, anorexia nervosa and the person within.* New York: Basic Books.

Crisp, A. H. (1995). *Let me be.* London: Psychology Press.

Davis, W. N. (2005). *The Renfrew Center: Current treatment perspectives.* Unpublished manuscript.

Johnson, C. (2005, November 7–10). *Something new, something old.* Paper presented at the Fifteenth Annual Renfrew Center Foundation Conference, Philadelphia, November 7–10, 2005.

Levenkron, S. (1982). *Treating and overcoming anorexia nervosa.* New York: Scribners.

Lock, J., LeGrange, D., Agras, S. W., & Dare, C. (2001). *Treatment manual for anorexia nervosa: A family-based approach.* New York: Guilford Press.

Ravussin, E., & Bogardus, C. (1992). A brief overview of human energy metabolism and its relationship to essential obesity. *American Journal of Clinical Nutrition, 55,* 242–245.

Strober, M., Freeman, R., & Morrell, W. (1997). The long-term course of severe anorexia nervosa in adolescents: Survival analysis of recovery, relapse, and outcome predictors over 10–15 years in a prospective study. *International Journal of Eating Disorders, 22,* 339–360.

Sullivan, H. S. (1953). *The interpersonal theory of psychiatry.* New York: Norton.

U.S. Department of Health and Human Services. (2006). *Evidence report/technology assessment, number 135: Management of eating disorders* (HRQ Publication 06-E010). Rockville, MD: Agency for Healthcare Research and Quality.

Witton, N. S., Leichner, P., Sandhu-Sahota, P., & Filippelli, D. (2007). The research directions survey: Patient and parent perspectives of eating disorders research. *Eating Disorders: The Journal of Treatment and Prevention, 15,* 205–217.

chapter four

Developing Body Trust
A Body-Positive Approach to Treating Eating Disorders

Deb Burgard

Introduction

Of the many cruelties inflicted by an eating disorder, surely one of the worst is the steady corrosion to the sufferer's partnership with her body. The demands of an eating disorder intensify the "normative discontent" experienced by women in Western culture. The split between the part of the self that identifies with trying to be thinner, and the unruly, embattled "body self," grows wider and more vicious with every cycle of bingeing and purging, every contested carbohydrate gram, every weight loss and regain, indeed, every body battle, won or lost.

The fact that current standards of beauty dictate that women be unusually thin means that most women will experience a dissonance between their biology and their desire to be socially powerful through conventional beauty (Rodin, 1993). If we plotted the body mass index (BMI) of a population of people practicing a healthy lifestyle, we would see that, like most other biological traits, BMI assumes the normal (bell) curve; that is, people practicing healthy lifestyles do not all weigh the same per unit of height (Bacon, Stern, Van Loan, & Keim, 2005). In other words, the desirable degree of thinness is the result of a healthy lifestyle for only a tiny minority of the population. The rest of the people are faced with a dilemma that is vaguely perceived but usually never faced directly: Either abandon a healthy lifestyle in favor of draconian and, possibly, frankly eating-disordered practices or figure out a way to have a satisfying life at one's genetic weight. Most people, even medical professionals, and sometimes even eating disorder specialists, do not see the choice in these terms, continuing to subscribe instead to the myths that we can choose our weight, that a healthy lifestyle will automatically lead to one's desired weight, and that failing to lose weight must mean there is something wrong with our bodies (Saguy & Riley, 2005).

The typical experience of dieting reinforces many of these myths. When one first begins a diet and motivation is strong, weight loss is the easiest. When the stresses of life inevitably intrude and maintaining a rigid eating plan becomes more difficult, or when there are emotional conflicts that claim the dieter's focus, lapses in dieting occur, often at just about the time one's body begins to mount a metabolic defense against further weight loss. As a result, it can seem like the cultural teachings are true about fat being the "evidence" of unacceptable feelings breaking through discipline, and how if one could just stay in that disciplined, confident mood, one could diet easily. And, it can seem true that one's body is the enemy, searching for a lapse in vigilance to sabotage the goal of being thinner. Even though the process is the same for the overwhelming majority of dieters, each dieter individually maintains the belief that the diet's failure is a personal one, confirmation that she is not strong enough and vigilant enough to vanquish the body's agenda to make the shameful fat self visible to all. So, we convince ourselves that if this is what happens to all women who diet, it must be true that there is something inherently shameful and wrong about women's bodies.

The Cultural Context

Many ideas in Western patriarchal culture form the context for a pervasive distrust of women's bodies and desires. Most significantly, fat is symbolic of a negative feminine archetype, representing neediness, depression, passivity, lack of control, and lack of vigilance (Gard & Wright, 2005). Even many men who are fat experience their fatness as feminizing, and therefore shameful, in the same way our heteronormative world feminizes and derides the sexual orientation of gay men. One reason why thinness is so prized in the gay community may be to ward off the danger of being seen as feminine. The prizing of leanness is certainly one important reason why eating disorder pathology seems to be so common in the gay men's community (Russell & Keel, 2002).

Eating disorders are complex—they could not exist without a cultural context that sets up a dissonance between biology and social norms that overvalue thinness; indeed, they might not exist at all in a cultural context that did not connect shame and femininity, yet they do not happen for every person in spite of prevalent cultural messages. The development of an eating disorder seems to require the internalization of these norms as gospel truth. When a person believes the "good" self is active, disciplined, and confident, feelings of being inert, out of control, or vulnerable are likely to be relegated to a "bad," unwanted self. If the culture teaches that these "negative" feelings are embodied in and represented by fat, the stage is set to assume that, in fact, the bad self is essentially the fat self. This is why most American women know the meaning of "I feel so fat today," even though "fat" is not a feeling. If the negative female stereotype is associated with being out of control, and fat means female, the corollary is that by controlling one's fatness, one can control the fat/bad self, both its internal experience and its visibility to others.

Moreover, the internalization of these antifemale and antifat attitudes means that girls and women are likely to blame their own bodies and appearance for the painful interpersonal events they experience. It is a small logical leap to believe that perfecting one's body into a lean, minimally fat shape will protect you from social humiliation and hostility, if not make you the envy of other girls, respected and admired for this accomplishment.

In light of these deeply entrenched cultural attitudes, it is no surprise that eating disorders are more pervasive than ever. What is interesting to note, however, is how little attention is given in most eating disorder treatment protocols to the relationship with one's body. Indeed, the concept of the sufferer's relationship with her body is notably absent from most definitions of recovery as well. But, an unsolved adversarial attitude toward one's body, even in the absence of eating disorder symptoms, undermines a woman's well-being in numerous ways. It is like remaining in an abusive relationship: Even if there is no overt physical violence, the loss of the richness and security of what could be is devastating.

Process and Goals of Treatment

For there to be true recovery from an eating disorder, the relationship with one's body must be healed. In this respect, I am probably much more ambitious for my clients than the typical eating disorder specialist. I am not aiming for simple "symptom relief." I want to help my patients heal the relationship with their bodies, to trust their bodies as a treasured partner in living a good life.

No single chapter can convey the variety and richness of the actual therapeutic process with individuals, but I try to pull out the "body positive" thread of theory and experiential work that is usually part of my work. I am giving much too little space to the development of a therapeutic alliance, the actual relationship, the use of the patient's particular historical experiences, and so much more. I hope that this particular thread concerning a person's relationship with her body, and the process of building trust, will combine with the insights of the other authors in this book to create a tapestry that conveys the poignancy and complexity of eating disorders treatment.

In the beginning of treatment, I am getting to know the person, and we are looking for patterns together, defining the focus for our work, talking over what the vision of "better" might look like. I make a point of reminding a new patient that I cannot tell by looking at her what she might be doing with food or exercise, and that in my experience, symptoms of restricting, bingeing, and purging have been present in people at every conceivable weight. Sometimes, this is the first time the person has been explicitly told that it is her unique experience, not her body size, that will be the focus of our interest.

I am listening to her and also weaving in a lot of theory and information about the science of eating disorders, mammalian weight dynamics, cultural history, relationship dynamics, and so on. I am relating the principles of a health at every size (HAES) approach (Burgard, in press), which takes a person's day-to-day practices as the centerpiece of consideration rather than the number on the scale. HAES assumes that the size a person is when she is doing the practices that support health is, by definition, her healthy weight. The number on the scale is an outcome that we cannot know ahead of time; we cannot choose the number, we can only choose our day-to-day practices and be honest about what is sustainable in our unique lives.

I usually give the person a set of assessments to take home to get a better idea of her history, attitudes, and symptoms. I include a questionnaire that asks the things I have not yet found on standardized assessment forms. Among these are the following:

- Her own goals for therapy.
- Medical concerns she believes are related to her weight.
- Intent to lose weight now.
- Weight (and weight loss) history.
- Her explanation for why she is at her current weight.
- Things she is postponing until she reaches a different weight.
- How much she believes that she can choose her weight.
- What she thinks would happen to her weight if she ate according to body cues.
- Whether she can allow her weight to fluctuate during recovery.
- The attitudes of important people in her life about her weight.
- The body sizes of biological relatives and her own body size as a child.
- Experiences of discrimination or stereotyping.
- The extent to which she has body experiences that are typical of someone below or above her set point.

- How much she uses her body to make choices about when to start and stop eating, and whether she tends to eat before or after those cues or stop before or after those cues and why.
- How much she eats when distracted.

Because we are focusing on replacing the eating disorder symptoms with the day-to-day practices that will support her health, I also ask about

- How much she enjoys physical activity and sees herself as person who likes to move.
- The quality of her sleep (since a significant minority of my patients *across the weight spectrum*, when urged to get tested by me, have been diagnosed with apnea).
- Whether she feels like she can need other people and whether they are reliable supports.

After the person fills out and returns the questionnaire, her experience with it and her responses become the core of further discussions. She is also bringing in her day-to-day experiences and concerns for exploration and guidance. We tend to return over and over to a few extremely important conceptual matters, such as (a) a more productive way to think about body image; (b) the challenge of weight neutrality; (c) the renunciation of the fantasy of being thin; (d) dealing with the cultural attitudes in the media, family, and friends; and (e) how to eat.

Rethinking Body Image

Most models of body image have looked at either the mental picture of one's body size and shape or the attitude about its size, shape, or parts. But, it seems more useful to think of body image as the relationship with the part of the self that identifies with the body. When women stand in front of the mirror and make disparaging remarks about their thighs, butt, and belly, they act like no one is there to hear it. But they are hearing it, and the part of them that feels a sense of ownership for those thighs, butt, and belly is shamed.

The relationship between our conscious self and our "body self" is like any other; it can be functional or not. Most people assume that to alleviate their body image distress, they should work on making their bodies prettier and therefore easier to accept. This might be termed "makeover mind," and it is the basis for innumerable magazine articles and TV shows. But, consider this demand in the context of a relationship: "I can't like you, I won't take care of you, and I won't stop insulting you unless you lose weight." It would be more likely to cause alienation than inspire cooperation and affection.

The feelings of despair, hostility, sabotage, and frustration, which are so typical of eating disorders, are all predictable consequences of this demand to lose weight to be acceptable. What exactly are the possible responses to "Lose weight so I can find you acceptable"? Any or all of the following may occur within the psyche of the eating disorder sufferer: "OK, I'll try to be acceptable to you" (e.g., try to restrict, be perfect, lose weight, tone up); "Screw you" (i.e., get angry and binge); "Please accept me for who I am" (i.e., feel anxious when weight loss does occur); "I want you to love me as I am" (i.e., regain weight to see if the love is unconditional and reliable); "I'm so lonely" (i.e., feel depressed and alienated); or "Fine, then I won't need anything from you or anyone" (i.e., pretend you aren't hungry, display your bones to the world as evidence that you can live on air alone). By looking at what is going on in a relational way between the parts of self, we can understand why simply meeting the demand of becoming thinner does not solve anything.

Weight Neutrality

The HAES approach to treating eating and weight concerns is perhaps most controversial in its refusal to make the pursuit of weight loss a central focus. Instead, the focus is on the development of lifelong practices that support health and contribute to quality of life. In this respect, HAES is built on a trust that an individual's healthiest weight is the weight at which her body settles when she is living a healthy life. Practitioners of HAES do not shy away from the fact that most people need to choose *either* their health or the "desirable" number on the scale and will not be able to have both. HAES is weight neutral in this regard; unlike medical recommendations about what to weigh based on large population studies, HAES allows each individual to do the experiment of taking care of themselves and finding out what they weigh when they do. If what that person would need to do to have an "ideal" weight is not healthy, how can that be her healthy weight? HAES treatment models body trust in this way: The therapist is not undermining the development of a process-oriented solution by protesting that there should be a different weight result.

Relinquishing the Fantasy of the Thin Future

Because our culture is so relentless in its message that all problems can be solved with weight loss, most people seeking treatment for eating disorders have to confront the way they have poured all their hopes and dreams into the "solution" of being thin. The project of perfecting the body robs girls and women, and increasingly boys and men, of a normal developmental life path. The rich lessons in understanding one's self, trying out different interests, solving interpersonal problems, and learning to contribute to the world are sacrificed to the day-to-day rituals of counting calories, fat grams, carbs, and reps; monitoring the scale; anxiously thinking about threats to the rigid plan for the day; and so on. Any hopes and dreams about the future are tied to the achievement of this perfect body, which can somehow solve every uncertainty and danger.

Giving up this bulwark against the unknown threats ahead is terrifying and requires a long, slow process of going back and "growing" whatever got skipped, ignored, or neglected in the person's developmental history. It is only the real skills of life that trump the eating disorder symptoms and provide a lasting strategy for coping. Giving up the fantasy of the thin future may also feel like giving up the hopes and dreams that a person has associated with it, and this can be a source of considerable grief. But, finding out that one's dreams do not have to depend on a thin future is one of the most exciting and liberating aspects of recovery.

Dealing With Cultural Attitudes

Most of my patients obsess nearly constantly about the meaning, whether accurate or not, that they imagine their body size projects to other people. It is enormously helpful to acknowledge the fact of stereotyping and stigma based on weight across the weight spectrum. One patient may elicit the stereotype of the "perfect girl" because she is blonde and slender, while another patient elicits the "bookish loser" because she is fatter and wears glasses. During treatment, we talk a great deal about "stereotype management skills" or, more simply, lessons in coping mechanisms for people who are members of stereotyped groups.

In keeping with the focus on the body, I use an analogy to the immune system called the "emotional immune system." Like the physical immune system, our emotional immune system deals with threats, asking the question, "Is this foreign or familiar?" If a person has internalized the outside attitudes against female and fat bodies, it is more likely that the interpersonal and environmental insults to her will pass the emotional immune system's boundary and wound her more deeply than a person who has recognized those attitudes as external, noxious, and rejectable. Having a sociocultural perspective allows the person from the stereotyped group to recognize the insult as "foreign" and mount an emotional defense. It may sting, but it will not pass the internal boundary and resonate with one's own truth, which would be immeasurably more damaging.

The other category of stereotype management skills constitutes the ability to show up through the fog of the stereotype. One of the most exciting developments in the recovery of a person with an eating disorder occurs when she stops trying to be accepted by meeting the agenda of the other person and instead pours her energy into showing up as her real self in order to be truly known. This also is a process that starts with her knowing her own truth. Having her body as a partner is essential to this goal because it is within her body that she experiences her feelings, her yearnings, her anxiety, and her appetites. It is also essential to experience her body's logic and legitimacy as an initial model for the self.

It should be noted that stereotyping can create different kinds of demands on patients with eating disorders. A woman might have a body that meets the cultural standard for attractiveness, but there is no guarantee that this makes it easy for her to show up. In fact, quite a few patients have historically already been slender and gotten trapped into eating disorder behavior to be even thinner. They talk about believing that having a perfect body will solve everything, so if they feel lousy about themselves, they must need to weigh even less. When these people eat according to their bodies, they are likely to stay thin and be deemed acceptable by their culture. Their task may be more to find a sense of entitlement to be their unique selves, someone other than who was prescribed. If you look like a homecoming queen, can you really allow yourself to be a physics professor? A lesbian? Unhappy or unsettled? Anything except what your dear parents are hoping for? Can you let yourself know who you are and risk the loss of the pretty-girl privilege?

On the other hand, if your healthy body size is larger than culturally prescribed, like most women, you may have had the repetitive experience of being marginalized. Many of these people have dieted into socially acceptable weight ranges and then regained weight. There may be a fundamental sense of not belonging, and to eat according to your body cues means you will have a larger-than-acceptable body. How do you claim that body and take good care of it? How do you value your own experience enough to go against the myths of the culture? How do you value your self that is being devalued by stereotyping? How do you attribute the diet-induced binges to the process of dieting rather than being intrinsic to your own body when the culture is saying that your body's appetites are dangerous, and you must have no self-control if you are not thin?

Remedial Eating

One practical difficulty during eating disorders recovery is to learn how to make decisions about food that are not related to weight loss. Most of my patients have extensive nutritional knowledge but little memory of the skills they were born with in determining hunger and satiety. Interestingly, the use of body cues to decide about when to stop and start eating, and what to eat, can be an important vehicle for healing the relationship with one's body. Instead of seeing the body as a saboteur of the mind's agenda to be thinner, the body can be experienced as a reliable moderating influence on the wild swings originating in the mind's psychology between being good or bad, in or out of control, compliant or rebellious, and so on.

The definition of what is normal for eating is surprisingly elusive. Most eating disorder treatment protocols rely on a nutritionist to define a plan for the patient and rarely delineate what kind of eating patterns constitute evidence of "recovered" eating. I have always shared this conceptualization with patients:

> Normal eating is being able to eat when you are hungry and continue eating until you are satisfied. It is being able to choose food you like and eat it and truly get enough of it—not just stop eating because you think you should. Normal eating is being able to use some moderate constraint in your food selection to get the right food, but not being so restrictive that you miss out on pleasurable foods. Normal eating is giving yourself permission to eat sometimes because you are happy, sad or bored, or just because it feels good. Normal eating is three meals a day or it can be choosing to munch along. It is leaving some cookies on the plate because you know you can have some again tomorrow, or it is eating more now because they taste so wonderful when they are fresh. Normal eating is overeating at times: feeling stuffed and uncomfortable. It is also undereating at times and wishing you had more. *Normal eating is trusting your body to make up for your mistakes in eating* [emphasis added]. Normal eating takes up some of your time and attention but keeps its place as only one important area in your life. In short, normal eating is flexible. It varies in response to your emotions, your schedule, your hunger, and your proximity to food. (Satter, 1987, pp. 69–70)

Again, "Normal eating is trusting your body to make up for your mistakes in eating." This sums up what is missing from most attempts to define normal eating in terms of the frequency and content of meals and the types and amounts of calories. If we see our bodies as the enemy, there is no room for "mistakes" since only our will can rescue us. But, our bodies are actually quite good at regulating around homeostatic points for temperature, hydration, and yes, weight. If our culture did not set up a dissonance between our biology and our aesthetics, perhaps eating would be as uncomplicated as any other biological need that occurs throughout the day. What if a woman demonstrated control over her wayward body by only urinating once a day? Perhaps then we would have a diagnosis for peeing disorders, peeing disorder treatment programs and research on peeing disorder prevention and psychotherapy.

Finding the Parent Within

One of the exciting things about eating disorder treatment is that using the body's hunger and satiety cues is both an alternative to eating disordered thinking and a way to heal the relationship between one's self and body. If one is not going to do whatever it takes to be a certain weight because what it takes is throwing up, fasting, or excessive exercise, then how does one decide when to start and stop eating? The answer is turning within, to the entity that was most distrusted. This process is usually fraught but rewarding.

It should be noted that "listening to your body" is not just about developing awareness of hunger and satiety; it is also about taking action based on that awareness, that is, being responsive or attuned. A person might protest that she does not want to become aware of when she is hungry or full because she would be unwilling to act on it anyway, and so she feels there is no point in knowing. Or, she might be quite aware of her internal cues but determined to demonstrate to her unruly body self that its needs are irrelevant. This is like a parent who has an agenda independent of the child, who cannot coordinate his or her actions with his or her child's demands. Whatever is causing a person to take this stance is worth investigating further; it could be a reenactment of the person's own experience of her parents or representative of how she parented herself during a neglected childhood. Hopefully, the exploration will lead to the meanings that are driving the behaviors and, as a result, a chance to try something new.

For some patients, the process of listening to one's body becomes a new diet rule. They set up physical hunger as the sole justification for eating and unleash the familiar self-punishing thoughts if they eat for other reasons. This type of response to the body is also a reflection of a person's capacity to parent herself. I might remind someone in this situation about Satter's definition of normal eating (1987) and reiterate the importance of trusting her body to make up for "mistakes" in much the same way that a parent has to trust that their child will be "okay" if the child falls down. Sometimes, patients are not willing to avoid self-policing activities long enough to discover whether their fears are realized (e.g., whether their weight will change), so their fear of gaining weight (or the way they will feel if they do) remains in place. For these people, evidence that the process can be trusted comes ultimately from the recognition that when they try to be kinder to themselves, their eating disorder symptoms calm down. They can see that something relational is happening, and the metaphor of parenting oneself makes intuitive sense.

Frequently, it is when people have the opportunity to experience a nurturing, caregiving self that they can begin to loosen the grasp of the internal dictator. This can happen, for example, when someone risks breaking a rule and then is able to deal with the ensuing punitive thoughts in a different way. One Rice Krispies treat too many? Two pints of ice cream after husband went to bed? Whatever it is, it does not matter. Many times a person reports an angry, critical reaction, such as, "You lazy fool, WHY did you do that?" But then, we use the event as an opportunity to actually be curious. I try to change the frame to engage the person in a gentler, collaborative process. "What if you were really trying to find out why you did that? It seems important to know why. Let's assume you must have a good reason, even if it is one that remains hidden to the part of you that is so mad right now."

Many people have come back to therapy the following week and said, "It can't be that simple, that I just need to be kinder to myself." They are surprised at how much better they felt when they showed themselves that their feelings are worth investigating. It gives hope to the part of them that is painfully aware of what it feels like to communicate in the behavior of the eating disorder: hope that this is not the only way to communicate and not the only way to be cared for.

Most people with eating disorders expect to be told in therapy that they are too self-indulgent, and they express the hope that therapy will make them better dieters, more able to restrict without bingeing, or better at needing less to live on the planet. In fact, most people with eating disorders are starving for what they really need, regardless of what their body size might be. They need help developing all the other ways of caring for themselves that humans have discovered. Having a body is the most concrete way to be reminded that we need, that we are not machines and not spirits living off air. Learning to respond to one's body is an essential first step to developing a functional relationship with one's self.

After some time of using hunger and satiety cues, most patients begin to reliably experience a sense of their body's agenda. They are usually surprised at the modesty of their body's demands, especially in light of the perceptions they had held of their body's unpredictable and wild appetites. Gradually, it becomes clearer when their bodies are not the source of the urge to eat. The demand is there, but for something else: a need that is going unmet, which may have nothing to do with food.

Listening to our bodies in making eating decisions is like throwing a pebble in a pond. We start with the question, "Am I hungry?" but the inquiry ripples and is unlikely to end there. Once there is a responsive, interested internal parent and a more definite self that has opinions that can be known, the sky is the limit. For example, "I'm not hungry but I am tired. Maybe I need to take a nap." Or, "Do I want to go out tonight or stay in?" "Do I really want to be pre-med?" "What was that uneasiness I felt with that guy yesterday?" "Who do I love?" "What is my purpose on the planet?"

Throughout treatment, my patients and I regularly return to the themes of the self and the body self, or the internal parent and the internal child, but of course each person is actually experiencing both sides of the interaction. Perhaps it is the more benign, mutually enhancing dynamic of their interaction that is the real source of healing. The self that is responding to the body's hunger with food is reliable and caring; the body that is predictable in its needs and a constant partner in the quest to enact one's human will is a precious companion and literal home for our time on Earth. Wherever we were before we were born, and wherever we are going after, while we are here we depend on our bodies to make it possible.

References

Bacon, L., Stern, J., Van Loan, M., & Keim, N. (2005). Size acceptance and intuitive eating improve health for obese, female chronic dieters. *Journal of the American Dietetic Association, 105*, 929–936.

Burgard, D. (in press). Health at every size. In S. Solovay & E. Rothblum (Eds.). *The fat studies reader*. New York: New York University Press.

Gard, M., & Wright, J. (2005). *The obesity epidemic: Science, morality and ideology*. New York: Routledge.

Rodin, J. (1993). Cultural and psychosocial determinants of weight concerns. *Annals of Internal Medicine, 119*, (7 Pt. 2), 643–645.

Russell, C. J., & Keel, P. K. (2002). *Homosexuality as a specific risk factor for eating disorders in men. International Journal of Eating Disorders, 31*, 300–306.

Saguy, A. C., & Riley, K. W. (2005). Weighing both sides: morality, mortality and framing contests over obesity. *Journal of Health Politics, Policy and Law, 30*, 869–921.

Satter, E. (1987). *How to get your kid to eat … but not too much*. Palo Alto, CA: Bull.

Effective Clinical Practice: Methods

chapter five

Holistic Integrative Psychiatry and the Treatment of Eating Disorders

Barbara Wingate

Introduction

The heart and soul of holistic integrative medicine is a commitment to knowing and treating the patient as a whole person, embedded in, and influenced by, a particular social context. The practice of this kind of medicine takes time and a spirit of open-mindedness. Too often, traditional medicine omits or glosses over a patient's context, rushes through assessment, or encourages an "expert," top-down, noncollaborative model for implementing treatment. Interventions are too frequently given and received in a managed care, time-restricted world, dominated by technical and pharmaceutical interventions.

Interventions with women with eating disorders must consider the multifaceted feelings of "dis-ease," reflecting the contributions of both genetic loading and environmental triggers. Traditional medicine often fails to offer much that can lead to the full restoration of health and an overall sense of well-being in these patients who suffer as much spiritually as they do physically and emotionally. This chapter discusses some specific ways that nontraditional methods for psychiatric practice can be incorporated into the treatment for patients with eating disorders. Moving beyond diagnosing pathology and prescribing medications, these nontraditional conceptualizations and the subsequent treatments can enable eating-disordered patients to tap into their spirit, replenish their joy, feed their mind, and accept their imperfect bodies. These nontraditional adjuncts to care are most frequently referred to as complementary and alternative medicine (CAM).

About Holistic Integrative Medicine

The goal of holistic integrative medicine, including the subspecialty psychiatry, is to help each person reach the highest health potential using the most appropriate modalities of CAM and integrating them with the best of traditional medicine. Mischoulon (2005) estimated that about 35% of the United States and 70% of the world's population used some form of CAM. Comprehensive accounts of the development and practice of CAM include *The American Holistic Medical Association Guide to Holistic Health* (Trivieri, 2001), *Alternative Medicine, The Definitive Guide* (Trivieri & Anderson, 2002), and *Integrative Medicine: Principles for Practice* (Kliger & Lee, 2004).

The major difference between traditional medicine and holistic medicine is that the former focuses primarily on eliminating illness, while the latter emphasizes the promotion of health. Further, in contrast to traditional care, holistic work is committed to creating a collaborative partnership with patients and planning an individualized approach to physical, emotional, and spiritual health.

Many organizations are dedicated to holistic care but perhaps the oldest and best known is the American Holistic Integrative Medical Association (AHIMA). Founded in 1978 by neurosurgeon Norman Shealy, the name was just changed in 2008 from AHMA (American Holistic Medical Association) to AHIMA to include to concept of integrative as well as holistic care. Shealy helped to develop the 12 core principles of holistic care after finding traditional medicine too narrowly focused on the mechanics of the physical body. Robert Ivker (2001), a recent past president of AHMA, stated that the most critical principle is, "Unconditional love is life's most powerful medicine" (p. viii). Unlike traditional medicine, practitioners focus on heart-centered solutions. "Holistic physicians, engaged in the business of caring, guide their patients in a healing process of learning to nurture themselves physically, environmentally, mentally, emotionally, spiritually and socially" (Ivker, 2001, p. viii). In addition, holistic caregivers are encouraged, in fact mandated, to love and care for themselves. Everyone deserves love and caring, but how can medical professionals teach it unless they practice and experience it? In other words: Physician, heal thyself. Just like psychotherapists who have experienced the challenges and benefits of their own therapy, those who have "walked the walk" of holistic healing are going to be better partners for their patients.

Psychiatrists working with eating-disordered patients are challenged by a formative resistance toward wellness, present when the disorder is at its most virulent state. Psychiatrists easily shut down and close off their hearts when faced with the repetitive frustrations of patients refusing to take medication, clinging to frightening low levels of weight, and compromising every aspect of the body's regulatory systems. Medically trained to fix or "cure" the problem, many psychiatrists become impatient when eating disorder symptoms are not easy to relieve. The nature of the path to healing for this population is slow and requires tremendous patience and tolerance for the ups and downs inherent in the recovery process. A psychiatrist grounded in holistic integrative medicine is more likely to maintain open-heartedness in the face of these fears and obstacles.

Traditional Medicine and Holistic Integrative Psychiatry

Two historical trends had a significant impact on the development of conventional medicine and the subsequent emergence of holistic integrative psychiatry. In the 17th century, during the era of Descartes, the idea that mind and body could and should be studied and understood separately became a dominant belief (Lee, Kliger, & Shiflett, 2004). Over the next 200 years, traditional medicine discovered, and steadily improved on, an array of methods to more closely examine the inner workings of the body. These discoveries reinforced the notion that the body could be assessed and treated in its own right, as a "thing" responsive to the findings of medical research. At the same time, study of the mind received relatively less scientific attention. Its connections to, as well as its interactions with, the body were largely ignored in the rush to find new ways to influence physical health.

Growing out of this singular emphasis on the body, and driven in part by the ever-rising costs required to relieve its ills, traditional medicine has increasingly embraced the concept of "evidence-based" practice: the conviction that only those medical treatments that have been proven effective by means of empirical research are eligible for insurance reimbursement (Lee et al., 2004). Evidence-based practice is commendable in that it focuses on what is likely to be successful. This approach, however, generally stresses evaluating separate aspects of the body and discounts the premise that the whole is more than the sum of several parts. It depersonalizes treatments and treatment relationships; focuses on specific, isolated interventions to test for credibility; and ignores less-tangible and less-measurable treatment resources. Similar tensions have existed within the realm of practicing psychotherapy. Systems that stress measurable behavioral outcomes simultaneously withhold credibility for those treatment methods that rely more on relationships and nontraditional approaches such as meditation and eye movement desensitization and reprocessing (EMDR).

Because psychiatry has lagged behind other medical fields in the development of diagnostic tests for both the definition and the treatment of disease entities, mental health issues have historically been considered less valid. This is clearly indicated by the lack of parity in mental health reimbursement. However, the last decade has witnessed an increasing awareness of the need to integrate treatment of the body and mind, and the idea of "mind-body" medicine has become a noteworthy topic for both physical and mental health specialists. For example, managed care now routinely challenges internists and family practitioners to recognize somatic symptoms of depression and anxiety instead of testing endlessly for "real illness" and wasting valuable health insurance dollars. Physicians are coming to understand that the depression that can follow a heart attack, the "mania" of a cancer patient on steroids, or the anxiety that can grip an asthmatic on high doses of bronchial dilators are all predictable care issues. Psychiatrists are being trained to understand the influence of innate biology on conditions such as depression and eating disorders and are pushed to focus on pharmacologic solutions.

Eating disorders epitomize mind-body disorders. Eating-disordered patients are particularly challenging because they need many modalities of treatment at the same time: psychotherapy, including individual, family, and group modalities; nutritional rehabilitation; medical monitoring, sometimes from several different specialists in addition to the primary care provider; psychotropic medications; body-oriented and expressive therapies. It is essential that these providers communicate, develop collegial connections, and work as an interdisciplinary team. Without forging these relationships, many patients will fall through the cracks of our current health care systems, in which physicians are too often overworked and disconnected from other professionals outside their immediate networks.

Clinical Perspectives on Holistic Integrative Psychiatry

There are several noteworthy pioneers quite active in the field of integrative psychiatry: psychiatrist James Gordon, author of *Manifesto for a New Medicine, Your Guide to Healing Partnerships and the Wise Use of Alternative Therapies* (1996), and James Lake, the current chair of the American Psychiatric Association's Caucus on Alternative Care and author of *Textbook of Integrative Mental Health Care: Foundations and Clinical Applications* (2006). Wood (2007) provided a user-friendly guide to the practice of holistic integrative psychiatry in *Ten Steps to Take Charge of Your Emotional Life*, conceptualizing the patient as architect of her own healing plan, a core principle of holistic care. She reminded patient and healer that care must begin with a thorough assessment and diagnosis of both physical and emotional conditions and the need for medications. Holistic psychiatrists have a unique role here by virtue of their physically oriented medical education and

ongoing mental health training. This background provides for a comprehensive assessment of body-mind interaction, including an understanding of the underlying biology, the myriad somatic and behavioral aspects
of both psychiatric and comorbid illnesses, and the impact of medications
on cognitive and emotional functioning in ongoing treatment.

Despite the fact that conventional medicine has begun to address the
importance of mind-body assessment and treatment, the ever-increas-
ing popularity of CAM is testimony to the many patients who still feel
their needs cannot be met by traditional practitioners. At the same time,
people seek a healing of the body and mind and an elevation of spirit.
Intuitively recognizing the synergy of body, mind, and spirit healing,
they are searching for a way to heal the "whole" being and are open to the
use of prayer, nature experiences, art, meditation, music, color, and sound
healing. Patients are turning to other systems such as folk medicine,
homeopathy, osteopathy, Chinese medicine, Indian aryuvedic systems,
and naturopathy that address the spirit and healing of the whole being.
They are exploring variations of what is known as energy or vibrational
medicine that works with natural biofields and uses hands-on manipulation, massage, and electromagnetism for treatments, such as acupuncture, Reiki, and healing touch (Gerber, 2000). They are looking for natural
alternatives to many of the traditional psychiatric medications, including
vitamins, supplements, and herbs, to promote overall health and not just
to treat specific psychiatric states such as anxiety, depression, insomnia,
or mood swings.

Holistic integrative psychiatrists must master the core set of evidence-
based diagnostic and treatment tools and be familiar with the CAM interventions particularly relevant to psychological and emotional difficulties.
During treatment, they attempt to foster a collaborative exploration of
various CAM techniques to determine which aspects seem to be uniquely
effective for their patients.

Spirituality

Wood (2004) brought psychiatric holistic treatment into sharp focus by
using the analogy of a three-legged stool. One leg stands for body, another
for mind, and the third for spirit. When the three legs are sturdy, a person
sits in good health.

Frequently, spiritual health is the most neglected leg of the stool for the
patient as well as the caregiver. Many studies demonstrated that physicians, especially psychiatrists, are less likely than the general public to
look to God or another form of higher power as a genuine source of healing (Levin, 2007). For years, mainstream psychiatry has viewed religious
and spiritual beliefs as akin to fantasy coping skills, a form of benign

denial at best, and at worst, clear evidence of frankly delusional functioning (Levin, 2007).

A refreshing and highly significant movement in a new direction was highlighted in *Psychiatric Annals, a Journal of Continuing Psychiatric Education.* An entire issue was devoted to the topic of spirituality in clinical practice. The journal editors introduced the issue with the following comments:

> There is a quiet revolution going on in psychiatry that euphemistically is described as psychiatry's remembering, if not discovering, "the forgotten factor," the patient's spiritual or religious commitment. The thrust of this quiet revolution, a clinical paradigm shift, is that religion and spirituality are now frequently seen as potential sources of strength in a person rather than as evidence of psychopathology. (Josephson, Larson, & Kitjamo, 2000, p. 533)

Hand in hand with the paradigm shift, psychiatrists and other mental health caregivers are challenged to explore and become comfortable with the sources and vicissitudes of their own spirituality. Doing so will almost certainly increase their comfort to properly assess and incorporate the role of spirituality in the health of patients.

An eating disorder is truly a dis-ease of the soul. Johnston (1996) and Johnston and Antares (2005) artfully used story and metaphor to address the soul's hunger for meaning as a vital aspect of eating disorders recovery. Particularly for people with unfathomable trauma in the form of neglect, abuse, or loss, psychological and psychiatric approaches cannot reach deep enough to address body, mind, and spirit. Viewed from a spiritual perspective, many of the challenges faced in life are actually necessary and important ways to grow into one's most divine self. This elevation to spiritual health is in contrast to pathologizing the painful experiences one may encounter on life's journey.

Given the ways that patients with an eating disorder risk their health and life itself, it is necessary to identify and explore the patient's philosophy of living and dying; their beliefs are always there but frequently go unexamined. Similar to therapists who engage in their own psychotherapy, it is very helpful for holistic caregivers to make inquiries into their own beliefs. Do you have a religious or spiritual orientation that guides life decisions? Do you believe in sin? Do you believe in revenge? Do you believe in forgiveness? What inspires awe in your life? Do you believe in an afterlife? Do you believe in reincarnation, in a life "purpose," in karma? As psychiatrists, knowing our own spiritual needs and beliefs, our experiences of love, faith, hope, and awe, and our own spiritual or religious traumas makes it possible to collaborate more effectively and help patients to incorporate their own "spirit" into a search for well-being. Richards, Hardman, and Berrett (2007) provided a multitude of assessment tools for caregiver and patient in their unique and comprehensive book, *Spiritual Approaches in the Treatment of Women With Eating Disorders.*

Yoga and Meditation

The behaviors and symptoms associated with an eating disorder distract sufferers from knowing their wounded soul by burying it from consciousness. Yoga, which always includes small amounts of time devoted to meditation when practiced in full, is an ideal vehicle to help guide awareness of body and mind, helping to ground the patient in the here and now and move them toward union with the soul.

Western medicine lacks awareness about the complexity of this ancient healing technology that addresses the interweaving of body, mind, and spirit through the classic eight limbs, also known as ashtanga yoga (Cope, 1999). These eight limbs are (a) *yamas*, right ethical actions; (b) *nyamas*, right daily practices; (c) *asanas*, physical postures; (d) *pranayama*, breath work; (e) *pratyahara*, quieting of the senses; (f) *dharana*, concentration; (g) *dhyana*, meditation; and ultimately (h) *samadhi*, oneness of self experienced as bliss. Unfortunately, understanding the language, techniques, and philosophies are beyond the scope of this chapter.

Not unlike the many types of psychotherapies, there are many forms of yoga, and a working knowledge of the various types is helpful to assist in guiding your patient. For example, the rigorous asana-based forms of yoga, such as Bikram hot yoga, ashtanga, and power yoga, would be contraindicated for physically compromised anorexic patients. A yoga focused more on breath work, meditation, and gentle restorative postures is good for most patients who are anxious, weary, and at war with themselves. Holistic integrative psychiatrists should encourage patients to find a class or style that suits them and, most importantly, a compassionate teacher who focuses on self-acceptance and awareness of self in the moment, highlighting basic needs such as positive self-talk, eating, and resting. Both invigorating and restorative, at its core yoga is noncompetitive, does not demand any external standard of perfection, and celebrates inner beauty. The language used by most yoga instructors lends a compassionate voice for resisting judgments and offers constructive alternative words for replacing the critical, demeaning ones that dominate the eating-disordered patients' inner self-talk.

The physical practice of yoga, asana work, often releases emotions from nonverbal body-centered memories. Through focus on breath and attention to body sensation, a person struggling with an eating disorder can have ways to experience herself in the present that may help build a bridge to a deeper level of connection with self. Awareness that comes through breath work can help patients ground themselves to a deeper core level of self and spirit and a sense of being in connection with a universal life force.

Yoga's ability to promote better balance of the sympathetic and parasympathetic nervous systems is critically important to overall health and well-being. It helps the hormones from the endocrine system collaborate with the neurotransmitters of the central nervous system and assists the body mechanisms responsible for detoxification (such as the kidneys, lungs, skin, and the digestive system). Yoga also reduces cortisol and adrenalin levels, thereby decreasing stress and increasing resilience, and strengthens the immune system through mechanical movement of the lymphatic system. The body's immune system is guarded by a connecting network of lymph nodes, the collectors of toxic waste and cellular debris. Lymphatic waste is moved to its cleansing destination only through intentional physical movement, unlike heart-motivated blood circulation and lung-motivated air/breath circulation. Exercise in general enhances this cleansing process, but with its systematic practice of twists, inversions, and bends, yoga is particularly effective.

In the past decade, psychological literature has burgeoned with books on meditation, separate from the practice of yoga, with a focus on mindfulness meditation in the treatment of depression and anxiety (Germer, Siegel, & Fulton, 2005; Segal, Williams, & Teasdale, 2002; Williams, Teasdale, Segal, & Kabat-Zinn, 2007). A wide variety of Buddhist-based meditations address forgiveness and loving kindness directly. More and more psychologists and clinical social workers are seeking training to learn how to incorporate Eastern philosophy and treatment tools into their clinical practice, with homage give to Judith's classic, *Eastern Body, Western Mind: Psychology and the Chakra System as a Path to the Self* (1952). Psychiatrists are finally opening themselves to the usefulness of these ideas and inviting those trained in these areas to present at their continuing education programs and contribute to their journals.

McGee, clinical instructor in psychiatry at Harvard Medical School (2008), presented an up-to-date overview of the many types of meditation now considered helpful with a variety of psychiatric illnesses. He indicated two factors in the meditation process that assist in managing a mental illness marked by extremes in all regards: extremes of negativity, rigidity, distorted thinking, perfectionism, self-degradation, shame, and obsessiveness, all hallmarks of an eating disorder. First, meditation practice offers an opportunity to provide a daily ritual (to replace the many rituals available in the form of an eating disorder); next, by engaging them to notice their minds' thoughts without judgment, patients learn to cultivate an internal resource that can assist them to make sense of things and respond in less self-destructive ways.

Natural Alternatives to Psychiatric Medication

When treating eating disorders, holistic integrative psychiatrists can also recommend the use of supplements, herbs, and amino acids as adjunctive treatments. Many of the traditional medications used to treat psychiatric conditions have weight gain as a side effect, a particular challenge for patients with eating disorders who face the very difficult task of developing new eating habits and healthier body image while struggling with distortions and obsessions about both. Neither traditional nor CAM choices offer treatment specifically for eating disorders; however, the vast majority of these patients end up on medications that treat anxiety, depression, or mood instability.

Holistic integrative psychiatrists offer natural alternatives to treat depression and mood disorders, including omega-3 fatty acids; St. John's wort; S-adenosyl-L-methionine (SAM-e); B_{12}; and folate (Wood, 2007) as well as 5HTP (5-hydroxy-tryptophan) (Ross & Emory, 2007). Like anything else we ingest, these over-the-counter supplements can affect individuals quite differently and warrant collaborative monitoring. I favor SAM-e for depression in conjunction with B_{12} and folate to promote an adequate supply of necessary neurotransmitters with minimal side effects. SAM-e is a naturally occurring molecule in the body. I often include it in doses of 200–1200 mg to lessen the need for high-dose antidepressants or in some cases eliminate the need for antidepressant medication. Like Wellbutrin, SAM-e does not promote weight gain; however, it can induce mania, just as all the antidepressants can, and should be monitored similarly.

I often suggest omega-3 supplementation in the 1000–2000 range for those with mood disorders, including bipolar disorder, as it has some documentation for reducing depressive symptoms and mood swings. Although there is growing literature on the use of inositol for panic, anxiety, obsessive-compulsive disorder, and bulimia, the research is preliminary and variable (Belmaker, Benjamin, & Stahl, 2002).

I remain cautious but optimistic about the primary use of supplements to treat significant psychiatric comorbidities. Since these cannot be patented like drugs, there is not the same incentive to develop these alternatives; therefore, evidence-based results are still minimal. The National Institute of Health's Complementary and Alternative Medicine Center (www.nccam.nih.gov) continues to research a variety of nontraditional psychiatric alternatives, albeit at a snail's pace. Subsequently, we will see more tailor-made eating plans that address the specific and often-challenging eating needs of patients with substance abuse, autoimmune dis-eases, celiac disease, diabetes, depression, and binge eating (Gordon, 1996; Khalsa, 2003), and it is hoped, our biggest challenge, anorexia nervosa.

Clinical Perspectives on Holistic Integrative Psychiatry and the Treatment of Eating Disorders

Case vignettes best illustrate how holistic integrative psychiatry works in the assessment and treatment process and how the respect for the patient must always guide the work.

Assessing Carefully

The following two clinical examples highlight the importance of accurate diagnosis in the treatment of eating disorders. In the early 1990s, while I was attending psychiatrist on an inpatient general psychiatry unit, a middle-aged woman was admitted with a diagnosis of anorexia nervosa and depression. Due to my experience diagnosing and treating eating disorders, I was concerned with her lack of the hallmark obsessions about weight and body image. Although mildly depressed, she was not unhappy to have lost weight and claimed it was not purposeful. Despite the reticence of the patient's gastroenterologist, I advocated a repeat of the gastrointestinal diagnostic tests that were unremarkable 6 months earlier. This time, sadly, a tumor of the pancreas was revealed, which accounted completely for her weight loss and lack of appetite. She was soon discharged from the psychiatric unit to receive appropriate medical care. Her case speaks to the need to integrate psychiatric and medical data when forming a diagnosis; we must work hard to see the whole person despite the prominence of specific symptoms, such as drastic weight loss in combination with other psychiatric symptoms.

The second case involves a young woman I saw as an outpatient. She began treatment with a long history of binge eating disorder, punctuated by occasional episodes of purging. Her history was complicated by treatment-resistant bouts of depression and social anxiety stretching back into childhood. The patient's physical presentation was remarkable for unusual fat deposits on her neck, shoulder, and abdomen as well as areas of darkened skin. These symptoms were related to a childhood diagnosis of polycystic ovarian disease (PCOD). She had not had any recent follow-up with an endocrinologist, and no one had explained to her that severe carbohydrate cravings and subsequent weight gain are associated with PCOD. I was able to relieve some of her anxiety and depression over weight gain just by informing her that these problems were part of the picture of PCOD. We worked together to find a caring endocrinologist who was knowledgeable about eating disorders while compassionately addressing her food cravings. Eventually, the patient was prescribed the drug metformin to stabilize her blood sugar and carbohydrate metabolism. In addition, she was diagnosed with celiac disease, a life-threatening allergy to gluten. Appropriate adjustments to her diet led to improvements in physical and emotional health.

Case Example: Accessing the Healing Power of Love

Zoe was a patient in her early 40s, recently discharged from an inpatient eating disorders program, where she had been treated for anorexia, depression, and post-traumatic stress with dissociative features. She was married with three children and in the process of divorcing her husband of 20 years. While in treatment, she acknowledged memories of severe childhood sexual abuse by parents and others, often in a religious setting. She had been physically abused by her husband and was terrified and shamed by what she was coming to understand as the truths in her life. Restricting calories and obsessive exercising had become a life-threatening set of coping mechanisms for the intolerable feelings of shame and anxiety.

In the first year, she was frightened for her safety and for the safety of her previous therapist, a kindly well-boundaried male psychologist whom her husband now blamed for their separation. Unable to make eye contact and often speaking in whispers, she could barely stand to eat and was acutely suicidal. She required the full support of her outpatient team, with her internist playing a key role in keeping her calories at a weight-maintenance level.

Zoe would use my emergency number to call and literally moan or cry about her need to kill herself. She adored her children and was tormented by fears that in a dissociated state she might have allowed them to be abused by relatives or her husband. Although raised in a traditionally religious home with family and siblings active in the church, she rejected God and was filled with pain and anger. Her love for her children offered the only reason to live or to eat. Her maternal instincts were strong, loving, and life saving.

My efforts to recognize and repeatedly speak to Zoe's strength and gift of love for her children were instrumental in allowing us to establish a base of trust and openness. Psychiatry training so often focuses on solving the presenting problem or ailment that it often provides little guidance in how to develop relationships with patients, the actual critical component for any treatment plan to be effective. Getting to know the fuller self of the patient is the path to building an alliance that allows for healing. Zoe's willingness to try and then benefit from both antidepressants and antianxiety medications happened because she believed that I was an ally and not one more person out to get her. As long as she did not lose weight, I treaded lightly on getting her to reduce her running, despite the fact that she was injuring her feet significantly. It took years for her to stop running, with unavoidable foot surgery finally stopping her.

Over the course of 10 years of therapy, Zoe and I often had conversations that questioned the meaning of life and the presence and nature of God, and she often questioned me about my own beliefs. She found few joys in life outside of babysitting infants. I let her know how I saw her love of babies as inspirational and joined her in acknowledging the real miracle of babies, recognizing how they nourished her soul and helped her heal from the depth of her despair and deep wounds. As I became more involved in yoga and developed an expanded vocabulary to understand God as a universal force, Zoe also became intrigued and began more expansive study into other spiritual teachings that offered some comfort and distance from her earlier religion-associated pain. Eventually, she became trained in obstetrical care nursing and in pre- and postnatal yoga training, giving her a healthy community to connect with and to support her continued recovery from the self-hatred spurred on by her eating disorder. Along with my consistent recognition of her life force, these practices allowed her to grow in faith and restore hope. Eventually, she allowed herself to eat. She gained to a healthy weight with an enjoyment of food. She thrived well beyond either of our wildest dreams. I know that my being a real person to Zoe, dependable, loving, and boundaried, was a key to her recovery. She remains an inspiration to me and a reminder of the power that comes when we allow for connection with one's deeper spirit. Interestingly, Zoe picked the name to be used in this chapter: Zoe means "full of life."

Case Example: Healing Deep Wounds: The Power of Pets

Sara, a patient referred for a psychopharmacology consultation, chose to see me because she knew I was a Kundalini yoga teacher, and she also taught yoga. Sara had been diagnosed with bipolar disorder and was struggling with being significantly overweight. She had a history of bulimia along with a history of severe depressions. At the time of our consultation, Sara was overwhelmed with a recurrence of suicidal ideation, a deepening depression, and worry over her inability to curb her compulsive overeating. As our first session ended, she asked if she could bring her dog, Sam, when she came back. I am very interested in the healing power and joy of animal connections, so I urged her to do so.

As Sara and Sam arrived for the second session, it was immediately clear that the two of them were devoted to each other. Knowing that Sara needed to experience being seen far beyond her depression and weight symptoms, I asked for a brief history of Sam, a 6-year-old German shepherd. With pride, she explained how she had rescued Sam from a local pound. His family had abandoned him when they moved abroad, and he was scheduled to be put down. Sara herself had been abandoned emotionally by her mother many years ago, and just several months before she adopted Sam, her mother announced that she did not want to have any further contact. This rejection led to an increase in Sara's binges and a deepening of her depressive mood. It was clear to me that Sara would be very alert for signs of rejection or dismissal. I sensed that I needed to meet her at a personal level, and that our relationship would be critical to her healing process.

As I asked about her relationship with Sam and invited her to feel comfortable with him in the boundaries of my office, I learned that Sam's arrival had changed many things for her. A parallel healing process was at play, for, as she rescued Sam, she connected with a living being that could in turn help her to rescue a part of herself. Sam's love and affection toward her and his willingness to receive her care and devotion gradually released her from obsessive eating and suicidal thoughts. In fact, it was her interest in Sam's well-being that caused her to seek out psychiatric help as she was worried over who would care for Sam if she was hospitalized or successful with a suicide attempt.

Starting with my respect for her relationship with Sam, Sara and I were able to create a therapeutic connection. This in turn allowed us to proceed with the difficult and traditional task of finding which medications might help stabilize her mood disorder and be the least conducive to weight gain, not an easy proposition given her medical needs. Interestingly, although it was a mutual interest in yoga that brought us together, yoga was the more superficial part of our deep healing connection. Our real connection crystallized over the understanding of who Sam was to her and how he eased her deep hurts with unconditional love, something that she had not known in her family life. After months of working together, Sara told me that my reaction to her relationship with Sam was what helped her to feel comfortable revealing the depth of her despair and loneliness. We continue to explore the ways that she can heal her deep wounds, when she must rely on traditional medications for stability, and which alternative natural substances might fortify her natural resilience.

Final Thoughts

The goal of holistic integrative care is to promote overall health and well-being and thereby prevent the need for the "dramatic saves" that traditional medicine occasionally provides. When illness does strike, it uses a well-integrated patient-involved approach. Holistic healing, both in general medicine and psychiatry, requires that caregivers have compassion for themselves and their patients and the will to make the time, effort, and discipline that health requires. When we take a loving, compassionate view of ourselves and work on our own healing, our patients sense this and are emboldened to make the effort in their own journey. Health is not about perfection. It is an ongoing process that encompasses many lessons of love, pain, resilience, connection, and growth.

Caregivers who treat eating disorders can benefit from specific knowledge about CAM. Holistic integrative psychiatry in conjunction and collaboration with other healing modalities has a great deal to offer a patient suffering with these conditions and the multitude of "dis-eases" they reflect.

References

Belmaker, R. H., Benjamin, J., & Stahl, Z. (2002). Inositol in the treatment of psychiatric disorders. In D. Miscloulon & J. R. Rosenbaum (Eds.), *Natural alternative to psychiatric medications* (pp. 111–122). Philadelphia: Lippincott, Williams, and Wilkins.

Cope, S. (1999). *Yoga and the quest for the true self.* New York: Bantam Books.

Gerber, R. (2000). *A practical guide to vibrational medicine.* New York: Quill.

Germer, C., Siegel, R., & Fulton, P. (2005) *Mindfulness and psychotherapy.* New York: Guilford Press.

Gordon, J. (1996). *Manifesto for a new medicine, your guide to healing partnerships and the wise use of alternative therapies.* Reading, MA: Perseus Books.

Ivker, R. (2001). Introduction. In L. Trivieri, Jr. (Ed.), *The American guide to holistic health: Healing therapies for optimal wellness* (p. viii). New York: John Wiley & Sons.

Johnston, A. (1996). *Eating in the light of the moon.* New York: Birch Lane Press.

Johnston, A., & Antares, K. (2005). Eating disorders as messengers of the soul. In S. G. Mijares & G. S. Khalsa (Eds.), *The psychospiritual clinician's handbook: Alternative methods for understanding and treating mental disorders* (pp. 97–114). Binghamton, NY: Haworth Press.

Josephson, A. M., Larson, D. B., & Kitjamo, N. (2000). What's happening in psychiatry regarding spirituality? *Psychiatric Annals: A Journal of Continuing Psychiatric Education, 30,* 533–541.

Judith, A. (1952). *Eastern body, Western mind: Psychology and the Chakra system as a path to the self.* Berkeley, CA: Celestial Arts.

Khalsa, D. S. (2003). *Food as medicine.* New York: Atria Books.

Kliger, B., & Lee, R. (2004). *Integrative medicine: Principles for practice.* New York: McGraw-Hill.

Lake, J. (2006). *Textbook of integrative mental health care: Foundations and clinical applications.* New York: Thieme Medical.

Lee, R., Kliger, B., & Shiflett, S. (2004). Integrative medicine: Basic principles. In B. Kliger & R. Lee (Eds.), *Integrative medicine: Principles for practice* (pp. 3–25). New York: McGraw-Hill.

Levin, A. (2007, October 5). When it comes to religion psychiatrists are different. *Psychiatric News*, p. 10.

McGee, M. (2008). Meditation as psychiatry. *Psychiatry, 5*(1), 28–41.

Mischoulon, D. (2005). *Natural remedies for psychiatric disorders, considering the alternatives.* Cambridge, MA: Home Study Compact Discs, Harvard Medical School Department of Continuing Education.

Richards, P. S., Hardman, R. K., & Berrett, M. E. (2007). *Spiritual approaches in the treatment of women with eating disorders.* Washington, DC: American Psychological Association.

Ross, C., & Emory, H. (2007) Alternative approaches to treating eating disorders. In C. Costin (Ed.), *The eating disorder sourcebook* (pp. 283–294). New York: McGraw-Hill.

Segal, Z., Williams, J., & Teasdale, J. (2002). *Mindfulness-based cognitive therapy for depression.* New York: Guilford Press.

Trivieri, L. (2001). *The American Holistic Medical Association guide to holistic health.* New York: John Wiley & Sons.

Trivieri, L., & Anderson, J. (2002). (Eds.) *Alternative medicine, the definitive guide.* Berkeley, CA: Celestial Arts.

Williams, M., Teasdale, J., Segal, Z., & Kabat-Zinn, J. (2007). *The mindful way through depression.* New York: Guilford Press.

Wood, E. (2004). *Medicine, mind and meaning: A psychiatrist's guide to treating the body, mind and spirit.* Tuscon, AZ: One Press.

Wood, E. (2007). *Ten steps to take charge of your emotional life.* Carlsbad, CA: Hay House.

chapter six

Countertransference in the Psychotherapy of Patients With Eating Disorders

Douglas Bunnell

Introduction

Emotional and affective reactions to patients are a rich source of information to the experienced clinician. Over the course of their clinical experience, therapists can develop increasing accuracy in differentiating their common and expectable emotional responses from unique reactions that often signal an important development in the therapeutic moment. Awareness of one's breadth of emotional reactions, broadly defined as *countertransference*, is an important component of the psychotherapy of eating disorders. The patient's relational patterns, developmental facets, and attachment style emerge in the context of interaction with the therapist, and the therapist's emotional reactions to these interactions provide vital information about the patient's life and experiences. Making use of these reactions to enhance therapeutic empathy and attunement can be challenging and fraught with risks to the treatment relationship. Yet, with the self-awareness derived from experience and self-exploration, countertransference reactions can foster important therapeutic shifts.

Importance of the Therapeutic Relationship

There is an increasing awareness that the quality of the therapeutic relationship may be the most important factor in the outcome of psychotherapy (Ablon & Jones, 1999; Blatt, Quinlan, Pilkonis, & Shea, 1995; Fairbairn, 1952; Mitchell, 2000; Safran & Muran, 2000; Stern, 1985; Stolorow & Atwood, 1992). According to Diener, Hilsenroth, and Weinberger (2007), for example, therapist facilitation of a patient's affective experience is associated with marked clinical improvement over the course of psychodynamic therapy. In their opinion, a combination of symptom stabilization, knowledge of the patient's unique history, and "implicit relational knowing" as enacted with the therapist represents the curative power of psychotherapy.

Regarding the treatment of eating disorders, even in spite of research reinforcing the supremacy of cognitive-behavioral therapy for bulimia nervosa (Fairburn, 2002), recent investigations indicated it may be more beneficial to mix directive behavioral approaches with a more relational focus on the therapeutic alliance (Thompson-Brenner & Westen, 2005a, 2005b). While no comparable data exist for anorexia nervosa and related eating disorders, it seems reasonable that the ability to engage and sustain patient motivation, which is likely the result of a positive therapeutic relationship, strongly influences length and outcome of treatment.

Countertransference and Projective Identification

Therapists, new or experienced, need to develop skills that enhance connection to their patients. Skillful use of countertransference reactions provides one important way to connect. But how can therapists be sure their reactions reflect what is happening in the relationship with their patients rather than their own idiosyncratic or unique personal experiences? This question has persisted from Freud's day. The original, "narrow" view of countertransference saw therapists' emotional reactions as by-products of the therapists' own psychopathology. Effective technique required therapists to filter out these reactions from their ongoing communications with patients. In contrast, the prevailing view in most current psychoanalytic models is that these reactions are important signals, and that therapists need to learn how to manage and use them for therapeutic advantage (Gabbard, 1995). This "broad" definition conceptualizes countertransference as the whole set of feelings and emotional reactions evoked in therapists by their relationships with patients (Abend, 1989; Slakter, 1987).

Winnicott (1949) described three different categories of countertransference reactions: objective, common, and idiosyncratic. Objective reactions refer to relatively straightforward and expectable reactions to general characteristics of patients, such as age, gender, size, class, and race. Common reactions are the set of "usual" reactions that therapists accumulate over the course of their therapeutic work. In other words, they constitute those reactions that therapists learn they are likely to feel in any particular clinical situation. Only after therapists acquire a confident sense of their own set of usual or probable reactions in therapeutic relationships can they identify those that are novel, unique, and "idiosyncratic."

Idiosyncratic reactions are a particularly rich source of understanding. They occur at the intersection of the patient's transferential perceptions and longings and the corresponding perceptions and longings within the therapist (Tansey & Burke, 1989; Wooley, 1991). For example, a patient might communicate her expectation that I will shame her by subtly activating within me an urge to reject her. Alternatively, I might experience a strong desire to tell her there is nothing she cannot tell me. In either case, I am responding to what gets activated within me as a result of the interaction in that very moment.

These interactional pressures are driven by a process called *projective identification* (Gabbard, 1995; Grotstein, 1981; Ogden, 1979), by which patients "project" their own experience into the experience of the therapist. Projective identification is therefore a particular kind of countertransference. Modern definitions of projective identification stress interpersonal aspects (Kernberg, 1980; Ogden, 1979; Sandler, 1987; Tansey & Burke, 1989) of the therapist-patient interaction. In effect, it is viewed as a mechanism for relational connection since patients can evoke feelings and experiences in the therapist that correspond with or complement the patient's own experience of herself.

For example, patients who have been sexually traumatized may evoke in the therapist an experience of being the perpetrator or the actual victim. No patient projection will result in, or create, an interactional pressure on the therapist unless the projected material is "taken in" psychologically or introjected by the therapist. Furthermore, therapists' experiences of projections can be influenced by their own self-experience. Consequently, in these complex moments, therapists can be pulled into interactions in which they carry projected and disavowed aspects of patients as well as residues of their own past history.

While a rich and nuanced literature on the intricacies and clinical use of projective identification is available (Grotstein, 1981; Kernberg, 1980; Ogden, 1979; Sandler, 1976), it is much more than can be summarized here. In short, projective identification is a major force in the psychotherapeutic relationship. The concept offers a language to describe and explain how patient and therapist influence one another. With considerable effort and self-awareness, therapists can learn to understand this language. Of particular significance for effective use of projective identification is the capacity to know when countertransference feelings are the product of the projection-introjection process as opposed to feelings based primarily on a therapist's past history. While years of professional experience can help clarify the distinction between "personal" reactions and the projective identification experience, newer therapists can develop awareness by routinely exploring whether their emotional responses might reflect something about the immediate interaction with their patient. If you notice that you are angry or frustrated, you should ask yourself how it might serve your patient to make you feel this way. Distinguishing your own personalized reactions from projective identifications in the moment is difficult. For less-experienced therapists, personal therapy and close supervision are essential components in the development of this awareness and use of this approach.

Special Aspects of Eating Disorder Treatment

The American Psychiatric Association's (APA's) *Practice Guidelines for the Treatment of Eating Disorders* (2006) emphasize the importance of the therapeutic alliance as the foundation of effective psychotherapy. The guidelines encourage therapists to "adapt and modify" their treatment approaches as the nature of the therapeutic alliance evolves. The guidelines also encourage therapists to be cognizant of their own countertransference reactions since their judicious use can deepen the therapeutic alliance and help therapist and patient decide on treatment choices and goals. Awareness of countertransference experiences are particularly important insofar as it can help guide the timing and nature of attempts to focus on symptom and behavior change. Directive interventions to stabilize symptoms and change eating disorder behaviors, an extremely important and frequently necessary aspect of the treatment, are truly the art of eating disorder psychotherapy.

In contrast to most other clinical conditions, the nature of eating disorders, in fact the core elements of the psychopathology, complicates the process of therapeutic engagement, creating the "raw material" for any number of difficult treatment relationships and a great many premature terminations. At the outset of treatment, patients frequently are suspicious, overtly or otherwise, about the motivation of their therapists. Many are fearful that therapists want only to make them gain weight. Most, to one extent or another, are ambivalent about recovery. In essence, this is because the idea of giving up the symptoms of an eating disorder almost always feels like losing a very significant relationship, as if to surrender something that has been a defining, reliable, and integral part of the self.

A number of other patient attributes make the development of a positive therapeutic alliance a challenging task. By temperament and experience, many patients with eating disorders come into therapy believing that they are not worthy of understanding, acceptance, or empathy, making it hard for them to accept and utilize therapists' efforts to be comforting and supportive. Characteristics such as perfectionism, low self-esteem, obsessive-compulsiveness, asceticism, and a low tolerance for novelty, all common in patients with anorexia nervosa, are not a good foundation for trust and relatedness and consequently represent considerable obstacles to therapeutic engagement (Kaplan & Garfinkel, 1999). Furthermore, eating disorders rarely travel alone; instead, they are associated with a high degree of psychiatric and medical comorbidity. Anxiety and depression are diagnosed in up to two thirds of patients with bulimia nervosa or anorexia nervosa (Bulik, Sullivan, Carter, & Joyce, 1996; Haas & Clopton,

2003), and many patients enter treatment with complicated and compromising medical conditions.

Many practical factors, external to ongoing individual psychotherapy, also increase the risk of therapist frustration, fatigue, demoralization, and anxiety and contribute to less-than-ideal therapeutic relationships. For instance, many patients will need access to higher levels of care. While patient resources are often limited, programmatic treatment is usually expensive, lengthy, and sometimes difficult to locate. As a result of financial and insurance limitations, an appropriate level of care can be out of reach, causing undue anxiety for even the most experienced therapists. Also, in outpatient settings, therapists must frequently spend time and energy constructing functional treatment teams, involving physicians, nutritionists, psychopharmacologists, and family therapists. Similarly, collateral contacts with teachers, other family members, coaches, and insurers can take enormous amounts of extra effort. Moreover, many therapists working with patients with eating disorders will need to review medical reports, dietary charts, thought/feeling logs, and meal plans as well as coordinate input from family members and other professionals. Add to all this the need for supervision, peer consultation, continuing education, and personal psychotherapy, and the level of demand on eating disorders therapists is even greater. Sometimes, a combination of these factors intensifies the therapist's anxiety to the point at which the therapist is pushed to press for behavior change prematurely, resulting in damage to the therapeutic alliance and the patient's progress.

Concern over medical stability is yet another special feature of eating disorder treatment. Anorexia nervosa has the highest mortality rate of any psychiatric diagnosis (APA, 2006). The ability to listen empathically can easily become compromised by the therapist's worry over safety issues. This is especially difficult when therapists sense a wide discrepancy between their own high anxiety and their patients' apparent lack of concern. It is a taxing dilemma when the therapist ends up holding the total sum of anxiety in the therapeutic relationship. As can be true for the burdens exerted by practical issues, holding all the anxiety can pressure therapists into taking too much responsibility for the need to change eating disorder symptoms and behaviors. However, resisting pressure to act can create the space that is required to explore the patient's disavowal of concern. Is the patient "placing" the anxiety in the therapist? Could this represent a reenactment of another important relationship? Questions such as these often yield important answers and provide guidance for treatment. The ability to ask them is built on therapists' awareness of the therapeutic interaction and their capacity to contain the pressure to act.

The psychotherapy of patients with eating disorders is subject to an unusually high level of scrutiny. Many therapists comment that it feels as if a third person (a parent, friend, or in many cases, the insurance company) is always in the treatment relationship. As a result, in contrast to psychotherapy with other kinds of patients, eating disorder therapists may feel held, or in fact hold themselves, to particularly high, exacting performance standards. Differentiating reactions to external scrutiny from more internally derived expectations can be difficult and confusing. Therapists who struggle with worries about the judgment of others and those who tend to feel overly guilty are likely to press for more rapid improvement than is realistic or therapeutically appropriate, causing treatment to be derailed or end prematurely.

Personal psychotherapy helps therapists differentiate feelings evoked by eating-disordered patients from feelings derived from personal history and psychodynamics. If they intend to use countertransferential experiences as sources of clinical information about their relationship with patients, therapists must make this essential distinction. Therapists' personal experiences with loss, trauma, attachment, eating patterns, weight concerns, discrimination, invalidation, anger, anxiety, class, and culture, all of these and more, can come into play during the course of eating disorder treatment.

Countertransference in the Psychotherapy of Eating Disorders

Given the evidence that quality of the therapeutic relationship has a marked impact on psychotherapy outcomes, eating disorder therapists need to develop the ability to empathically connect with their patients. Empathic attunement is enhanced when therapists pay close attention to their emotional, affective, and cognitive reactions to patients since doing so provides important and highly personalized information regarding the patient's relational style, internal world, and developmental level. Of particular importance, therapists have to be attuned to the forces that can leave them feeling devalued or idealized, essential or ineffective, worthwhile or worthless. Any of these feelings, and they clearly cover a wide range, may be important communications that represent patients' prior treatment or early life experiences.

Perhaps the most predictable countertransference or projection/introjection experiences that occur during eating disorder treatment cluster around feelings of frustration and impatience (Zerbe, 1998). As patients seem to resist the process of treatment or struggle to find control over their eating disorder symptoms, therapists may feel a growing internal pressure to "deliver" results. More often than not during these situations, it is most helpful to do nothing other than simply describe the scenario.

Indeed, in many cases the most effective therapeutic intervention is to stay centered, listen quietly, and consistently contain the feelings of pressure and anxiety that stimulate an urge to take some action.

In this regard, it seems important to refine therapeutic language and expectations to help ourselves, and our patients, understand the slow process of change. For example, what does it really mean when a patient is said to be "resistant"? This very common assessment of patients with eating disorders may reveal more about the clinician's state of mind than anything else. *Resistant* is often a code word for "frustrating" and implies that the patient is actively evading responsibility for the need to change. When the slow pace of change is understood to be entirely a function of resistance, the enormous importance of the patient's attachment to her symptomatic self is unfortunately minimized and disregarded.

There are many perspectives on patients' powerful ambivalence about recovery. From a psychodynamic perspective, for example, the need to maintain a relationship with the destructive eating-disordered self stems from the fear that any attempt to commit to a new self will, inadvertently, revive the very same terrors and anxieties initially soothed by disordered behaviors. In effect, the development of the eating-disordered self serves to split off, or disavow, destructive and unwanted experiences and longings. Fairbairn (1952) stressed that disavowed longings actually build psychic structure. That is, the drives and relational needs bound up by the eating disorder can lead to an organized and resilient self-structure that can be very difficult to change.

Therapists' countertransference reactions to their patients can signal early clues about potential new self-organizations. Summers (2005) talked about the importance of creating a space in the therapeutic relationship where patients can risk new self-expressions, encouraged by therapists' empathic nonjudgment and their sensitivities to nascent clues about facets of a new self-organization. This is an especially useful notion while working with patients with anorexia nervosa. These patients, even after weight restoration, are often painfully constricted. The range of possibilities for self-definition and expression is narrow, limited by a temperamental preference for familiarity and a reluctance to try new things. Perhaps the greatest benefit effective psychotherapy offers is the space for trying out new aspects of the self: direct, spontaneous, creative, greedy, hungry, impatient, lazy, or angry aspects, as reflected in therapists' countertransference experience. For example, the first time a therapist begins to feel angry toward an anorexic patient may be the first sign she is starting to explore or develop an angry part of herself. Or similarly, the first time a therapist feels teased during a session may signify the patient is starting to experiment with a sense of her own power.

Throughout treatment, the concept of projective identification helps to explicate the meaning of therapists' countertransference reactions. For example, should a therapist feel helpless or powerless during a session it is worth wondering about those relationships in which the patient has felt as if she had no ownership or ability to take charge of her life. When a therapist feels burdened by anxiety and responsibility, it is important to consider whether, and when, the patient herself has felt she held too much responsibility. At such a moment, one potential therapeutic response is to disclose a feeling of burdensome anxiety and then invite the patient to think out loud about how such a feeling might actually represent a way for her to manage similar feelings in herself. The therapist might say:

> "I'm sitting here increasingly aware of my own anxiety. I don't usually feel that way with you, so I'm wondering what might be happening in this moment. Can you think of any other relationship where you've felt like the other person was way more anxious about things than you were? If not, I wonder if my anxiety might be telling us something about how scared you're feeling about things, even if you can't quite say it out loud."

During therapeutic moments when you find yourself feeling angry at a patient, or at her eating disorder, it is important to contain this reaction and examine the interactive process. Are you being impelled by her projections to collude in her own feeling that she should be criticized for being "bad"? Or, if you begin to feel defensive during a session, could you be experiencing your patient's projection of feeling overly criticized and unable to defend herself? Tolerating confusion about the potential meaning of your irritation can be a major challenge when your patient is severely underweight, bingeing and purging a great deal, tormented by her negative body image, or unable to self-regulate her eating. As suggested, these kinds of projection/introjection dynamics can cause therapists to try to resolve their own uncomfortable feelings by "taking charge" and trying, prematurely, to structure and control eating disorder behaviors.

The question of how much significance to give to symptomatic improvements, and perhaps especially the pace of weight gain in anorexia nervosa, can be strongly influenced by personal issues that therapists carry with them into their offices. Sometimes, there is a clear choice regarding whether to sit quietly and listen or to start talking about the need to decrease food restriction to lessen food binges. Other times, however, this moment of choice involves the therapist's own feelings and attitudes, both neurotic and realistic, about performance, competition, evaluation, and self-worth. Inevitably, personal characteristics such as these are simultaneously in play as therapists attempt to construct an understanding of the therapeutic situation.

All eating disorder therapists have the responsibility to know as much as possible about their individual predispositions to distort aspects of the therapeutic relationship and the overall clinical situation. Doing so is critically important for success in distinguishing countertransference reactions based on early life experience from those based on projections/introjections and, therefore, to the capacity to direct treatment in a clear, forward-moving direction.

By way of illustration, I have recognized over the years that, due to my own past experiences, I have a particular sensitivity to the way young women with anorexia nervosa communicate their sense of never being "good enough." In my work with one particular 18-year-old, I noticed that I often felt on the verge of tears when she spoke. Yet, she rarely spoke of negative experiences, and it was unusual for her to express any sort of dissatisfaction or sadness. Instead, she described, at great length, her compulsion to be the best, to make others proud, and her own pride that she could make do without a lot of affirmation or praise. Although I knew very well my usual connection to the anorexic dynamic of not being good enough, my tearful reaction was atypical. During one session, I thought that the tears signified a nonverbal, perhaps preverbal, experience of feeling unloved, desperately unworthy, and bad beyond reconciliation. This forbidden and disavowed self-experience was thoroughly shielded by my patient's asceticism, self-sufficiency, and other anorexic symptoms. It, and my tearful feelings, had become part of our relationship through projection/introjections in interaction with my personal countertransference. I used my awareness to craft this response:

> "I've just felt some tears in the back of my eyes. I wonder if this has something to do with how sad you feel. As if you can never be good enough to make up for how bad you felt about wanting so much."

We sat quietly for a moment, and her eyes slowly filled with tears. She asked me:

> "How did you know that?"

I told her, with my eyes also filling a bit:

> "I'm not really sure; it just felt like I really 'got' what you were feeling."

Our connection in that moment generated real treatment progress. It was the product of my being able to make therapeutic use of my internal sensitivities interacting with this young woman's self-experience.

As mentioned, for a variety of reasons, both within the therapeutic relationship and without, there are likely to be pressures to act, to control, to direct, or to prescribe during the course of treatment. Therapists need to be aware of the sources of these demands and work continuously to monitor their sensitivities to them. Aggressive or poorly timed attempts to stabilize eating disorder symptoms and behaviors, in the context of ignoring or misreading the psychodynamics and projections/introjections that are present in the therapeutic relationship, can lead to increased treatment dropouts and symptom exacerbation (Bulik & Kendler, 2000). While directive and behavioral techniques are essential and appropriate therapeutic responses, they are likely to be most effective when the patient is open to the therapeutic dialogue and motivated to attempt change.

The following case example illustrates how my own anxiety about therapeutic outcome led to a premature attempt to change behavior and a temporary disruption in treatment. During an apparently routine session, early on in the treatment of a mature woman with a relatively recent onset of anorexia nervosa, we were exploring her reluctance to gain weight. She needed to gain only a small amount to comply with a treatment contract that would keep her out of the hospital. I was aware of the financial pressures she and her family faced, and I was also conscious of being the new therapist on her treatment team. She had discontinued a long-term relationship with a prior therapist, and I was the first one she had consulted since that time.

In the session of note, I opened up what I believed was a fairly innocuous review of where she stood with her weight and then gently pushed her to gain even more. After a brief silence, she looked at me and mentioned that she was concerned that her boyfriend would start "touching" her if she gained weight. In that moment, her entire demeanor changed. She shrank into the couch, pulled her legs under her body, and gradually turned her eyes away from me. Silent and frightened, she began to hang her head in her hands. After a long moment of charged silence, she reported that she felt her father was on top of her.

In this complicated therapeutic moment, a number of issues converged. Perhaps my sensitivity to the financial issues, the comparison with her prior therapist, and her boyfriend's expectations made our relationship vulnerable to a projective/introjective miscue. In retrospect, I believe I pressured her about her weight because she evoked in me an unconscious perception that she was someone I could control and command. In that moment, she served my need to be gratified, and together we colluded in a reenactment of her being smothered by unwanted contact.

In subsequent sessions, we explored her profound guilt and shame for feeling cared for, cherished, and loved by her father's sexualized contact. Our "forced contact" revealed important aspects about her experiences of closeness, need, and dependence. At the same time, this particular interaction helped us to explore novel features of her eating disorder, that is, its protective function. Informed now by a better appreciation of the meaning of her symptoms, we were able to make gradual changes in her eating behaviors. While doing so, we discussed how the difference in her eating patterns affected her sense of safety in her relationship with me, her boyfriend, and her father.

Nonetheless, her symptomatic improvement and her increased sense of being understood was not without its price. My rush to control had, at first, provoked a substantial regression and even a period of dissociation. Right after I made the initial effort to get her to increase her food intake, she had missed several sessions and spent several weeks withdrawn and isolated. During that time, she reverted to old eating patterns, avoided her two children, and complained of feeling frightened and vulnerable around her boyfriend and other friends.

During the treatment of eating disorders, therapists continually confront a difficult dilemma. How can they directly address symptom change in ways that patients will experience as tolerable and beneficial? Overly directive approaches may provoke unanticipated reactions and resistance, while simply waiting for attunement and empathy to lead to behavior change is usually ineffective. Once again, it is worth emphasizing that therapists' awareness of the source of their own emotional reactions can provide significant guidance about the timing of interventions. For example, had I understood my urge to direct the pace of my patient's weight gain as a projected aspect of her own feelings I might have chosen to intervene in the following manner:

> "I'm aware of an urge to tell you how important it is for you to eat more and gain weight. I haven't felt this so strongly with you before, so I'm wondering what it might mean. Do you have any ideas? What would it mean if I tried to take control that way? Is it possible that it would remind you of your relationship with someone else in your life?"

At the same time, in this hypothetical scenario, I would have added a strong statement about how essential it was to eventually eat more and gain weight. Therapists working with countertransference and projective identifications should not ignore the need for symptom change. Rather, the use of these factors should enhance the patient's receptivity to the need for change.

Planning to Use Countertransference Reactions

As an essential first step in making judicious use of countertransference, therapists must be able to recognize their own emotional reactions as they interact with patients. This is more difficult than it might seem. Many therapists are trained to be overly watchful of themselves lest they disclose or be influenced by unexpected feelings or desires that can disrupt ongoing treatment. As a result, they strive to be relatively disconnected from their emotional responses, so simply learning to tolerate the full range of reactions can be a significant challenge.

Second, it is important to keep in mind that countertransference reactions only become serious problems when they are extreme or enacted (Gabbard & Wilkinson, 1994) or, in other words, when such reactions involve major boundary violations around dual relationships and erotic contact. On a lesser scale, countertransference enactments can include excessive or inappropriate self-disclosure, inappropriate affective responses, inconsistency in scheduling or length of sessions, as well as the setting of overly rigid boundaries. Wisely, Gabbard and Wilkinson (1994) stressed the general importance of opting for containment of countertransference reactions until therapists develop some clarity about their source and significance. As with most things in psychotherapy, timing is essential, and it is inevitable that mistakes will happen. However, as Susan Wooley (1991), a great observer and thinker regarding the nuances of treatment with eating disorders, noted: Mistakes are only mistakes if they are repeated.

Working with countertransference reactions requires a high degree of tolerance for ambiguity and uncertainty. Nonetheless, tolerating the uncertainty and sloppiness of emotional reactions provides therapists with multiple opportunities to explore and enrich the therapeutic process. Before making a decision about how or when to use a countertransference reaction in communicating with a patient, therapists should (a) name the feeling in question; (b) identify whether the reaction is objective, common, or idiosyncratic (Winnicott, 1949); and (c) attempt to identify the function and the meaning of the reaction. Exploring these issues before acting protects patients and helps to better understand how patients experience themselves in relationships.

In addition, and equally important, disclosing countertransference reactions at an appropriate time can help therapists create a new kind of relationship with their patients. According to Wooley (1991), the disclosure of emotional reactions can serve to nourish and sustain human connection. As noted, the quality of therapist-patient connections may be the most important curative factor in psychotherapy. The choice to disclose should be made with a plan in mind, or at least a hunch, about how the disclosure might enrich the relationship. New therapists should seek consultation when considering this kind of intervention. In my experience, disclosing a countertransference reaction works best when I describe my reactions as something I would like my patient's help in understanding.

Final Thoughts on the Unique Tool of Countertransference

Increasing sophistication and confidence in the careful use of countertransference reactions inevitably enriches the psychotherapy relationship and contributes to positive treatment outcome. In the field of eating disorders, a number of special considerations complicate the nature and intensity of countertransference. Therapists need to be aware of all these considerations and carefully monitor their treatment responses, particularly when certain patient characteristics, or characteristics of the clinical situation, trigger interventions based on personal history or current struggles. Ongoing self-exploration and self-awareness are the most powerful antidote for inappropriate countertransference reactions. The most effective use of countertransference depends on the ability to distinguish idiosyncratic reactions and empathically explore their meaning. Therapist interventions directed at eating disorder symptoms are often a result of countertransference pressures. On the other hand, many of the most important and influential interventions, including those related to symptoms and other eating disorder behaviors, occur during therapeutic moments characterized by empathically attuned countertransference reactions.

References

Abend, S. M. (1989). Countertransference and psychoanalytic technique. *Psychoanalytic Quarterly, 58*, 374–395.

Ablon, J. S., & Jones, E. E. (1999). Psychotherapy process in the NIMH collaborative study of depression. *Journal of Consulting and Clinical Psychology, 67*, 64–75.

American Psychiatric Association. (2006). *Practice guidelines for the treatment of eating disorders* (3rd ed.). Arlington, VA: Author.

Blatt, S. J., Quinlan, D. M., Pilkonis, P. A., & Shea, T.M. (1995). Impact of perfectionism and need for approval on the brief treatment of depression: The National Institute of Mental Health Treatment of Depression Collaborative Program revisited. *Journal of Consulting and Clinical Psychology, 63*, 125–132.

Bulik, C. M., & Kendler, K. S. (2000). "I am what I (don't) eat": Establishing an identity independent of an eating disorder. *American Journal of Psychiatry, 157*, 1755–1760.

Bulik, C. M., Sullivan, P., Carter, F., & Joyce, P. (1996). Lifetime anxiety disorders in women with bulimia nervosa. *Comprehensive Psychiatry, 37,* 368–374.

Diener, M. J., Hilsenroth, M. J., & Weinberger, J. (2007). Therapist affect focus and patient outcomes in psychodynamic psychotherapy: A meta analysis. *American Journal of Psychiatry, 164,* 936–941.

Fairbairn, W. R. D. (1952). *Psychoanalytic studies of the personality.* London: Tavistock.

Fairburn, C. G. (2002). Cognitive-behavioral therapy for bulimia nervosa. In C. G. Fairburn & K. D. Brownell (Eds.), *Eating disorders and obesity: A comprehensive handbook* (2nd ed., pp. 302–307). New York: Guilford Press.

Gabbard, G. O. (1995). Countertransference: The emerging common ground. *International Journal of Psychoanalysis, 76,* 475–485.

Gabbard, G. O., & Wilkinson, S. M. (1994). *Management of countertransference with borderline patients.* Washington, DC: American Psychiatric Press.

Grotstein, J. S. (1981). *Splitting and projective identification.* New York: Aronson.

Haas, H. L., & Clopton, J. R. (2003). Comparing clinical and research treatments for eating disorders. *International Journal of Eating Disorders, 22,* 413.

Kaplan, A. S., & Garfinkel, P. E. (1999). Difficulties in treating patients with eating disorders: A review of patient and clinician variables. *Canadian Journal of Psychiatry, 44,* 665–670.

Kernberg, O. (1980). *Internal world and external reality.* New York: Aronson.

Mitchell, S. A. (2000). *Relationality: From attachment to intersubjectivity.* Hillsdale, NJ: Analytic Press.

Ogden, T. G. (1979). On projective identification. *International Journal of Psychoanalysis, 60,* 357–373.

Safran, J. D., & Muran, J. C. (2000). *Negotiating the therapeutic alliance: A relational treatment guide.* New York: Guilford Press.

Sandler, J. (1976). Countertransference and role-responsiveness. *International Review of Psychoanalysis, 3,* 43–47.

Sandler, J. (1987). *Projection, identification, projective identification.* Madison, CT: International Universities Press.

Slakter, E. (1987). *Countertransference.* Northvale, NJ: Aronson.

Stern, D. (1985). *The interpersonal world of the infant.* New York: Basic Books.

Stolorow, R., & Atwood, G. (1992). *Contexts of being: The intersubjective foundations of psychological life.* Hillsdale, NJ: Analytic Press.

Summers, F. (2005). *Self creation: Psychoanalytic therapy and the art of the possible.* Hillsdale, NJ: Analytic Press.

Tansey, M. J., & Burke, W. F. (1989). *Understanding countertransference.* Hillsdale, NJ: Analytic Press.

Thompson-Brenner, H., & Westen, D. (2005a). Naturalistic study of psychotherapy for bulimia nervosa, Part 1: Comorbidity and therapeutic outcome. *Journal of Nervous and Mental Disease, 193*(9), 573–584.

Thompson-Brenner, H., & Westen, D. (2005b). Naturalistic study of psychotherapy for bulimia nervosa, Part 2: Therapeutic interventions in the community. *Journal of Nervous and Mental Disease, 193*(9), 585–595.

Winnicott, D. W. (1949). Hate in the countertransference. *International Journal of Psychoanalysis, 30,* 269–274.

Wooley, S. (1991). Uses of countertransference in the treatment of eating disorders: A gender perspective. In C. L. Johnson (Ed.), *Psychodynamic treatment of anorexia nervosa and bulimia* (pp. 245–294). New York: Guilford Press.

Zerbe, K. J. (1998). Knowable secrets: Transference and countertransference manifestations in eating disordered patients. In W. Vandereycken & P. J. V. Beumont (Eds.), *Treating eating disorders: Ethical, legal and personal issues* (pp. 30–55). New York: New York University Press.

chapter seven

Family Therapy With Eating Disorders
Creating an Alliance for Change

Anita Sinicrope Maier

Introduction

Eating disorders are family disorders. They have a direct or indirect effect on each and every member of the family system. As family members develop anxiety concerning the ill member's state of health, the "identified patient" becomes the focus of constant attention. Communication becomes guarded and distant, and family members grow fearful of saying the wrong thing or prompting a confrontation, especially when the person denies her illness (Sinicrope Maier, 1996).

Mothers worry that they have somehow failed in their mothering. Fathers either obsess about taking control of the situation and solving the "problem," or they may distance themselves from the entire issue and let the mother take responsibility for the daughter's care. Feelings of frustration, guilt, and anger can overwhelm parents as all their efforts seem to have no impact on their daughter's behavior.

Siblings and other family members often feel neglected and resentful as the ill member moves into what appears to be a position of power. She may be seen as manipulative, demanding, and willful through either her overt or covert actions. If she experiences mood swings and emotional outbursts, a chaotic environment emerges in the household, and people begin to "walk on eggshells" to avoid conflict. If she becomes quieter and isolative, efforts to coax and include her in activities may increase, potentially causing her to withdraw even more. The family's normal activities and schedules often get disrupted to accommodate her needs. Routines may be abandoned and social contacts diminished.

Mealtimes with anorexic members become battlegrounds filled with tensions and conflicts around eating, food choices, and preparation of the meals. In the case of bulimia, missing food, messes in the kitchen or bathroom, vomit odors, hidden food, and stealing money for the next binge create a surreal environment. The many forms of lying and the secretive behaviors concerning food often breed mistrust, anxiety, and anger among family members.

Women (and men) of all ages can experience eating disorders. Family involvement therefore may go beyond the parent and sibling systems. When a partner of an adult woman discovers that his loved one has anorexia or bulimia or a similar eating disorder, he is filled with confusion regarding how to respond and how to be a support. He often feels that his love and protestations of her beauty should be enough to make her get well, and when it does not, he feels impotent and ineffectual. Intimacy and affection may be withheld from him as the illness progresses, decreasing her libido and increasing body image distress. Partners are at risk of feeling abandoned and insignificant as the spotlight of their partner's attention becomes obsessively focused on eating disorder symptoms.

Families experience a plethora of emotions concerning the illness, including guilt, shame, fear of stigma, anger, despair, bewilderment, and worry. Loss of what is, and of what might have been, fill their thoughts. Extended family and friends often do not understand the complex nature of the illness and may try to simplify the issue, placing judgment on the parents for not solving the "problem" quickly by either getting her to eat or getting her to stop other behaviors, such as purging. Partners are torn between knowing whether to take a tough stand or to turn their heads and give unconditional love. Amidst a daily fear of impending death (while also feeling misunderstood, alone, helpless, and hopeless), families begin to isolate and question whether their lives will ever return to "normal."

A Historical View

In 1978, Salvador Minuchin and colleagues revived interest in a family approach to the treatment of anorexia nervosa and coined the concept of a "psychosomatic family" (Minuchin, Rosman, & Baker 1978). Minuchin's (1974) systems model of structural family therapy analyzed the behavior and psychological makeup of the individual by emphasizing the influences family members had on each other. In this model, symptoms are seen as expressions of family dysfunction, and treatment seeks to free the "identified patient" and restore homeostasis in the system.

Around the same time, Palazzoli (1996) and her colleagues in Milan developed the Milan systems family therapy. This model maintains that members in the system hold particular positions and follow a series of rules that govern and maintain the homeostasis of all family interactions. Palazzoli described eating disorder families as exhibiting a clear display of drama and suffering. They would do anything, she believed, to help the patient, but they often withheld important information to maintain a respectable front. The therapist's task is to unearth unconscious secret rules that perpetuate the family's malfunction and change the rules, thus changing the functional modality of the system.

In the early 1980s, Cecchin and Boscolo expanded the Milan method and developed a hypothesis that each family with a problem has a basic premise unique to them that must be resolved. With anorexia, food becomes a way of indirectly communicating about unrecognized problems in the family. Siblings become important figures in their work. The Milan team urged the family to react to the anorexic as a human being, not a sick person, and they encouraged continuous feedback between the individual who changes and the system itself (Boscolo, Cecchin, Hoffman, & Penn, 1987).

A gentler approach to working with families is the Maudsley method. Professor Gerald Russell led a team (originally composed of Ivan Eisler, Christopher Dare, and George Szmukler) at the Maudsley Hospital in England, which created a model for the treatment of adolescents with anorexia nervosa. This model moves away from blame and causation and instead views the illness as a medical condition for which the family must take responsibility to care for the sick child (Eisler, 2007). It recognizes that in the acute stages of starvation, an adolescent is unable to utilize insight until after the process of refeeding occurs. Parents are engaged to act as doctors by feeding their child. Food is seen as medicine. The therapist serves as a coach and support to the family. When the child reaches 95% of her target (ideal) body weight, she begins individual therapy focusing on issues and anxieties associated with adolescence, exploring her identity and independence, while learning to construct clearer family boundaries (Lock & le Grange, 2007).

Studies showed that this approach is less effective for older adolescents (over 18), and it is not recommended as treatment for adults. It is also not appropriate for those who binge and purge or those who have highly controlling, critical, or abusive parents (Lock, 2001). Treasure, Eisler, and colleagues have more recently developed multifamily groups that provide families of both adolescents and adults with intensive "trainings" on how to be more effective carers (Treasure, 2007).

Overview of Family Dynamics With Eating Disorders

These approaches to family therapy encompass just a small sampling of many models studied in the treatment of eating disorders. The consensus of opinion is that we have a long way to go in researching which family therapy approaches really work with this population (Eisler, 2007).

Family therapy is often used as an adjunct to individual treatment. In my own practice, I take bits and pieces from different models and try to match them to the therapeutic problems that families present. The eating disorder therapist must have a big "bag of tricks" to honor individual and family differences. By understanding the complexity of family structure, history, and experience with the illness, then stepping back and taking an "isn't that interesting" attitude, one increases the likelihood of uncovering a wealth of useful information: family secrets; hidden agendas; issues of contradictions, rigid roles, and rules; as well as spoken and unspoken expectations (Vanderlinden & Vandereycken, 1997).

As families watch their loved one transform before their very eyes into someone who may bear only a mere resemblance to who she was before the illness, fear of what lies ahead seeps in and paralyzes their every thought and action. Not knowing where to turn or whom to call may be overshadowed by the initial hurdle of breaking through their personal denial.

Many stressors, including resistance to treatment, lack of insurance coverage, or difficulty finding qualified expertise in treatment, may deplete the family before they ever walk through the door for treatment. A family in crisis does not necessarily reflect lasting family pathology. Instead, begin with the assumption that families do their best, yet they may be lacking in essential problem-solving capabilities. All types of family problems or disturbed interactions can be both the cause and the consequence of the eating disorder (Vanderlinden & Vandereycken, 1997).

Sometimes, the client herself may call for treatment without having ever divulged to another individual her shaming secret. She may not want to involve her loved ones in her problem, and she may reject the therapist's urging to solicit family support. In this case, one may continue to discuss the pros and cons of family involvement at different intervals during the treatment to help alter her view of inviting family members to participate in therapy (Yager, 2007b). The therapist must also assess whether it is best to do the family work in conjunction with individual therapy or to add a separate family therapist to the team.

Family denial can be a major obstacle to recovery, and sometimes the therapist must reach out more aggressively to confront the system. It is often said that the healthiest member of the family is the one who presents for treatment, and that family resistance to joining in the therapeutic process is a strong indication of systemic dysfunction. Parents or partners may be afraid that if they join in therapy, they will be blamed or made to feel guilty or that their own weaknesses or illness could be uncovered. This fear may be a strong enough motivation for them to say, "Why should *we* be involved in her therapy? It is *her* problem, not ours." In this situation, one may need to back off and then try again to engage them later as the therapy progresses. If the therapist does not have the skills or empathy to lead family work, it is best to refer the family to someone who does. The nature of these potentially life-threatening illnesses, with the daily issues relating to food and body, make interfacing with family members necessary, even with adult clients.

My personal and professional experiences support the notion that therapists must always try to join the family, encouraging stronger, healthier, and more intimate relationships rather than projecting blame or taking positions that could cause alienation. An exception might occur when abuse, major addictions, or mental illness are present in the family system. In that case, the client may need to be protected from the dysfunction as it may indeed be a contributing factor to her illness. If only one or two members are willing to participate, it is worth bringing them into sessions or groups. In systems theory, when one or more members of a family make a change, the whole system changes, and new relationships, roles, and communication become possible (Minuchin, 1974).

Remember, no matter how chaotic, enmeshed, or controlled the system may appear, it is the system that has survived thus far. Psychiatrist Ruth Kane (personal communication, 1993), an important mentor, taught me that the "crazier a family may look upon presentation, the more likely it is that they cannot get along without each other." Beware of trying to separate the client from a family before her ego strength enables her to create her own social supports.

Beginning Stages of Treatment

I usually see clients alone for several sessions before bringing the family in for treatment. It is imperative to engage and get the client's trust before she is put into the stress-provoking situation of family work. If a family member brings a client to a first session, however, I will ask my client permission to bring that person in at the end of the session (10–15 minutes) to answer any questions he or she may have of the "therapeutic process." This is always done with the client present and is especially important if the client is young or still living at home and dependent on the family for her care. The parent or caretaker is generally filled with trepidation and confused about his or her role in the process. The one who initially brings her to sessions is often the person most supportive of therapy and the one who also possesses the most concern.

Being empathic of the family's needs is important in generating their trust. Families need to be taught about eating disorder symptoms and guided through the recovery process. I want individual clients to understand that family concerns should be asked in her presence, and that I will not talk to family members behind her back or without her permission. Establishing trust and confidentiality with my client is crucial. I explain to the family that these guidelines will help their loved one progress in recovery. They are told that they may come to an occasional family session to address concerns as they arise. Their response (verbal and nonverbal) to this declaration tells me a great deal about their willingness to be involved. For instance, a mother might say that she would love to come, but that her husband does not believe in therapy. Or, a father may say that his wife is angry and will not participate. Communication patterns and family relationships are instantly apparent through such responses.

Initial meetings need to assess the presence of eating disorders within the extended family, other psychiatric disorders, alcoholism, and substance use in both family and important nonbiological role models (Yager, 2007a). It is especially important to know of any suicide history in the family, as well as histories of abuse and neglect. Although we can ask clients about these issues in private, family members can often embellish with information or inform us of situations that the client may not know because of family secrets.

Families enter therapy believing that the focus of attention will be about their daughter's or partner's illness and how to deal with eating disorder symptoms. Encouraging them to attend a multifamily group or support group helps them address these important topics. If the client enters therapy after an intensive inpatient stay, the family may already possess a good deal of information about the illness. If education about the illness and symptoms has not been addressed, this information will need to be discussed in the first couple of sessions; after all, they face these problems every day. Recovery is a process that most typically may take years, with numerous stages to pass through and many different and distinct problems to master. Symptoms pertaining to food, body image, and eating may not be the first to go away; therefore, they must continue to be addressed simultaneously with other issues.

The educational focus must be not only about eating disorders but also about depression, anxiety, and low self-esteem, concomitant factors with so many eating-disordered individuals. Personality disorders, bipolar disorder, and obsessive-compulsive disorder may also be part of the client's spectrum of illnesses and need to be evaluated. Many families are relieved to learn of the genetic transmission of eating disorders (Bulik, Sullivan, & Tozzi, 2006) as it draws the attention away from accusation of bad parenting and moves toward an understanding of an inherited predisposition that creates a higher vulnerability to developing eating disorders.

A good starting point in family work (usually less threatening) is to analyze the communication styles and try to improve on the communication process among members. Through individual sessions with the client, therapists will develop a general understanding of the way she communicates, whether passive, aggressive, or assertive in her responses to family, and how her family communicates in response. But, it is only when they are together in a session that a therapist can determine if the client's perception is indeed accurate. The hypersensitivity and self-deprecating thoughts of many people with eating disorders lead them to expect criticism and internalize shame even when the family never intended such a message.

When a client or family member describes conversations they have had, I will ask them directly, "Did you really say that?" Most often, the answer is, "No, but I wanted to," or "That's what I was thinking," or "Well, not exactly in that way." I again question the actual words reported to be used and then try to restructure the interchange by making suggestions, adjusting the language, and urging the speaker to talk assertively from her heart rather than from a position of blame, anger, or frustration. This directive allows words to be heard rather than blocked. A slight change in the wording, inflection, or purpose can make a huge difference in the communication process. The therapist's modeling of an effective way of speaking can help to promote change. As one member begins to speak in a more appropriate manner, the possibility of change increases.

Understand that a client's initial response to family therapy is one of fear. She may anticipate a chaotic scene of temper and lashing out. It is your role, as therapist, to assure her that you will not allow that to happen. Indeed, she may have experienced such a session in the past, especially if it was led by an inexperienced therapist who believed that sessions should replicate exactly what happens at home. By guiding and facilitating a calmer, more assertive, and direct way of communicating, the session is used as a training ground for future situations that occur outside the therapeutic realm. The following rules help to avoid anyone feeling "ganged up on" and to prevent scapegoating:

- Only one person may speak at a time.
- Each must use assertive "I" language (I think, I feel, I believe).
- No one should speak for another.
- Each person must talk directly to the person about whom they are speaking.

Be prepared to hear a client express concern that her family will be on their best behavior and will try to "con" the therapist into believing that they are the "perfect" family. I always assure her that I expect that to happen, and that I will, as a result of my experience, be able to see past any deception. I let her know that while I will be in the process of engaging them to get them to be open and nondefensive, I will still be her advocate and supporter. I also explain that I will become an impartial observer to the family communication process and a "decoder" of the spoken and unspoken language in the system.

Often, before a family session, my client and I may "script," even rehearse, what she needs to say to her family members. I ask:

- What do you want your family to know or understand?
- What, at this given time, is important to functioning better as a family?
- What needs to be clarified?
- What misunderstandings may exist?

By role-playing the anticipated responses, the client is empowered to feel more capable of responding in an assertive and prepared manner.

Coordinating everyone's schedule is a dilemma most therapists face. Family members may be met, and worked with, in a piecemeal fashion. I often have a separate mother-daughter session and then a father-daughter session before coordinating attendance by more members. This can strengthen the bond of each relationship and promote trust with some family members before the entire group appears. Generally, mothers, seen as the primary caretakers in the majority of families, seem more naturally willing to attend sessions than fathers. Fathers' work schedules often make them unavailable, or at least this is the way the situation is presented. When clients are old enough and able to drive to sessions, I encourage them to bring their teenage or older siblings to a session without their parents. Broader pictures of the family structure and roles open up when sisters and brothers attend sessions. Their view of the parents may not be the same as the client, but in any case it will either validate or provide another perspective of the family functioning. When involved in the therapeutic process, siblings can act as reliable consultants and excellent "cotherapists" (Vandereycken & Van Vreckem, 1992).

Many families believe that younger members should not be involved in treatment because they either do not know about the illness or parents think they are too young to understand. As most siblings actually do know that something is very wrong with the client and worry about her silently, it is advisable to meet with them and answer any questions that reflect their concerns. All too often, siblings are "put on the back burner" during the acute stage of the illness, only to be left with feelings of fear, anger or neglect. In such a situation, they may develop a variety of problems resulting from unintentional neglect. In the case of my own family, 25 years ago our younger daughter never spoke of her sister's illness and her fear that she might die until a school counselor noticed mood changes and encouraged her to speak about her complicated feelings and worries. Despite our love for her, immersed in the crisis of dealing with an eating disorder, neither her father nor I had understood how she also was suffering.

Therapeutic Issues

Treatment for eating disorders is like peeling an artichoke; it requires peeling away each leaf, giving it attention and credence while knowing that it may be a long time until one gets to the tenderest heart. Eating artichokes requires patience just as treating eating disorders does. Recovery is a process, and it also requires patience. When we tell the family that eating disorders are not about food, eating, and body size, they become confused and want to know, "So what are the issues?" Therapists must try not to minimize or generalize with cliché answers such as those about low self-esteem, perfectionism, culture, biology, control, depression, anxiety, and even genetics, although these issues are likely to be present. It is important to keep the questions open and offer previously stated issues as contributing factors but not the whole explanation.

Some therapists believe that we should not even try to get to the underlying issues. They believe it is enough to just treat the symptoms and help improve eating and body image issues. I am not one of those therapists. Backing away from dealing with deeper issues increases the likelihood for relapse.

Family therapy will not fix all family issues. The main treatment goal is to help improve the clients' relationships and environment to make them more conducive to supporting lasting health and recovery.

Separation-individuation issues always lie at the heart of the eating disorder (Vanderlinden & Vandereycken, 1997). The most well-meaning and loving parents have shielded their daughter from mistakes and disappointments by intervening on her behalf, telling her what must be done, or doing it for her. This intensifies the daughter's feelings of incompetence and compromises her decision-making ability. Consciously or unconsciously, she fears separating, and when the vital milestones of development are reached (such as leaving home for college or a job), her illness may intensify as she does not believe she can survive or succeed on her own. I take note of how a mother talks about situations that her daughter may be facing and her use of terms such as "we" instead of "she," suggesting that the boundaries between them are nonexistent or weak or that she may be living her daughter's life as her own. I point out that if she feels the situation so acutely, her daughter may not be able to take responsibility for her own feelings, behaviors, or decision making. This in turn may lead her to feel personally impotent and increase her need to numb and avoid feelings. When enmeshment is high, daughters often withhold problems to protect mothers from feeling their pain. It is important that separation and individuation issues be resolved slowly, compassionately, and carefully without leaving either client or parent feeling abandoned.

Parents may possess personality traits of perfectionism and overachievement similar to those of their daughters. Inadvertently, they may be at risk of falling into the trap of identifying with their child in these areas or needing her to fulfill some need of their own. This is especially true of fathers. When their "little girl" reaches puberty and leaves childhood behind, along with the bonding activities they shared of sports and play, fathers often feel uncomfortable with her growing into a young woman (Maine, 2004). The potential for feeling loss is inevitable for many. When parents are unable to understand and support healthy separation, daughters often feel abandoned and even ashamed of their changing body and interests. Fathers are often confused by the tumultuous emotional state of early female adolescence and, in their frustration, can pull away emotionally and sometimes physically. A growing state of emptiness and "father hunger" may begin to emerge in daughters at this time (Maine, 2004).

If the adolescent can remain connected to her dad via achievements in sports or academics, she may have a better chance to hold his positive regard. A desperate need to be the very best, and thus prove herself worthwhile in his eyes, may push her to her highest limit or even above it. The cost for reaching these standards might require her to leave her comfort zone and enter a constant state of anxiety or exhaustion.

Throughout the normal process of separation and individuation, arguments and oppositional behavior may increase. The fighting may be an unconscious drive by both parent and child to make the separation easier and more justified. The emotional chaos and disagreements with mother may overshadow and deflect from the loss of dad, or it may be that mother is safer to oppose and battle because her love is felt to be unconditional (Sinicrope Maier, 2000).

Fathers often withdraw further as the bickering increases. They do not recognize that this dance of separation and individuation (done differently by females and males) is a normal and necessary stage of development. I help parents recognize the process of adolescent development and their changing roles. Parents are vulnerable to feeling irrelevant and not needed, so long-term changes in development are important to explain.

The longer I practice, the more I realize the role of shame in the development and maintenance of the disorder. A family style may overwhelmingly focus on the negative rather than the positive. Well-meaning and loving parents often judge, scold, accuse, intimidate, and criticize in hope that they can save their loved one from the pain that they may have themselves experienced (Bradshaw, 1988). Unknowingly, this predisposes a child to mature with a heightened feeling of shame about herself. As adolescence approaches, her sense of shame increasingly centers around her body.

Treating the client's illness may present a golden opportunity to mobilize the family to address sexual, emotional, physical, or substance abuse issues among its members. Gently testing the waters, in a nonaccusatory way, is the best way to proceed. These issues are not easily uncovered or talked about in family sessions. The environment must be perceived as safe for the client to be willing to discuss them even in individual sessions. These topics are usually not addressed early in the therapeutic alliance as they might lead to more family disruption (Vanderlinden & Vandereycken, 1997). If the abuse is within the immediate family and is still continuing, therapists need to do their best to get it to stop or get the client out of that environment and they must know and follow the state laws regarding reporting abuse. Sometimes, the client is afraid or unable (financially) to leave and may need help from extended family or friends. Healthier families have the ability to cope when abuse issues are uncovered, and they often lend significant support toward healing.

Partners

Little research or writing is available concerning partners of adult women (and men) with eating disorders. In my experience, this dyad is often the most important and most effective in providing support, not only with food and eating, but also in developing a healthier self-image. Feedback on how a client looks, and a realistic appraisal of her body size, is dismissed when it comes from family or female friends. Distrust causes her to believe that a family bias, female jealousy, or competition may underlie supportive comments. She may be more willing to trust male friends and significant others when they share how they see her.

In educating significant others, it is important to address issues like intimacy (both emotional and physical), sex, trust, companionship, and power. Husbands and partners struggle with how to be effective supports and often feel powerless. Guiding, modeling, and scripting about double-binding issues such as answering the question, "How do I look?" are important for successful recovery.

Interest in, and pleasure from, sexual activity usually decreases when the client is in the grips of depression, anxiety, and an eating disorder. Hugging, back rubbing, and nonsexual touching can also be problematic, especially if the client has suffered from sexual abuse in her past. Lesser forms of intimacy may be avoided (even if she craves it) simply because of the fear of it "going further."

If the disorder began after the relationship was forged, the partner may be steeped in guilt that he caused it, or indeed, he may truly *need* to accept some responsibility for being part of the problem. If the disorder was present before they met, the therapist may examine whether he was attracted to her because she was passive, people pleasing, malleable, and dependent. In that case, these qualities may have been serving his need for power and control; this raises concern about the relationship's ability to continue should the client get healthier. If his self-esteem is driven by caring for her, being needed, "saving" her, or being able to "make it all better," the relationship may be at risk if she recovers and his help is no longer needed. If she does not recover, will he be willing to stick it out for the long haul or be angry at what may be perceived as resistance and a slap to his ego (Sinicrope Maier, 2004)?

Teaching couples how to "fight fair" may enable the client to be less afraid of conflict and instead look at confrontation as a way to achieve resolution without rejection or abandonment. Therapists need to be curious regarding whether the arguments, disagreements, and hurts are replications of ones they had in their families of origin and need to help couples discover differences in their relationship to develop new ways to solve problems (Sinicrope Maier, 2004).

Therapy cannot guarantee happy endings in these relationships. The process of recovery requires a great deal of patience and dedication. Many couples are unaware of their marital difficulties until the client begins to recover, and they see that, in the absence of the disorder, the relationship is still chaotic and dysfunctional. Often, her illness has been blamed for an abundance of problems they have faced as a couple, and her guilt and shame have allowed her to accept the blame. As she learns new communication and assertiveness skills through treatment, the defects in a couple's communication may become glaring. When only one person is willing to change and grow, the couple's future may become at risk.

Multifamily Therapy and Support Groups

Psychoeducational and multifamily groups are very useful adjuncts to individual and family therapy, but they are not universally available. The multifamily groups may be composed of parents and spouses of your own clients and others who have been screened to be appropriate members. Many of the topics discussed in individual sessions can be effectively addressed in these groups. Although the client may not want parental involvement in her own therapy, she often welcomes them getting information and support through this modality.

Discussions in the multifamily groups involve a wide range of topics depending on the needs uncovered as a result of individual sessions with clients. In this type of group, I limit discussions about food and eating and often call on the "experts" (those "seasoned" members of the group) to share how they dealt with the various problems encountered in the course of their illness (either successfully or unsuccessfully). We explore parental roles and family relationships often in the context of the participants' experience in *their* family of origin and how the current situation with their loved one may necessitate a different approach. As a facilitator, I add comments, point out differences, or correct misinformation, always in a manner that empowers the parent to experiment with new approaches to being supportive.

The psychoeducational support group is less structured and personalized since people from the general community may attend. Our groups are open to people with the disorder, families, and friends. Meeting bimonthly for 90 minutes, a professional specializing in eating disorders leads them, often with a cofacilitator who is in recovery. The success experienced in my 25 years of using this model suggests that combining a diverse population helps each group member improve their understanding of eating disorders and their impact on the entire family. This may be the first opportunity that attendees have for obtaining information or guidance. This group is not a substitute for therapy but rather an adjunct service for those in therapy. If people are not already in therapy, the most important service the group may provide is to encourage and support participants to seek therapy and provide a referral for treatment (Sinicrope Maier, 1995).

Families: The Silver Lining in a Dark Cloud

Regardless of how many family members a therapist may have contact with or what modality may be used as the therapeutic tool, it is important to treat all family members with respect and empathy. They are going through a very difficult time in their lives and may be depleted, both emotionally and financially. Legitimate fear will inevitably be present concerning their loved one's health, and they may question whether their progress is sufficient. It is necessary to frame recovery as a very long and rocky road, with many ups and downs, forward movement countered by regression at times. Keeping the family calm and validating the important changes in both client and family will help to keep them on track through the challenging process of recovery.

It would be dishonest to say that working with families is not a difficult task. The work is sometimes painful and stressful. Seeing the family communicate more effectively and function in an emotionally healthier way, however, makes this work both exciting and rewarding, for the therapist and families alike, and provides a silver lining in the dark cloud of eating disorders.

References

Boscolo, L., Cecchin, G., Hoffman, L., & Penn, P. (1987). *Milan systemic family therapy: Conversations in theory and practice.* New York: Basic Books.

Bradshaw, J. (1988). *Healing the shame that binds you.* Deerfield Beach, FL: Health Communications.

Bulik, C. M., Sullivan, P. F., & Tozzi, F. (2006) Prevalence, heritability and prospective risk factors for anorexia nervosa. *Archives of General Psychiatry, 63,* 305–312.

Eisler, I. (2007, May 5). *Plenary session III, working with carers of adolescents with eating disorders: Use of multi-family group therapy to support carers.* Presented at the International Conference on Eating Disorders: Eating Disorders: Complexity, Progress and New Directions, Baltimore, MD.

Lock, J. (2001). Eating disorders: Innovative family-based treatment for anorexia nervosa. *The Brown University Child and Adolescent Behavior Letter, 17*(4).

Lock, J., & le Grange, D. (2007). Family treatment of eating disorders. In J. Yager & P. S. Powers (Eds.), *Clinical manual of eating disorders* (pp. 149–170). Washington, DC: American Psychiatric Association.

Maine, M. (2004). *Father hunger: Fathers, daughters, and the pursuit of thinness.* Carlsbad, CA: Gurze Books.

Minuchin, S. (1974). *Families and family therapy.* Cambridge, MA: Harvard University Press.

Minuchin, S., Rosman, B., & Baker, L. (1978). *Psychosomatic families: Anorexia nervosa in context.* Cambridge, MA: Harvard University Press.

Palazzoli, M. S. (1996). *Self-starvation: From individual to family therapy in the treatment of anorexia nervosa.* Northvale, NJ: Aronson.

Sinicrope Maier, A. (1995). A psychoeducational eating disorder support group for individuals, family and friends. *Food for Thought,* special edition.

Sinicrope Maier, A. (1996, Spring). Engaging family in the process of recovery. *Food for Thought.*

Sinicrope Maier, A. (2000). Mothers, Daughters, and eating disorders. *Food for Thought, 15,* 4.

Sinicrope Maier, A. (2004, November 6). *What's love got to do with it?* Paper presented at the Fourteenth Annual Renfrew Center Foundation Conference, Philadelphia, PA.

Treasure, J. (2007, May 5). *Working with carers of adults with eating disorders.* Paper presented at the International Conference on Eating Disorders: Eating Disorders: Complexity, Progress and New Directions, Baltimore, MD.

Vandereycken, W., & Van Vreckem, E. (1992). Siblings of patients with an eating disorder. *International Journal of Eating Disorders, 12,* 273–280.

Vanderlinden, J., & Vandereycken, W. (1997). *Trauma, dissociation, and impulse dyscontrol in eating disorders.* Bristol, England: Brunner/Mazel.

Yager, J. (2007a). Assessment and determination of initial treatment approaches. In J. Yager & P. S. Powers (Eds.), *Clinical manual of eating disorders* (pp 31–59). Washington, DC: American Psychiatric Association.

Yager, J. (2007b). Management of patients with chronic eating disorders. In J. Yager & P. S. Powers (Eds.), *Clinical manual of eating disorders* (pp. 407–449). Washington, DC: American Psychiatric Association.

chapter eight

Sacred Circles
Feminist-Oriented Group Therapy for Adolescents With Eating Disorders

Beth Hartman McGilley

Introduction

Feminist-oriented group therapy for eating-disordered adolescents attempts to identify, address, and eradicate the embodiment of oppressive physical, social, and political forces by providing sacred healing grounds within which self-awareness and transformation can occur. Unlearning silence, starvation, and solitude, the sanctioned developmental milestones in Western girls' adolescence, is fostered by creating "alternative relational and dialogical spaces" (Piran, Jasper, & Pinhas, 2004). Communication and creative resilience strengthen when safety and respect are experienced in the context of the therapeutic group relationship.

Group therapy emerged as a mainstream therapeutic medium in the 1940s, and its practice has undergone radical transformations while its benefits have been widely applauded. Significant changes in group practices have mostly occurred in "front characteristics," such as the structure, membership, content, leadership style, duration, setting, and theoretical orientation, whereas the core elements of group therapy, the "bare-boned mechanics of change" have demonstrated remarkable constancy (Yalom & Leszcz, 2005, p. xiii). This chapter highlights these essential group elements, provides a brief overview of fundamental feminist-oriented therapeutic concepts and illustrates the integration of these core features within the "lived experiences" of adolescent girls in an eating disorders recovery group.

Overview of Group Therapy

The distinct advantages and therapeutic possibilities that group treatment confers have been well documented (Bloch & Crouch, 1985; MacKenzie, 1990; Yalom & Leszcz, 2005). In general, the potential benefits of group treatment include the eradication of shame and isolation of individual members; improved social support; opportunities to improve communication skills (listening, articulation, and reflection); leadership modeling and training; vicarious and experiential learning; and experiencing healing and growth in connection (Yalom & Leszcz, 2005). Feminist-oriented group therapy borrows from these general benefits while also providing a process for group interaction sensitive to issues of gender, agency, and social oppression (Butler & Wintram, 1991; DeChant, 1996; Lakin, 1991; Seu & Heenan, 1998). The invaluable therapeutic benefits, relative cost-effectiveness, and short-term duration of many groups arguably distinguish this healing modality as a critical and primary source of therapeutic intervention (Yalom & Leszcz, 2005).

The global, economic, and diverse applications of group psychotherapy also render it vulnerable to misapplications and mismanagement. This introduction will focus on three fundamental aspects of group therapy vital for clinical effectiveness: patient assessment and preparation for group; group cohesion; and core group therapeutic factors (Harper-Giuffre & MacKenzie, 1992; Yalom & Leszcz, 2005).

Assessment and Preparation for Group

Establishing a patient's appropriateness and readiness for group may be the single most predictive factor of therapeutic outcome. Patients need to clearly demonstrate the interest, willingness, and initiative to attend meetings on time, as scheduled, and to their completion. Most dropouts occur in the first few weeks of a group because one of the above criteria was not met (Harper-Giuffre & MacKenzie, 1992). Given these criteria, group therapists can use a treatment contract delineating these requirements, allowing patients to make informed commitments and holding them accountable to their peers and group facilitators. Psychoeducational and didactic groups provide a more topic-oriented focus and can be an ideal stepping stone for patients pursuing more subjectively oriented process groups. A brief, introductory didactic group meeting explaining therapeutic principles would be an ideal primer for these purposes.

New members should be indoctrinated into the concept of the group relational process as the "source" for, and "container" of, therapeutic changes, as well as be informed about the themes, issues, and dynamics likely to emerge over the course of group therapy. If possible, offering new members the opportunity to talk to a current or previous group member may greatly enhance their "buy-in," improve readiness for group treatment, demystify common fears, and clarify misunderstandings regarding its process (e.g., not fitting in or being judged).

Another critical group assessment variable involves establishing that patients have the intellectual, cognitive, and emotional capacity to effectively integrate and utilize the rich and often-provocative material generated in a process-oriented group. As noted in this chapter, eating-disordered patients who are critically emaciated, malnourished, metabolically unstable, or profoundly depressed will not be able to make effective use of group therapy. Similarly, patients with certain personality features (e.g., borderline, paranoid, or narcissistic) or erratic, impulsive behaviors that preclude their ability to resonate with, receive feedback from, or consistently attend to the group process will unlikely benefit from group therapy and may potentially compromise it.

Group Cohesion

Group cohesion, or developing feelings of "groupness," is the first critical task of an emerging group. Through this sense of community, members derive the initiative, conviction, and accountability essential for therapeutic change to occur. Once consolidated, the healing ties that bind group members are synergistic, and the sacred space created within their circle ideally percolates with a powerful restorative potential. To the degree members operate with integrity, honoring the defined structures of the group (i.e., attendance, confidentiality, consistency) while thoughtfully indulging the boundless properties of their union (i.e., self-disclosure, risk taking, authentic presence), profound growth and change can occur.

As a rule, traditional models of group leadership are more autocratic in the sense that leaders are presumed to be the experts and to function much like conductors, tasked with orchestrating, if not actively directing, the rhythm and flow of the group process. Extra group social contact is thus generally discouraged because the facilitator is not present to "manage" or observe the interactions and because of concerns that issues such as enmeshment, competition, or conflict could develop outside the group context that could dilute the working relationships of members within it (Harper-Giuffre & MacKenzie, 1992). In contrast, feminist-oriented groups view power and leadership as being shared among members and facilitators who are all considered to be experts of their own experience (Butler & Wintram, 1991; DeChant, 1996; Enns, 2004; Seu & Heenan, 1998). Relationships are considered a potent resource for therapeutic experimentation and change, thus extra group contact is supported, even encouraged as a vital healing tool.

Core Therapeutic Factors

Drawing from the extensive body of literature provided by Yalom and Leszcz (2005) and Bloch and Crouch (1985), Harper-Giuffre and Mac-Kenzie (1992) suggest clustering curative group therapy factors into four categories: supportive factors, self-revelation factors, learning from others factors, and psychological work factors. Metaphorically considered, these are the kindling elements that provide the source of the healing energy group therapists are challenged to ignite, stoke, and tend to cultivate the group's ultimate curative potential. It is through the vibrant, energetic exchange of these elements—the rub of a dynamic membership and the breadth of new considerations—that therapeutic combustion occurs.

Supportive Factors

Supportive factors include the instillation of hope, acceptance, universality, and altruism. Joyce Carol Oates (personal communication, 2007) is credited with saying that, "Hope is the healer that helps us survive when our soul is as thin as a playing card." Healing without hope is like wet matches: Devoid of the spark of possibility, however slight, even the most resilient of us cowers in the dark. Groups have the added healing property of exposing members to hope's healing in action by witnessing and participating in other member's growth processes. Experiencing empathy while observing other's dysfunctional thought and behavioral dynamics can diminish internal derision while instilling motivation for personal change. Conversely, as with engendering hope, experiencing other's acceptance, despite self-loathing, can eradicate the shame and social isolation pervasive in this client culture. As Yalom and Leszcz (2005) poignantly described, "The phenomenon [of universality] finds expression in the cliché 'we're all in the same boat'—or perhaps more cynically, 'misery loves company'" (p. 6). In fact, empathic resonance appears to be neurochemically mediated. Recent research on mirror cells in the anterior cingulate demonstrated that the brain cannot distinguish real from perceived pain, suggesting that "feeling another's pain" is indeed not just a metaphor. Dubbed the "Dalai Lama" cells, this discovery reveals we are literally wired for connection (Ramachandran, 2006).

Altruism functions in group therapy by way of redirecting clients' exhausting and deriding self-focus, providing opportunities for making meaningful contributions in others' lives. Shifting seamlessly between roles as help receivers and providers, group members expand their sense of self, effectiveness, and interpersonal worth.

Self-Revelation Factors
These factors include the therapeutic benefits of self-disclosure and catharsis. Timing of self-disclosure is key, and group leaders are charged with assisting members to share judiciously with regard to their own and the group's capacity to emotionally integrate and to make effective use of shared material. Catharsis, the expression of highly charged emotions, must be paired with cognitive learning to reap its therapeutic rewards (Yalom & Leszcz, 2005). Simply stated, insight is not curative. Clients must translate, integrate, and channel their insights and abreactions into directed, persistent behaviors to achieve sustained improvement and meaningful change.

Learning From Others
Interpersonal instruction factors, most vital early in the group process, include modeling and vicarious learning (Harper-Giuffre & MacKenzie, 1992). Members will mimic and follow therapists' lead when it comes to risk taking, such as self-disclosure and interpersonal support (Yalom & Leszcz, 2005). Developing the skills and willingness to contend with fear and anxiety, the twin torments of contemporary culture, may also be facilitated through group interaction. Group members learn vicariously as others describe their successful recovery efforts as well as their responses to relapse. "Confronting traumatic anxieties with active coping (for instance, engaging in life, speaking openly, and providing mutual support), as opposed to withdrawing in demoralized avoidance, is enormously helpful" at the interpersonal, intrapsychic, and neurochemical levels (Yalom & Leszcz, 2005, p. 11).

Psychological Work Factors
Receiving feedback, trying out new behaviors, developing insight, and experiencing corrective emotional experience are core factors in long-term, process-oriented groups (Harper-Giuffre & MacKenzie, 1992). Establishing the proper balance of structure and spaciousness provides a fertile environment for members to experiment with new manners of understanding and "innerstanding" (Kimura, 2004). The variety of membership and shared vulnerability offer extensive opportunities for members to practice new behaviors; receive immediate, constructive feedback; and experience and offer validation of perceptions. Groups become both a social microcosm and a kaleidoscopic panorama of one's family constellations. Herein lies one of its unique advantages. Members eventually "show up," relating and exhibiting the same maladaptive patterns,

insecurities, and unfinished business learned in their families and their broader social contexts. In Yalom and Leszcz's (2005) terms, "there is no need for them to describe or give a detailed history of their pathology: *they will sooner or later enact it before the other group members' eyes*" (p. 32). Processing these dynamics is the harbinger of insight and the foundation for corrective emotional experiences. Through well-informed and thoughtfully directed interactions (e.g., Gestalt techniques), groups can effectively challenge members to rework and release their hold on inhibiting or destructive vestiges of the past.

Feminist Theory and Therapy

The infusion of feminist theory into clinical practice has radically contradicted, if not altered, both fundamental principles of human development and functioning and theoretical models of change on which the foundations of clinical practice were informed. Central, organizing shifts in perspective include reformulations of adolescent female development; relocating concepts of pathology from the individual into the cultural context; and revitalizing the power and necessity of connection and mutuality while diminishing patriarchal emphasis on competition and individualism, presumed to be the "natural" and necessary dynamics of male development (Jordan, Kaplan, Miller, Stiver, & Surrey, 1991; Miller, 1976). Key feminist concepts of particular relevance to therapy with eating-disordered adolescents include (a) recognition that gender and gender roles are socially constructed (Smolak & Murnen, 2004); (b) conceptualization of power as intrinsically relational, incorporating a dramatic shift from a "power over" to a "power with" model in the treatment relationship (Surrey, 1991); (c) helping women to find their own "voice," speak it, and in so doing legitimize their personal authority (Gilligan, 1982); (d) reconceptualizing adolescent development as occurring in connection with and through relationship (i.e., self-in-relation theory; Jordan et al., 1991); and (e) exposing the traumatizing effects of the objectification and commodification of the female body (Anderson-Fye & Becker, 2004; Kilbourne, 1999; Maine, 2000; McGilley, 2004; Wolf, 1991).

Feminist-Oriented Group Therapy for Adolescents With Eating Disorders

Group therapy for eating-disordered adolescents provides opportunities to be "response-able to self and others, attend to one's own and collective well-being" (Brabeck & Brown, 1997). For 21 years, I have been the primary therapist for an adolescent eating disorder group. The group also serves as a training opportunity for new therapists. Uniquely, my current cotherapist is a former member of this group who went on to complete her graduate training in marriage and family therapy. Both of us have recovered from an eating disorder (neither a prerequisite nor an inherent advantage or detriment for group leadership). The issues of self-disclosure and personal recovery from an eating disorder have been previously discussed in the literature (Johnson & Costin, 2002; McGilley, 2000).

Group candidates are carefully screened for their readiness and capacity to benefit from the group experience. Patients are expected to be able to manage their eating disorder symptoms such that they are *relatively* medically and nutritionally stable. Given the variable course of recovery, it is common that members will go through bouts of physical or psychiatric instability. Members can maintain their group status as long as their compromise does not impair their ability to provide to, and profit from, the group process. Group readiness also requires that patients have overcome denial and view their eating disorder as a problem. If and when a member is unable, by virtue of relapse, resistance, or loss of conviction, to uphold the defining admission criteria, she will be asked to take a "time-out" until she and the group feel she has restored her commitment to recovery.

Group Format and Demographics

The group is open ended and process oriented, comprised of up to eight high school and college-aged youth, with a blend of eating disorder diagnoses. Weekly meetings are 2 hours, and confidentiality is strictly observed. Aside from my initial decisions on whom and when to refer to group, virtually all subsequent decisions involving the size, timing of adding members, and the process of the group are made by the group collective. Members are viewed as their own experts, emphasizing that "truth" does not rest in any external therapeutic authority. Group facilitators serve as guides and collaborators in healing. Members are encouraged to think and, literally, sit in circles instead of lines as a way to diffuse unnecessary competition, thus building healthy alliances and appreciation for individual differences and strengths. In this model, there is plenty of room "at the top" for all of their gifts; perfection is seen as an unrealistic and limiting goal, and the concept that "enough is plenty" is one of many healing mantras members use to source their recoveries (McGilley, 2006).

Group Process

Group begins with a "go around" the circle in which each member takes 5 minutes to update her symptom status (e.g., whether she is maintaining weight, self-harming, bingeing, purging, overexercising, without indulging specifics), followed by identifying whatever issue, theme, or circumstance she would like to further address in the group. For example, a member might state that she restricted over the weekend and wanted to work on confronting the friends whose behavior had triggered hurt and anger, feelings she elected to cope with by starving.

Following the go around, I review each member's request for help to set the agenda. The group is then open for the girls to direct their focus and energy as they see fit. This nondirective process allows members to practice their assertiveness, test out expressing their needs, and vie for their rightful place at the table. Since this is an open-ended group, there is always a blended membership of "newbies" and "crones." Crones inevitably assume leadership roles and tend to the kindling process of the group. For example, modeling the therapeutic tasks of finding their voice, negotiating self-in-relation, and risking conflict in connection, crones encourage newbies, who are apt to minimize their needs for group time, or confront members who overutilize group time in a manipulative or ineffective manner. Lastly, the content of group discussion is generally open, except with regard to members' weight and specific symptom management issues. These issues are relegated to individual therapy because of their potential iatrogenic and contagion effects.

Between-Group Contacts

The bonds that form between members, especially in these times of e-speak, Facebook, and MySpace, readily begin to extend beyond the confines of the therapy circle. It is distinctly through having new experiences inside and outside the group that they begin to see themselves in a different, redemptive light. One of our healing mantras, borrowed from Dr. Maureen Walker (2002), speaks directly to this: "Do not go out acting as if you don't have people!" The group understands this as a measure of their accountability to one another as much as a message of shared community.

It is completely unrealistic, in my experience, to assume group members (at least adolescents) will not have outside contact, so it is in the best interests of the group facilitator to help members effectively and appropriately tap into these connections. Members are invited at the outset to join a group e-mail list—none have refused. Inactive members (e.g., those away for college) often e-mail their updates to instill a sense of their "virtual" presence and continued investment in the group. Rather than diluting the connections between members, as cautioned by Yalom and Leszcz (2005), I have found that between-group exchanges, even when conflictual, can significantly deepen what occurs in a group or provide grist for the "therapeutic mill" in subsequent ones. Members are held to the honor system and are encouraged to bring e-mail interactions back into the circle for discussion. It is deeply embedded in our concept of a healing circle that our "Word" is ultimately all and everything we have to bring to our relationships. I have been heartened by the degree to which group members embrace and protect this covenant. A crone summed it up by writing:

> This is what GROUP therapy is about! Using each other as resources is the best way to stay grounded and sane during the week. These e-mails are like little booster shots of therapy for me.

Scheduling group outings and celebrations are other ways for therapists to capitalize on between-group contacts, further fostering cohesion and growth in environments otherwise commonly riddled with symptom triggers or emotional land mines. Playing laser tag, for example, can give members permission to practice spontaneity, competition, fear management, and rampant silliness while also allowing them to witness and relate to their group facilitators in alternative learning contexts. Last, the therapeutic benefits of group meals have been long practiced and well documented in the literature. Our group abides by three rules for group meals: no diet foods, no salads without protein, and no solo trips to the bathroom.

Group Duration and Graduation

Group members' attendance varies from months to years, with 3 years an estimated average length of stay. College-aged members attending school out of state often resume membership during summer breaks, even if this extends the group size limits. Graduation from group is discussed in advance, and members are encouraged to give candid feedback about the departing member's readiness to leave and indicators for relapse, as well as to honor her growth and contributions to the group. Importantly, graduations are also potent therapeutic junctures in which issues of loss, abandonment, unresolved grief, and conflict can be acknowledged and reworked. Graduations are celebrated in a manner of the member's choosing, such as the exchange of symbolic gifts or a "dress-up" dinner. Graduates are welcome to return for visits (e.g., over Christmas break) or if they have later need for treatment support (although this has been extremely rare).

Group in Action

From its inception, this group has been almost as much about educating new therapists as it has been about fostering patients' recoveries. For a workshop on the blessings and pitfalls of psychotherapy, I enlisted the group's help in providing true and intimate reflections on their experiences of the treatment process. The following dialogue is from the group enactment of the improvisation game called the Good, Bad, and the Ugly.

Improv exercises are intended to invoke the dramatic, and in this exercise, three people are given theatric license to expound on the good, bad, and the ugly qualities of whatever subject is chosen. What ensued in this group incorporates a blend of exaggerated "truths" about the best and worst of what happens behind therapy's closed doors. Rather than the improvisational nature of the exercise obscuring the virtues and pitfalls of therapy and recovery, it served to expose and highlight these aspects. This exercise can become intense and demoralizing for those in the "bad" and "ugly" roles. To close the experience from a position of true congruence, I eventually shifted the process and engaged them in a frank discussion of their current status in recovery and how it felt to "defend the illness" after working so hard to defeat it. Ultimately, the experience has proven itself to be humbling and gratifying, exposing the enormous efforts required to achieve the redemptive benefits of recovery. The following excerpts from the improv exercise have been chosen to illustrate various group and feminist concepts discussed in the previous sections. Dialogue has been edited for brevity and clarity if necessary.

Improvisation Reflecting Oppressive Social Contexts

In this exchange, centered on the theme of "recovery," three members adopted good, bad, and ugly perspectives as they spontaneously debated the liberating promise of healing vis-à-vis a hegemonic culture promising acceptance through compromise:

Good: In recovery, you are finally living your life. You aren't living the eating disorders life.

Ugly: Who cares what anyone says about recovery. Being thin and being pretty and having control—that's the only thing.

Good: What about your personality and your experiences? Don't you want to do more with your life than be thin and pretty? There is so much more to you.

Bad: The thing is I know how to do the eating disorder. It's easy, simple and convenient. Why not stay there?

Ugly: It makes me special. Everyone else has these needs [for recovery] but I know I don't need it. I'm stronger than them.

Good: Are you really stronger than anyone when you are 90 pounds and can barely walk around?

Ugly: Absolutely! And I'm the best at it.

Good: So you are the best at being sick? Don't you want to be remembered for helping others or being an amazing presence in a room?

Bad: Do people really look at those things? Let's be honest with ourselves.

Good: I think so. I think your personality is way more important than your outward appearance.

Ugly: Have you looked at a magazine lately?

Good: You can't live to the world's standards. You have to have higher standards. And that's what recovery teaches you—to have higher standards than the world.

At this point in the discussion, I jumped in to support the member promoting the good aspects of recovery:

Therapist: The good thing about recovery is, if you achieve it, it's the only way you are ever going to live real again.

Ugly: Reality sucks. Who cares if you are not living real?

Therapist: It is the only chance you've got.

Ugly: To do what?

Therapist: To be real! With your eating disorder, you have to be willing to risk that the only chance you've got is the one you never took ... that's what recovery gives you back.

Ugly: It's too much time, too much effort, too much consistency. Consistently changing everything. You're going to screw up sooner or later.

...

Good: But how much effort do you put into your eating disorder?

Ugly: Tons!

Good: So why not change the direction of that effort to recovery?

Improvisation Reflecting Issues of Empowerment

Empowerment is often an ambivalent achievement for eating-disordered patients, particularly those still wrangling with the "tyranny of nice and kind," who find unfortunate solace in acquiescence and conflict avoidance (Gilligan, 1982). It is a true marker of both a group's maturity, and an individual's recovery, when patients become decisive, risk taking, and contrary. The theme for this discussion was "therapists." Even as far along in recovery as most were in this group, the idea of valuing their health and restoration remained a troublesome dilemma:

Ugly: I think it's just a stupid job. Seriously, I listen to my friends all the time, and I don't have a degree and I don't get paid.

Good: But what if they have lived through it and have the degree?

Ugly: I've lived through stuff and give my friends advice, and I don't get paid.

Good: Don't you think they are a little more knowledgeable?

Ugly: I can get the same information from somethingfishy.com for free!

Good: I think the point is that connection, talking it out, it's so candid.

Bad: Well there might be a connection, but how does that make it easier to change? You can talk, but if you don't want to change, you are not going to.

Good: Right! Therapy changed my life because I was ready to change.

Supporting clients to find their own voice, trust their own perspective, and source their own experience for direction is another aspect of empowerment. There is no mistaking the longing in some, especially those earlier in the recovery process, to be "freed" from the bittersweet responsibilities and demands of being fully functioning and wholly present in their lives.

Good: My therapist says the right things at the right time. She lets me talk and cry, offers me advice that gives me the nudge I need to have the confidence to say, "Hey, I figured that out on my own!"

Ugly: She probably read it in a book somewhere!

Bad: I hate the silence part!

Good: Maybe silence is good? Letting you have your own space to figure some things out? God knows it isn't silent anywhere else in our lives!

Bad: Why do they have to talk in such secret code? Why can't they just come out and say it? Why do I have to figure it out for myself? Obviously, I don't know what I am doing wrong.

Ugly: I totally agree. They use secret talk! "How do you feel when that happens?" Okay. I'm obviously sick and I'm coming to you so why don't you tell me what I'm doing wrong? Don't let me figure it out for myself. Why stretch it out for weeks when you can tell me in 1 day what to do or what I'm doing wrong?

Improvisation Reflecting Issues of Voice and Self-in-Relation

The dialogue around the theme of "group therapy" revealed sentiments regarding the challenges and potential mixed blessing of a communal healing environment, including the potential lack of mutual empathy and the risks of resorting to the "underground" for shelter (Brown & Gilligan,

1992). Yalom and Leszcz's (2005) supportive factors (e.g., universality, instillation of hope, altruism); learning from others (e.g., modeling, vicarious learning); and psychological work factors (e.g., developing insight, receiving feedback) are also clearly reflected in this interaction:

Good: The best part of group therapy is that it shows you that you're not the only one feeling the way you are.

Bad: The worst is that everyone takes up your time. Everyone has their own agenda.

Ugly: Are you joking me? Blah blah blah! Let's get to me for once!

Good: Isn't that a little self- centered? I mean you can learn so much from others.

Bad: Yeah, everything to do wrong!

Good: You also see how other people have stumbled and how to avoid their mistakes.

Bad: Or you can be better at being the worst!

Ugly: Yeah—how about the competition? Every single girl in the room has the same disease. Let's just put it out on the table—everyone's in competition.

Good: But everyone is working toward the same goal. We all want to get better!

Bad: One of the bad things is that everyone isn't on the same page. We say we have the same agenda, but we don't. Then we get bogged down and lost!

Ugly: And what about the liars? They come in here, tell half the story, half the truth. Some are working their program, and others are totally holding back, not speaking the truth. They don't even want to get better.

Good: How do you know they aren't telling the truth?

Ugly: Through their behaviors. They come in weekly with the same symptoms, same excuses. Their words and actions don't line up.

Good: Shouldn't we be understanding? We have all been in their position. It takes more than just deciding to get better; it's a process.

Improvisation Reflecting Objectification and Commodification of Women's Bodies

Sadly, regardless of what topic the group was addressing, issues of body disparagement were replete in the discussion. Fortunately, despite their facility in promoting the "virtues" of seeking bodily perfection, its hollow victory was no longer lost on them. This exchange was about the pros and cons of "recovery:"

Ugly: I like my eating disorder. It's gotten me attention from modeling agencies. Why would I change that? My strengths and talents lie in my beauty.

Good: Recovery would argue that you're worth more then a price tag. In the end, do you want people at your funeral to say you were a million-dollar model?

Bad: At least I got my 5 minutes of fame. When I'm thin, the modeling agencies want me.

Good: You have to decide if you're going to play your life to an audience that values you as an object. They've [objectifying culture] got plenty of ways to make sure you're for sale. How do you want to distinguish yourself, be remembered; what's the difference you want to make? There are huge industries invested in keeping us at war within and between ourselves. Our challenge is to decide: What do we want to buy with our attention today?

Several group members joined in the discussion advocating for the benefits of recovery and embodiment:

Good: What if you recover and get 5 years of fame instead of 5 minutes? You'll never know if you don't try. The type of attention you get when you are recovered is much more meaningful than what you get from a modeling agency. It's more satisfying if someone looks at your heart and personality than your face or jean size.

Bad: What if I don't get attention either way?

Good: What if you keep living "what if?" That's the whole deal. Recovery gives you a way to stay out of that suspended place. Eating disorders offer excuses and keep you from being fully present. Decide if you're going to live a suspended life, or if you are willing to soar AND willing to crash. Are you willing to live into a full range of your experience? An eating disorder will only allow you to experience a fraction of what you're fully capable of. Remember our mantra? "As long as we're going to be alive, we might as well be amazing!"

A Path to Full*fillment*

Navigating the tumultuous and potentially treacherous terrain of recovery is a hearty challenge for both therapists and their patients. As with any therapeutic encounter, there are countless quagmires and countertransferential impasses. The group setting, with all of its equanimous and liberating potential, can also foster compromising collusions, resentments, and scapegoating dynamics. Even the most seasoned therapists will benefit from supervision to maintain rigorous and conscientious regard for their role in sustaining the sacred space that fosters a group's curative elements. Feminist-oriented therapy embraces the inevitability of conflict as further opportunity to teach new models of strength through vulnerability and growth through authentic connection.

In closing, the following quotation from my cotherapist summarizes the multiplicitous benefits of group for all those sharing in the process:

> A feminist-oriented process group has been transformative for me on two dimensions; first as an adolescent waning in the throes of my own eating disorder, then years later as a young recovered therapist just out of graduate school. Working as a co-therapist in this group afforded me renewed opportunities to experience the strength of shared power, to overcome fears associated with not being good enough, and to rediscover my voice and what it means to use it therapeutically. As I contemplate the life mantras of the group and the principles that drive therapeutic change, I am reminded of a quote by James Berrie: "Those who bring sunshine to the lives of others cannot keep it from themselves."

Group therapy for eating disorders, at its radiant best, sheds redemptive light on the path to recovery for those seeking its *full*fillment.

References

Anderson-Fye, E., & Becker, A. (2004). Sociocultural aspects of eating disorders. In J. K. Thompson (Ed.), *Handbook of eating disorders and obesity* (pp. 565–589). Hoboken, NJ: John Wiley & Sons.

Bloch, S., & Crouch, E. (1985). *Therapeutic factors in group psychotherapy.* Oxford, England: Oxford University Press.

Brabeck, M., & Brown, L. (1997). Feminist theory and psychological practice. In J. Worell & N. Johnson (Eds.), *Shaping the future of feminist psychology* (pp. 15–35). Washington, DC: American Psychiatric Press.

Brown, L. M., & Gilligan, C. (1992). *Meeting at the crossroads: Women's psychology and girl's development.* Cambridge, MA: Harvard University Press.

Butler, S., & Wintram, C. (1991). *Feminist group work.* London: Sage.

DeChant, B. (Ed.). (1996). *Women and group psychotherapy.* New York: Guilford Press.

Enns, C. (2004). *Feminist theories and feminist psychotherapies: Origins, themes and diversity* (2nd ed.). Binghamton, NY: Haworth Press.

Gilligan, C. (1982). *In a different voice: Psychological theory and women's development.* Cambridge, MA: Harvard University Press.

Harper-Giuffre, H., & MacKenzie, K. R. (Eds.). (1992). *Group psychotherapy for eating disorders*. Washington, DC: American Psychiatric Press.

Johnson, C., & Costin, C. (2002). Been there, done that: Clinicians use of personal recovery in the treatment of eating disorders. *Eating Disorders: The Journal of Treatment and Prevention, 10*, 293–303.

Jordan, J., Kaplan, A., Miller, J. B., Stiver, I., & Surrey, J. (1991). *Women's growth in connection*. New York: Guilford Press.

Kilbourne, J. (1999). *Deadly persuasion: Why women and girls must fight the addictive power of advertising*. New York: Free Press.

Kimura, Y. (2004). *The book of balance*. New York: Paraview Special Editions.

Lakin, M. (1991). Some ethical issues in feminist-oriented therapeutic groups for women. *International Journal of Group Psychotherapy, 41*(2), 199–215.

MacKenzie, K. R. (1990). *Introduction to time-limited group psychotherapy*. Washington, DC: American Psychiatric Press.

Maine, M. (2000). *Body wars: Making peace with women's bodies*. Carlsbad, CA: Gurze Books.

McGilley, B. (2000). On the being and the telling of the experience of anorexia: A therapist's perspective. *Renfrew Perspective, 5*(2), 5–7.

McGilley, B. (2004). Feminist perspectives on self-harm behavior and eating disorders. In J. Levitt, R. Sansone, & L. Cohn (Eds.), *Self-harm behaviors and eating disorders: Dynamics, assessment and treatment* (pp. 75–89). New York: Brunner-Routledge.

McGilley, B. (2006). Group therapy for adolescents with eating disorders. *Group, 30*(4), 45–60.

Miller, J. B. (1976*). Toward a new psychology of women*. Boston: Beacon Press.

Piran, N., Jasper, K., & Pinhas, L. (2004). Feminist therapy and eating disorders. In J. K. Thompson (Ed.), *Handbook of eating disorders and obesity* (pp.263–278). Hoboken, NJ: John Wiley & Sons.

Ramachandran, V. S. (2006). *Mirror neurons and the brain in the rat*. Retrieved January 6, 2006, from http://www.edge.org/3rd_culture/ramachandran06_index.html

Seu, I., & Heenan, M. (1998). *Feminism and psychotherapy: Reflections on contemporary theories and practices*. London: Sage.

Smolak, L., & Murnen, S. (2004). A feminist approach to eating disorders. In J. K. Thompson (Ed.), *Handbook of eating disorders and obesity* (pp. 590–605). Hoboken, NJ: John Wiley & Sons.

Surrey, J. (1991). Relationship and empowerment. In J. Jordan, A. Kaplan, J. B. Miller, I. Stiver, & J. Surrey (Eds.), *Women's growth in connection* (pp. 162–180). New York: Guilford Press.

Walker, M. (2002). 12th Annual Renfrew Center Foundation Conference: Feminist Perspectives on Body Image, Trauma and Healing. The Trauma of Racism: Embodying Disconnection. Philadelphia: Renfrew Center Foundation.

Wolf, N. (1991). *The beauty myth: How images of beauty are used against women*. New York: Harper Collins.

Yalom, I., & Leszcz, M. (2005). *The theory and practice of group psychotherapy* (5th ed.) New York: Basic Books.

chapter nine

Treating Eating Disorders
The Healing Power of Guided Imagery

Judith Rabinor and Marion Bilich

Introduction

In the beginning there was image. No words to express our feelings, our needs, our desires. Just image.

It takes years to develop language and give voice to our inner selves. For people who develop eating disorders, the ability to access and put feelings into words is blunted and poorly developed. Understandably, psychotherapy is difficult for these patients. The psychotherapy relationship is dependent on language, and the eating-disordered patient shies away from words, speaking of her inner pain and conflicts with her body. Inner turmoil is expressed in metaphors like bingeing and starving.

To meet this challenge, a wide range of techniques and approaches—ranging from insight-oriented psychotherapy, cognitive-behavioral therapy, art and dance therapy, to group and family therapy—have been developed to treat eating-disordered patients (Battino, 2007; Hornyak & Baker, 1991; Rabinor & Bilich, 2004). This plethora of treatments reflects the diverse needs of this heterogeneous population as well as the complexity of the disorders themselves. Guided imagery provides the clinician with a powerful tool that can be integrated into any of the commonly used approaches in treating eating disorders and facilitates healing by tapping into a deep level of consciousness often inaccessible through words (Singer, 2006).

We are two psychologists, each with decades of experience working with eating-disordered patients. We have found that guided imagery is a powerful but underutilized tool that can transform one's clinical work no matter what one's theoretical orientation (Hutchinson, 1985;

Kearney-Cooke, 1991). These techniques can be integrated into individual or group therapy, augmenting many commonly used approaches by offering an alternative entry point into the deeper levels of consciousness that require heightened use of the mind's imagination and the body's sensate experiences.

This chapter examines the nature of guided imagery and how it can be used in helping patients heal. We use the female pronoun since 90% of the eating-disordered population is female; however, this approach is applicable to clinical work with both genders. Through case examples, we demonstrate how these techniques have been used in our own therapy sessions. In addition, we offer guidelines for constructing and integrating guided imagery into clinical practice throughout a wide variety of settings.

What Is Guided Imagery?

Guided imagery is, simply put, focused imagination: a kind of directed reverie or daydream. Greeks, as far back as Aristotle and Hippocrates, believed that imagery was capable of releasing spirits in the brain that arouse the heart and other parts of the body. Navajo and other Native American Indian groups created healing circles where guided imagery was used to bring people into states of spiritual awareness. Focused imagery, in a relaxed state of mind, has been shown to positively affect medical conditions such as cancer, to improve self-regulatory capacities such as heart rate and blood pressure, and to enhance performance in a wide variety of fields (Naparstek, 1995). Guided imagery is often referred to as *visualization* or *mental imagery*, but the use of these terms can be misleading since guided imagery can include *all* the senses: auditory, olfactory, kinesthetic, tactile, and visual (Battino, 2007; Naparstek, 1995; Singer, 2006). Guided imagery techniques can be classified in a variety of ways, but for the purposes of this chapter we classify them in terms of both origin and therapeutic aim.

Types by Origin

Imagery can be spontaneous, generated by the patient. These patient-generated images often arise in the form of a metaphor or simile. For example, a patient may describe her eating disorder as like "a monkey on my back." The therapist may choose to go with that image, asking the patient to "talk" to that monkey and see what it is trying to tell her. Although the initial image arises spontaneously from the patient's unconscious, the therapist then guides a patient into a deeper, often-unconscious meaning. In other cases, the therapist will present predesigned scripted guided imagery to help a patient understand the underlying functions of her eating disorder. Examples of prescripted fantasies are given in this chapter.

Types by Therapeutic Aim

Imagery can be used diagnostically, as in the scripted fantasy mentioned; the therapist attempts to help the patient access unconscious material about the functions of her disorder. It can be used prescriptively as well. For example, in the patient-generated image of the monkey, a therapist might ask the monkey what the patient needs to do to get it off her back. Guided imagery is also helpful in skill building, such as strengthening tolerance for intense negative emotions or developing internal self-soothing mechanisms. For example, in Susie Orbach's *Fat Is a Feminist Issue 2* (1987a), patients are asked to review a binge incident as though watching a movie of that experience, re-creating the incident in vivid detail, becoming aware of all sensory aspects. Then, the patient is asked to observe the movie of the binge, frame by frame, and become aware of all the emotions she was feeling at the time. Finally, the patient is given the opportunity to rewrite the movie script and eliminate the binge. She is directed to stay with a new creation of the movie, this time with instruction to tolerate whatever feelings arise when she does not binge. This particular guided fantasy gives the patient a miniexperience of accessing and tolerating the emotions that underlie her eating in a safe, controlled therapeutic environment. It helps her build tolerance for the intense emotions that have often driven her to binge.

Why Imagery With Eating Disorders?

Imagery is the language of the unconscious. It has long been known that imagery techniques tap into that deep level of consciousness that cannot be accessed by words alone, giving voice to unconscious thoughts and feelings that may affect behavior (Assagioli, 1965; Jung, 2003; Leuner, 1969). Although we have learned to put words to many of our images, at the deepest levels of consciousness we continue to think in multisensorial images (Fezler, 1989). For example, when we remember a childhood incident, such as baking chocolate chip cookies with our mother or grandparent, we may recall not only a visual image but also the sounds in the kitchen as we prepared the batter, the sweet aroma of freshly baked cookies, the taste of the melted chocolate as we took our first bite, and the feel of that warm, melted chocolate on our tongues. People with eating disorders are frequently described as concrete, flat, and difficult to engage. Often, they report feeling empty inside. Disconnected from their inner worlds, they are isolated from themselves and others. Guided imagery techniques bridge the gap between that unknown inner world and the outer world of therapy. Despite the diversity of the eating-disordered population, the literature and our experience suggest that there are commonalities in the diverse categories of eating disorders, all of which are amenable to work with guided imagery.

Modulating Intense Emotions

People with eating disorders generally have difficulty dealing with intense emotional states. Binge eaters tend to binge when confronted with unacceptable or intense feelings. Those with bulimia will binge and purge, stuffing down and spitting out not only food but also feelings. Anorexics deny themselves food to exert control over their inner emotional worlds. In the context of a safe relationship with a trusted therapist, the eating-disordered patient can practice tolerating small doses of the very intense feelings eating disordered symptoms allow her to avoid.

A clinical example exemplifies this process. After a particularly angry encounter with her boyfriend, Ronnie, a 29-year-old bulimic, asked for "time off" from the relationship. "I need to think things over," she told him. After he left, she proceeded to spend the whole weekend bingeing and vomiting. In a therapy session, she realized that although she initially felt relief being assertive, she later caved in and turned to food. When her therapist suggested that perhaps her assertiveness scared her, Ronnie was surprised. "We need to work on strengthening this emotional muscle—your ability to be comfortable being strong," her therapist suggested and led her through the following imagery:

> "Take a moment to recall how sad you felt when Ben stormed out of the apartment. See yourself clearly, where you were sitting, and what you see when you look into your eyes. Allow yourself to feel your own pain. Now see yourself walking over to the refrigerator, but this time, see yourself taking a deep breath and walking out to the porch. Find a chair on the porch and see yourself sitting down. What is it like to sit with all the feelings Ben's leaving evokes? Let yourself feel it all and when you are ready, see if you can put your feelings into words."

Ronnie surprised herself. Through her tears, she said, "I'm so sad ... and angry." When the therapist suggested she express more, she said, "I hate being held captive by you Ben," and proceeded to express deep wells of anger and hurt.

Developing Self-Soothing Mechanisms

Many eating-disordered patients have not developed the capacity for self-soothing that allows for tolerating intense emotional states. This capacity is believed to develop through the internalization of early comforting or soothing experiences. In normal development, as children mature they are able to soothe themselves with fantasies, images, and memories of being soothed. Winnicott (1965) emphasized the importance of the empathic bond between mother and child as providing a "good enough" holding environment. He described how the internalization of early soothing experiences allows the child to separate and be alone. Early soothing experiences include use of stuffed animals, blankets, and favorite tunes. They are replaced by imaginary companions and fairy tales, and as an individual matures, by friends, lovers, and spouses. An impairment in this self-function may be indicated when bingeing and other eating-disordered symptoms develop as a response to inner pain, emotional discomfort, and loneliness. Hall, Hall, Stradling, and Young (2006) have described the use of imagery to create self-soothing mechanisms in emotional overeaters. Esplen, Garfinkel, Olmsted, Gallop, and Kennedy (1998) demonstrated the usefulness of using two different guided imagery techniques to help women with bulimia develop self-soothing abilities. "Imagine a special place, a natural environment where you can relax" is an example of a nondirective suggestion. Some individuals experience ambivalence or difficulty with nondirective suggestions and prefer a more direct approach (e.g., "imagine being by the beach on a warm summer day"), using their personal experience to help create an inner world of safety.

Uncovering Unconscious Material

Many eating disorder therapists (Bilich, 1983; Orbach, 1987b; Rabinor, 2002) have used guided fantasies to uncover the symbolic meaning of eating disorder symptoms. Hutchinson (1996) pointed out that the focused use of imagery is a powerful tool for accessing unconscious material often expressed symbolically in the symptoms of anorexia and bulimia. In addition, since eating-disordered patients are often distanced from and unaware of their deepest feelings, the healing process will need to include reconnecting with those feelings. Guided imagery techniques have proven invaluable in this regard (Bilich, 1983; Rabinor, 2002). Clinical examples presented in this chapter further explore this issue.

Principles and Assumptions: Integrating Imagery Into Psychotherapy

Guided imagery bypasses conscious defenses, thereby bringing feelings to the forefront, potently evoking profound affective experiences. Therapists should carefully assess whether its use is appropriate for specific patients. For example, the powerful emotions unleashed in a guided fantasy experience may overwhelm the fragile defenses of a low-functioning patient with a borderline personality disorder, but a higher functioning individual with some borderline features may work well with imagery techniques. The following principles need to be kept in mind when considering integrating guided imagery into treatment.

Psychoeducational Preparation

Because any psychotherapeutic technique has the potential to be intrusive and controlling, it is important that therapists explain the rationale for using imagery and the patient's right to use it or not, according to her own comfort. In keeping with a psychoeducational perspective that permeates our therapeutic approach, we introduce imagery by saying:

> "An eating disorder is always all about food—and not at all about food. It is more complicated than it may seem to be. Our work together will hopefully help you understand and appreciate what may lie behind your binging/starving/purging. Just as everything you are thinking or feeling matters, bodily sensations and images are powerful tools of healing."

Often, we refer to imagery work as "waking dream imagery," a term coined by Jerome Singer (1978) and Gerald Epstein (1987).

Relaxation

Guided imagery is facilitated by being in a relaxed, trance-like state (Naparstek, 1995). In a relaxed state, people slow down and are easily absorbed by vivid images or intense bodily sensations. Therefore, most guided imagery techniques are preceded by a short relaxation exercise. Each patient will have her preferred path to relaxation. For some, a few minutes of meditation or holding a yoga pose will bring about the desired state, while for others images of being in a calm, peaceful environment are most helpful. Together, therapist and patient can evaluate the options available and choose the best avenue.

One common relaxation exercise is to focus on breathing. Breathing plays an essential role in all inner-directed experiences. Breathing deactivates the thinking mind and takes us into our bodies. Breathing engages the body and focuses the mind on the automatic function of the body, thereby giving it a constructive directive. Our emotions live in our bodies and are registered in our patterns of breathing. For example, anger produces shallow inhalation and strong panting; fear creates rapid, shallow, ragged breathing. Guilt produces confined, constricted breathing. Just as our emotions are reflected in breathing patterns, breathing patterns can also alter emotions. Controlled breathing releases stress and allows the body to achieve a balance and emotional equilibrium. As psychotherapists, we have often been trained to rely on the verbal, on words and explanations, but when we tap into the body we can regulate our emotions by altering breathing.

The following is the transcript of a simple relaxation exercise based on breathing:

> "Close your eyes and focus your attention on your breathing and take slow deep breaths, in and out. ... Just focus your attention on your breathing ... pay attention to your body as you breathe ... in and out ... in and out ... just allow yourself to be with your natural breathing rhythm ... no place to go, nothing to do. Just breathe. In and out ... in and out ... just breathe. And as you breathe in and out, just notice where you are holding tension in your body and let it go ... and allow yourself to breathe, in and out. ... As you become more comfortable, more and more relaxed ... just feel yourself becoming more and more relaxed."

Imagery can also be preceded by a structured imagery relaxation experience, as illustrated by the following exercise adapted from Bilich's *Weight Loss From the Inside Out: Help for the Compulsive Eater* (1983):

> "Close your eyes and imagine yourself floating on a puffy white cloud. ... Just relax and enjoy the pleasant feeling of safely floating. ... As you float on this cloud, a pleasant feeling of peace and tranquility may come over you. ... You can feel your body becoming very relaxed as you float ... gently ... freely. ... You can notice the deep blue sky, as you float comfortably on this cloud ... the sun shining

> warmly on your face ... you can feel a gentle breeze
> blowing. ... All the noise and bustle of the everyday
> world is far away, and all around you is peace and
> calmness ... nothing to worry about and nothing to
> do ... just relax and enjoy the pleasantness of float-
> ing on a cloud." (Pause about 2 minutes.)

Creating Safety

The first step in beginning imagery work is to help each patient identify
and establish a safe place. Prior to the exercise, it is critical to explain:

> "Having a safe place is important because if scary
> or frightening thoughts, images or feelings arise, it
> is helpful to have a place to retreat to and take com-
> fort in."

The following is one of the exercises we use to help patients create that
safe place. After completing a simple breathing/relaxation exercise and
reminding the patient that she has a choice of keeping her eyes open or
closed, she is instructed to put her feet firmly on the ground to help her
center and feel grounded. We then say:

> "As you feel your whole body relax, take a moment,
> and see if you can bring to mind a place where you
> feel comfortable and relaxed, comfortable and safe."
> [Please note: The repetition is intentional because
> repetition breeds familiarity and comfort.] "It may
> be a familiar place, one you know well, or it may be
> a brand new place that you have never been before.
> Just take your time and let me know when you have
> found your safe place with a nod." [After patient
> nods, continue.] "Take a moment and breathe in and
> out ... in and out ... take all the time you need to
> sense whatever you know about this place. ... Just
> notice: What time of day is it, daytime or nighttime?
> And notice the temperature: Is it warm or cold, win-
> ter or summer? Just notice the sounds and smells
> that welcome you as you take a moment to be there,
> in this place, your safe place." [Maintain silence for
> a minute or two, then continue.] "Know that this is
> your relaxing, calm place, a place you can return to
> whenever you want or need to."

The Mind-Body Connection

People with eating disorders often express their emotional pain in their bodies. Therapists need to help patients become more mindful of how feelings are expressed and communicated in bodily movements and sensations. Helping patients notice their bodily movements is the first step. For example, Mia repeatedly twirled her hair in sessions. At first, she shrugged off the meaning of this behavior. Eventually, it became clear that "twirling" was a harsh and purposeful action: Whenever she articulated angry feelings, she punished herself for doing so. Uncovering this dynamic led to an insight: Purging was not really about eating the "wrong foods" but about thinking the "wrong" thoughts.

Not only are patients unaware of the ways their bodies hold discomfort, they are also unaware of the ways their bodies can provide comfort. In beginning a relaxation exercise, we often ask patients to do a slow body scan noticing how they hold messages of tension or vitality in their bodies. We affirm the power of the mind-body connection when reminding patients: "Go inside and see if you might notice something new that emerges."

The Principle of Amplification

Another way to acknowledge how bodies express pain often inaccessible to words and to emphasize the interconnection of the mind and body is to call attention to and exaggerate bodily sensations or movements. For example, Hindy frequently raised her hand to her mouth, blurring her speech. When her therapist began directing her to reenact this pattern, she realized how she selectively lowered her voice whenever she wanted to say something that she believed was not acceptable. Another patient frequently shrugged her shoulders. When the therapist asked her to exaggerate this movement, she realized she shrugged off and dismissed her hurt feelings.

Clinical Examples

Scripted Imagery 1: Favorite Food Exercise

Food has many meanings to each of us. It is linked to our earliest experiences of being loved, fed, and nourished. Our earliest experiences set the blueprint for how we expect to care for ourselves as well as how we expect others to care for and nourish us.

Eating-disordered patients come to therapy initially preoccupied with their fear of eating and dread of gaining weight. Often, they are obsessed with detailing what they eat and do not eat, oblivious to the symbolic meanings enacted in starving, bingeing, and purging. A primary goal of the initial stage of treatment is to help them become interested in the latent meanings encoded in their behaviors and to develop a deeper capacity for self-reflection. We have found that by focusing on their interests, such as food, dieting, eating, and not eating, we are able to meet their needs for mirroring, develop trust, and awaken their capacity for self-reflection. The following imagery exercise was developed to help group therapy patients begin to explore the roots of their feelings about food and eating:

"Close your eyes and imagine you are at a banquet, a banquet in the sky. Imagine there is a table before you, filled with food. Let your eyes sweep across the whole table as you look for your favorite food. Take your time, no need to rush, as you allow your eyes to sweep across the whole table, back and forth, as you look for your favorite food. Think about your favorite food. Perhaps a food comes to mind, and you are looking for that food now. Perhaps your eyes are sweeping across the table, going back and forth as you take your time, looking for, searching out, seeking your favorite food. Take a good look at all the foods that come into view as you let yourself see everything, as you search for a favorite, your favorite food.

"What is it like to see the table? How are you doing as you search, seek, and find your favorite food? Take a good look, and let your whole body— your eyes, your nose, your mouth, fill up with this food as you breathe into it, as you breathe in what it means to be with your favorite food. Soon you are going to eat this food. What kinds of feelings come up as you imagine eating this food? What are you feeling? Excitement? Joy? Terror? Dread? Take another breath and dip into yourself as you ask the question: What am I feeling as I sit with this food?

"Before you eat, take a moment and think about the first time you had this food. Allow a scene to come to mind: you with this food—the first time you had it. How old were you? Where were you? Can you recall the season—was it warm or cold, summer or winter? And now, think about the most recent time you had this food. When was it? Where were you? See yourself eating this food, the last time you had it. Think about the next time you will have this food. Do you know when that might be? Have you planned it? Or does it usually happen spontaneously, eating this food unexpectedly?

"Imagine we will be having it for lunch today. How would you feel about eating it here, today for lunch? Imagine tasting it. Do you pick it up with your hands? Touch it? Or use a fork and knife? Does it slide into your mouth? Is it gooey? Crunchy? Listen to the sounds you make as you taste it. Imagine smelling it. Does it have a particular odor? Is it strong or sweet? Pungent? Mild? Wild? Or does it have no odor at all? Taste it, imagine it entering your mouth. Do you eat it delicately? Do you feel prim and proper? Or do you eat it with enthusiasm and gusto? See it, taste it, listen to the noises you make as the food slides down your throat. Just let your whole body get involved as you allow yourself to be with your favorite food. As you see yourself eating it, see if there is any new information from way down deep that emerges—whether you come to know something new about yourself as you imagine being with your favorite food. Now, imagine putting your favorite food away. Wrap it in tinfoil, Saran wrap, or put it in a container—see what it is you will wrap it up in. Watch the food going into the box, the bag, the container. And now imagine putting the box, the bag, the container, in a shopping bag and having this shopping bag at your feet by your chair. When the bag is securely there, open your eyes, take out a piece of paper, and write about your experience in this exercise."

Discussion of This Exercise

Through a series of specific scenes, this exercise evokes unconscious sensory and affective material associated with food, eating, feeding, and nourishing oneself. It helps to awaken the latent and symbolic meanings encoded in eating behaviors. In addition, it evokes associative material that can be used clinically to understand how eating meets, and does not meet, nutritional, emotional, and spiritual hungers. Often, the imagery promotes the simple awareness that food and eating are pleasurable, allowing a new acknowledgment and validation of the right to feed oneself.

Processing This Exercise

When the imagery is complete, after journaling for a few moments, the group members are asked to introduce themselves as their favorite food, without having any side conversations during the introductions. To model the introduction process, the group leader provides an example, intentionally demonstrating how food is connected to both positive and negative experiences:

> "I'm lobster, Judy's favorite food. Judy eats me when she celebrates. She learned about eating me when she was a child at beach parties with her family. They were tons of fun. Judy still relies on me to celebrate. Sometimes she even treats herself to me if she feels sad. I'm lobster, Judy's favorite food."

Here are two examples of group members' introductions:

> "I'm hot fudge sundae, Marji's favorite food. Marji has a passive-aggressive relationship with me. Sometimes she loves me, sometimes not. The first time she met me she was very sad. She was a little girl, and her mommy and daddy gave me to her to feel better. Ever since, she has hot fudge sundaes whenever she is sad or lonely or unhappy. I give her the kind of comfort she isn't able to find from a real person. I'm hot fudge sundae, Marji's favorite food."

> "I'm mashed potatoes, Nina's favorite food. Although I'm Nina's favorite food, she doesn't eat me too often. How sad. She rarely gives herself what she really wants."

This exercise is designed to identify how one's attitudes and behaviors about food contain subtle attitudes toward life. For example, Marji realized food brought her the comfort she craved, and Nina realized that her self-starvation was not limited to food: She starved herself emotionally as well. Processing this exercise often allows participants to clarify the ways food expresses deep intrapsychic and interpersonal needs and conflicts. For example, food can help us feel special, sexy, and loved. What we eat, and how we eat it, can help us feel sneaky, entitled, or courageous. This exercise paves the way for reflection and skill building with the following kinds of questions: If you didn't use food, how else might you rebel? Comfort yourself? Be sexy? Feel special?

Concluding the group with a writing exercise offers an opportunity to process and integrate lessons from listening to others. In response to the instructions, "Say good-bye to your favorite food," one member wrote:

> "Dear spaghetti, You were there when I needed you, when I was alone, when I was lost and unable to ask for help, when my heart was breaking. You were there when others ignored me, teased me, laughed at me. I became so used to you that I thought you would always be there—until death do us part. Never in my wildest dreams did I think I would have to say good-bye or want to leave you behind. But I see, now, that you hold me back, hold me prisoner—I must move forward. I must take down the wall we built that shut out the world of pain, emptiness, and anguish. It's time now to take down the wall—brick by brick—and slowly let life in."

Scripted Imagery 2: The Inner Guide Exercise

This vignette was developed to help patients connect with their inner wisdom. It illustrates how a scripted imagery experience can be used, both diagnostically and prescriptively, with eating-disordered patients and can lead to greater understanding of and trust in their ability to function in the world without obsessions about food, body image distortions, or dietary restrictions.

In preparation, each patient thinks of a question she would want to ask if she had the opportunity to talk with the wisest of beings. In the imagery, patients meet and talk with an "inner guide," a being who is wise and all-knowing. Note that this guided imagery includes a built-in relaxation exercise designed to set the scene for meeting the guide and doing the inner work required. The basic transcript is as follows:

> "Close your eyes and imagine yourself in a beautiful, relaxing place. ... It could be a place you have been before, or it could be somewhere you would like to be. ... It could be real or imaginary ... make sure that it is a place that feels comfortable. ... Become aware of your surroundings ... make the place as real as you can, using all your senses ... be aware of the colors ... the sounds ... the smells ... the feel of the air on your skin. ... Try to make the image of this place as vivid as possible. ... Spend

a few minutes enjoying yourself in this beautiful, peaceful place.

"Now, in this peaceful place, imagine a golden white light of relaxing energy entering your body through your head ... a stream of beautiful energy flowing down through your head ... your neck ... your shoulders ... you can feel that golden white light bring peace and relaxation as it flows down your back and chest ... through your midriff ... down your legs ... and back into the ground. ... That golden white light has a clear path through your body, from your head to your toes, and back into the earth. ... Continue envisioning yourself in this place, with that golden white light running through you and around you, connecting you to all around you. ...

"Now, still envisioning yourself in that beautiful, peaceful place, become aware of the presence of a living being ... you may or may not 'see' that being, but somehow you will be aware of a presence ... you sense the presence of a loving, accepting, wise being ... you may begin to see your guide more clearly, or you may just hear a voice, or you may just continue to sense your guide is with you ... in any case you will sense the loving, caring and wisdom." [Pause at least 30 seconds.] "... This is your guide, your advisor, a link with your subconscious mind and your highest self ... your guide knows the answers to all your questions. ... Before you ask any questions, spend some time getting acquainted with your guide ... you might want to ask your guide's name ... your guide is to become your friend and advisor, so spend some time finding out more about who this being is and how your guide lives." [Pause 30 seconds.] "When you are ready, ask your guide the question you prepared or any other question that feels appropriate at this time. ... Be aware that your guide may answer with words alone, or you may be shown a picture or be given something. Your guide may make a gesture ... in some way your guide will give you the answer to your question." [Pause at least 2 minutes.] "... If you do not understand anything your guide says, ask your guide to explain, to be more specific." [Pause at least 2 minutes.] ...

"It will soon be time to say goodbye to your guide for now. ... Remember your guide is always with you, and you can come back to visit any time you wish. ... Before you leave, your guide will give you a gift, something to help you with your problem" [Pause at least 30 seconds.] "... Look at what your guide gave you and see if you can discover the significance of this gift ... you can ask questions about the gift. ... When you are ready, say goodbye to your guide and slowly come back to your existence in the room and open your eyes."

Discussion of This Exercise

For those who experience a visual image during this exercise, examining why the patient conceptualizes the guide as she does yields important information about her inner world. The guide may appear as a wise old woman or man, a religious figure, or a comic book character (most often an action figure). It can be very useful to help patients examine why their inner wisdom may have been conceptualized with that particular image. For example, Dotty saw her guide as Xena the Warrior. Then, she was asked to think of every word that came into her mind when she thought about Xena, and she chose words like big, strong, capable, smart. Dotty realized that she believed that she needed the physical and mental strength of an Amazon to get through her difficult life.

Esplen and Garfinkel (1998) suggested that imagery provided by a therapist (such as the therapist's taped voice) facilitates the connection between the patient and the therapist and may promote a "therapist presence" outside of therapy, creating a type of "portable transitional object." The therapist can create a recording of this inner guide imagery on tape or CD, allowing the patient to continue her inner work between sessions while also strengthening the connection with the therapist between sessions.

Processing This Exercise

Here are some of the most common difficulties that can arise while using the inner guide exercise, along with suggestions about how they can be addressed:

1. *"I couldn't find a guide."* Suggest that the patient keep trying. Usually, with persistence, a guide will "appear." It can help to explain that there is no right way to experience your guide. The guide may come in the form of a visual image, may be a disembodied voice, or may convey information through bodily sensations.
2. *"My guide wouldn't talk to me."* Often, it is helpful to suggest the patient ask the guide, "Am I not ready to hear what you have to say?" or "Do I not want to hear what you have to say?" When Paula's guide refused to communicate, she asked her guide why she was not talking, and having done so, Paula began to laugh. "She says I never listen to her anyway, and actually, she's right. No wonder she's not talking to me."
3. *"I don't understand my guide's answer."* More work may be needed to prepare oneself to deal with the meaning of the answer. If no information is given by the guide, it may be useful to have the patient ask her guide what she can do to prepare her to understand the answer.

Conclusion

In a novel by Herman Hesse (1961), Siddhartha, the seeker of enlightenment, ends up beside a raging river in India. A voice inside whispers to remind him to let the river of life be a teacher. Like the river of life, use of guided imagery offers patients an opportunity to stay with images that may be distressing, denied, disavowed, or displaced onto eating-disordered symptoms. Like the river of life, by staying with our images, we and our clients have endless opportunities for learning, growth, and accessing our inner wisdom.

References

Assagioli, R. (1965). *Psychosynthesis: A manual of principles and techniques.* New York: Hobbs, Dorman.

Battino, R. (2007). *Guided imagery: Psychotherapy and healing through the mind-body connection.* Bethel, CT: Crown House.

Bilich, M. (1983). *Weight loss from the inside out: Help for the compulsive eater.* San Francisco: Harper/San Francisco.

Epstein, G. (1987). *Healing visualizations.* New York: Bantam Books.

Esplen, M. J., & Garfinkel, P. E. (1998). Guided imagery treatment to promote self soothing in bulimia nervosa: A theoretical rationale. *Journal of Psychotherapy Practice and Research, 7,* 102–118.

Esplen, M. J., Garfinkel, P. E., Olmsted, M., Gallop, R. M., & Kennedy, S. (1998). A randomized controlled trial of guided imagery in bulimia nervosa. *Psychological Medicine, 28*(6), 1347–1357.

Fezler, W. (1989). *Creative imagery: How to visualize in all five senses.* New York: Simon and Schuster.

Hall, E., Hall, C. A., Stradling, P., & Young, D. (2006). *Guided imagery: Interventions in counseling and psychotherapy.* Thousand Oaks, CA: Sage.

Hesse, H. (1961). *Siddhartha.* New York: Bantam Books.

Hornyak, L., & Baker, E. (1991). *Experiential therapies of eating disorders.* New York: Guilford Press.

Hutchinson, M. (1985). *Transforming body image: Learning to love the body you have.* Freedom, CA: Crossing Press.

Hutchinson, M. (1996). Imagining ourselves whole: A feminist approach to treating body image disorders. In P. Fallon, M. A. Katzman, & S. C. Wooley (Eds.), *Feminist perspectives on eating disorders* (pp. 152–168). New York: Guilford Press.

Jung, C. (2003). *The psychology of the unconscious.* New York: Dover.

Kearney-Cooke, A. (1991) Reclaiming the body: Using guided imagery in the treatment of body image disturbances among bulimic women. In L. Hornyak & E. Baker (Eds.), *Experiential therapies for eating disorders* (pp. 11–33). New York: Guilford Press.

Leuner, H. (1969). Guided affective imagery (GAI): A method of intensive psychotherapy. *American Journal of Psychotherapy, 23,* 4–22.

Naparstek, B. (1995). *Staying well with guided imagery.* New York: Warner Books.

Orbach, S. (1987a). *Fat is a feminist issue 2.* New York: Berkley Books.

Orbach, S. (1987b). *Fed up and hungry: Women, oppression and food.* London: Women's Press.

Rabinor, J. (2002). *A starving madness: Tales of hunger, hope and healing in psychotherapy.* Carlsbad, CA: Gurze Books.

Rabinor, J., & Bilich, M. (2004). Experiential approach to body image change. In T. Cash & T. Pruzinsky (Eds.), *Body image: A handbook of theory, research and practice* (pp. 469–477). New York: Guilford Press.

Singer, J. (2006). *Imagery in psychotherapy.* Washington, DC: American Psychological Association.

Winnicott, D. W. (1965). *The maturational processes and the facilitating environment.* London: Hogarth.

chapter ten

BodyMind Treatment
Connecting to Imprinted
Emotions and Experiences

Adrienne Ressler

Introduction

The intangible reciprocal relationship between body and mind is a key element in the treatment of body image disturbance in clients with eating disorders. Body and mind are interrelated parts that form a cohesive whole. Our body movements are influenced by our thoughts, attitudes, and feelings, just as our thoughts, attitudes, and feelings are influenced by the rhythm and movements of the body (Rice, Hardenbergh, & Hornyak, 1989).

Throughout history, however, the contributions of psychology to physical health and disease have consistently been met with skepticism. Since the 17th century, science has split human beings into two separate but interacting entities of body and mind. A bargain made at that time between the French philosopher Rene Descartes and the Pope set the course of Western medicine for the next 300 years. To acquire the bodies needed for anatomic dissection, Descartes agreed to lay claim to only one aspect of human experience, the physical realm, while the church held exclusive domain over the soul, the mind, and the emotions of humankind (Pert, 1997).

Fortunately, through recent research findings in the fields of psychoneurology, neuroscience, yoga, dance/movement therapy, epigenetic medicine, sensorimotor psychotherapy, and meditation, the distinction between mind and body is revealed as merely an artificial dichotomy. Benson (2002, 2004), Weil (2007), Marks and Schultz (1992/2004), Forbes (2007), and Damasio (1994) are all well known for their groundbreaking work linking the relationship between the brain and the body. As Candace Pert stated in *Molecules of Emotion* (1997): "Mind doesn't dominate the body, it becomes body—body and mind are one. On the molecular level there is no difference between the body and mind" (p. 187). Or, as

Dawson Church (2007) stated: "Your body reads your mind" (p. 36). Even *Webster's New Collegiate Dictionary* (Merriam-Webster, 1970) recognizes the bodymind link, defining *emotion* (French from *emouvoir*, to stir up) as "a psychic and physical reaction subjectively experienced as strong feeling and physiologically involving changes that prepare the body for immediate vigorous action" (p. 271). Thus, bodymind treatment seems both necessary and natural when approaching the body image disturbance of clients with eating disorders.

BodyMind Integration

At the same time that our emotions and experiences are imprinted cognitively through our thoughts and language, they are imprinted physiologically in the very cells, organs, and musculature of the body. The body "freezes" with fear, "shrinks" in shame, "jumps" for joy, and "melts" with love. Whatever is happening in the mind is simultaneously stored in some part of the body. Chopra (1990) believes that, even on the cellular level, we hold the holographic memory of every experience we have ever had.

Somatic practitioners have long known that individuals split off from their emotions when they are unable to verbally process their feelings and split off from their body sensations when they are wounded emotionally, physically, sexually, or spiritually (McGeeney, 1988). The language used by Freud and Breuer (1893) described the memory of trauma as a foreign body that must be regarded as an agent continuing to work long after its entry. Terr (1990) described the return of trauma-related feelings triggered by stress long after the initial event as a form of psychophysiologic reenactment. It does not matter how "mental" the origins of post-traumatic psychophysiologic reenactment may be, the pains and bodily sensations that the victim feels are real. The link between body and mind remains unconscious to the survivor long after the incident.

Ironically, as obsessed as clients with eating disorders are about their bodies, they are not really "living in" or "grounded in" their bodies. The body is not used as a place to live or experience but as an object needing to be controlled. Clients often refer to their bodies as "it" or "this body." It is not uncommon to hear someone with an eating disorder describe her relationship with her body as that of one with a stranger or even an enemy (Kleinman & Hall, 2006). Often dissociating or rejecting the body parts they loathe or in which painful or frightening memories are held, they have no sense of the body being whole, having all of its parts. Their experience is one of detachment from the body and little sense of ownership.

As a result, clients are alienated not only from the body but also from the disowned parts of self and the experiences and emotions that the body holds. Individuals who are not connected to their bodies are cut off from identifying or accessing their feeling states. Thus, clients in treatment for an eating disorder or trauma often report having "frozen" feelings or being numb.

Many clients who suffer from eating disorders have dissociated from the body because for them the body holds pain and painful memories. "Ignoring internal states amounts to burying feelings, and the burial site exists in the body itself" (Kleinman & Hall, 2006, p. 2). Body loathing often starts at an early age as the result of taunting or teasing about body size, weight, or shape. Body dissatisfaction may be learned in the family or culture as a way of defining what it means to be "female." Some clients may carry a sense of shame over their body's response of pleasure to a violation of sexual boundaries and are left with a feeling that the body has betrayed them. Boundary violations often leave clients with a sense that someone else "owns" their body. An adversarial relationship with their body keeps clients from ever experiencing a sense of self that is integrated and whole.

When clients are disconnected from their body, they become split off not only from their life experiences but also from the parts of their body where those experiences and feelings are held. Reclaiming the body is an essential component in the recovery from an eating disorder. Woodman (1997) cautioned that the body's warning signs are to be heard and obeyed. The body must be attended to, rather than being ignored, starved, gorged, or made drunk. Feelings and actions can be trusted when they initiate from the body itself.

Culture and Identity

When individuals live their lives oriented to external, rather than internal, frames of reference reflecting the sensations and signals of the body itself, their sense of identity derives from the images seen in advertising, film, television, and the fashion industry. Identity becomes a cognitive concept only, not one that integrates body and mind. The individual is literally locked in her head. In *Betrayal of the Body*, Alexander Lowen (1967) stated that the feeling of identity arises from a feeling of contact with the body. Personal identity has substance and structure only insofar as it is based on the reality of bodily feeling (Montagu, 1971). Whitehouse (1999), too, believed that the head belongs to the body rather than the body to the head.

For most clients with eating disorders, the eating disorder itself acts as a substitute identity for the authentic self. "I am anorexic" is often heard, not "I am suffering from anorexia." This structure or framework serves to identify and organize the self. The negative ways in which clients perceive themselves become so familiar that, over time, they report: "It feels like me!" Females, young and old alike, seem to casually define themselves in harsh and punishing terms: "I am gross," "I am disgusting," "I am fat." Many repeat these "mantras" hundreds of times a day, reinforcing a negative body image identity until it becomes so familiar that they believe its message and embrace its persona.

As much as these women may claim to hate their negative/distorted identity, they get caught up in it, fearful of letting it go because it is "all she has." Like any other abusive relationship, the victim becomes identified with her abuser. Although clients are intimately familiar with their distorted body image identity, they do not really "own" it. That is, they have not really recognized how their relationship with self and others has been affected or how long the shadow is that gets cast on their life.

Several years ago, I facilitated a daylong body image workshop with 10 women, all suffering from eating disorders. The following dialogue is from an exercise designed to have them experience, in body and mind, how deep seated their commitment was to holding a distorted body image identity.

"Find a word that captures the essence of how you feel living in your body," I direct the group. It takes only a moment for each of the women to respond: fat, repulsive, jiggly, clumsy, gross, squat, a mess, hideous, a blob. (Two shared the blob identity.)

I have each of them, in turn, repeat their word and own it by saying: "I am ... ." in front of it. The group is uneasy; no one wants to go first. Having to say it aloud to others feels different from name-calling themselves. Putting the "I am" in front makes it more real. Jan goes first: *"I am repulsive,"* she says, staring at her feet. The rest of the group, one by one, claimed their negative body image identity. All agreed that it feels familiar, but not necessarily comfortable. I talk to them about identity, about how the words and images they reinforce get lodged into their minds until they become believed.

I then ask the group to imagine that they are all going to attend a party. Instead of introducing themselves by their given names, they must identify themselves by their negative body image. They must all meet everyone at the party. They laugh nervously. It seems ridiculous to them.

Initially, the room is buzzing. "Hi, I'm Squat." "Glad to meet you," says Hideous. She introduces herself back. Individuals separate and move on to the next person. The energy in the room becomes flat, the silliness gone, replaced by a heaviness in the air. When everyone finishes the task, they talk about the lack of connection to others that they experienced. They all felt the body changes, the drawing in, the shame, the fear of being found out. They talk about how trapped they feel in these identities. Not one of them wants to be who they think they are but feel they cannot change.

I continue with the exercise, but this time I advise them to identify a word that captures the essence of how they would like to feel living in their bodies. I advise them not to use a trigger word like "thin," "in control," or anything that has sent them to a bad place in the past. I instruct them to again place "I am ..." in front of their new identity word. "I know," says Repulsive. "I am elegant." As she speaks the word, she draws her whole body upward, suddenly appearing taller, longer. I ask her to define elegant for the group. "It means that I flow; I can glide through life."

Placing a hand on one hip, the next member grins wildly, "I am RED HOT SEXY!" The group responds with high fives and cheers. I ask her to explain what that would be like for her, to be living as "RED HOT SEXY!" She turns serious and goes quiet for about 30 seconds: "I think I would be terrified," she allows. We talk about how complex language is and how sometimes what we think we want is really not so great for us.

We mull over the identities each of them has chosen: Elegant, Grounded, Perfectly Me, Sleek, Playful, Vibrant, Glowing, OK, Flexible, Good Enough. They have an easier time calling up the distorted, critical self than they do claiming ownership of a healthier sense of self. "Another party is in order," I announce. I tell the group that the instructions are the same, but this time they will introduce themselves by their new positive body image word. The shift in energy is amazing. Connection and conversation flow as they move from person to person. Some laugh, some look a bit stiff and uncertain, but it is evident that they are all enjoying this. "Glowing" really is glowing. "OK" is standing up straight instead of slumping.

At the end of the exercise, they share their feelings. Most agreed it was fun, and they enjoyed how they felt in their bodies. "But it's not really me," says Elegant. I explain that it is really her. It is a part of her that she has kept in the background and not allowed to develop. I encourage the women to notice referencing themselves by their distorted body image identity and to say, "No, that's not me," when they recognize what they are doing. I instruct them to practice calling themselves by their positive identity name at least 100 times. I suggest that they write a list comparing the emotional and physical responses they experienced when playing out the embodiment of their positive and negative body image representations.

Before they leave, I remind the group that as good as this feels, feeling good is unfamiliar to them. For most of them, feeling in a way that is unfamiliar brings on anxiety. I explain that although the pain of the negative identity is diminishing, they are not used to living without it. We talk about ways to ease the anxiety and stay with the positive body image identity.

Body Image

Body image disturbance is one of the most intractable issues in the treatment of eating disorders. From an early age, the way females feel about their bodies correlates strongly with the way they feel about themselves. The experience of body image is inexorably woven into the very fabric of female identity. Consequently, most women have difficulty differentiating who they are from how they experience their appearance. Defined as having three components, body image is made up of the picture in their mind's eye of how they see themselves, the perception of how they believe others see them, and the experience of living in one's own body. In healthy individuals, a core body belief remains constant despite a bad hair day or increased number on the scale. This belief about oneself is relatively consistent with others' perceptions (Ressler & Kleinman, 2006). Individuals may lessen the severity of their eating disorder symptoms (or even stop them completely), successfully resolve family conflicts, and give up self-destructive behaviors, but if their connection to their body is not repaired, they may continue an adversarial relationship to their body, making them more vulnerable to relapse.

Body image is not a concept specific to eating-disordered clients; it is an integral part of human development proposed to begin before birth. Parents' perceptions of what their baby will look like, including what sex it may be, set the stage for a relationship based on expectation, acceptance, rejection, or indifference. The more compatible the imagined perception is with the actual infant, the more likely it is that acceptance and bonding will occur (Fisher, Fisher, & Stark, 1990). After the infant is born, the reciprocal relationship with the caretaker, strengthened by empathic parenting, touch, and eye contact (mutual gaze), promotes the development of trust, boundaries, and the capacity for connection. Body awareness in the child is produced through stimulation of the body, chiefly through the skin (Montagu, 1971).

The infant sees the world feelingly through touch and mirroring. If, over time, the synthesis of sensations experienced by the infant are basically pleasurable (empathic, affirming, nurturing), then the infant is likely to have a whole and integrated body image. If, over time, the synthesis of sensations are experienced as painful (e.g., holding touch is anxious, nervous, clutching, engulfing; gaze is critical, angry, unfocused; or the infant consistently experiences deprivation), then there will be gaps or distortions in the development of body image (Krueger, 1989). These individuals go through life experiencing feelings of emptiness and longing, with hungers that can never be satisfied.

The manner in which the child's needs are met registers in her consciousness as body sensations. The nature of her felt sensation will influence the relationship she comes to have with her body. The reject-ing parent deprives the child of the bonding needed for providing calm-ness and pleasure as well as the establishment of safety and boundaries. The possessive or intrusive parent denies the child the right to privacy and being separate, thereby depriving her from ownership of her body. Krueger (1989) explained that for individuals to experience a stable sense of self, it is essential that they first must have experienced the integrity of one's own body space and boundaries. When the infant's body boundar-ies are not consistently defined by touch, caress, or secure holding, the infant does not develop a reliable experience of internal body sensational affect or of body boundary and may later experience her body as incom-plete and her body image as distorted. It is useful to think of body image in terms of being on a continuum from whole or integrated to incomplete or disconnected.

Attachment

The latest scientific research demonstrates that our nervous systems are not self-contained: From earliest childhood, our brains actually link with those of the people close to us in a silent rhythm that alters the structure of our brains, establishes lifelong emotional patterns, and affects our capac-ity for relationship. The infant's brain is wired initially with the parent's brain so that, in an attuned attachment, the signals of one person are directly responding to the signals of another. When this does not occur, or when there is trauma to the developing nervous system, the result is emo-tional dysregulation, inability to soothe, and problems with attachment (Lapides, 2007). Allen Shore stated that psychotherapy works because it is an attachment relationship capable of regulating neurons and altering underlying neural structure (as cited in Lapides, 2007).

With clients who have eating disorders, it is essential to maximize rela-tional therapeutic strategies enhancing communication and trust to allow entrée into the inner world of the client. Rather than focusing primarily on diagnostic criteria and symptoms, emphasis needs to be placed on the "felt" sense of clients. The attuned relational bond established in therapy is paramount as it is there that we create the same type of mutuality that occurs in infancy when the "two brains" resonate together. "What is it like to be you?" I ask my client Suzanne, who suffers from anorexia nervosa. "How do you feel living in your body when you wake up in the morning? Help me understand, so that together we can work to help you feel better." Suzanne begins to relax when she senses that I genuinely am interested in "who" she is. I have begun to create a bridge into her world.

The function of the right, nonverbal hemisphere of the brain should be recognized for the important role it plays in treatment. Whereas the left hemisphere of the brain deals with explicit, verbal, and conscious processes as well as analytical and rational thinking, the right hemisphere is home to more intense emotions and provides the key to attachment, empathy, and self-regulation (Lapides, 2007). The right hemisphere may have a far greater role in the regulation of bodily and emotional states and in mediating social and emotional communication. The attunement between the right hemisphere of the client to the right hemisphere of the therapist may be crucial in establishing the secure attachment environment essential for effective therapy to occur. This environment can be achieved by therapists being authentic; asking open-ended questions that focus on feelings, sensations, and emotions; and revealing their genuine interest in their clients. This therapeutic process thus enables the therapist to serve in a similar role as an attachment figure and as a part of an interactive relationship.

As healers, we respond to our clients' stories, told to us both verbally and viscerally. As we react to their faces, bodies, voice tone, energy levels, and what we sense beneath, they react to us in kind. Often, they will express having a "sense" that something feels "wrong" with them but cannot specifically articulate what it is. In the service of preserving a false or inauthentic self and remaining distanced from their feelings, they attempt to give "right answers" and become adept at verbal repartee. When therapists have clients focus on breath and body, they experience the therapist's attunement, and the right brain becomes engaged. Engaging the right brain bypasses the client's anxiety and need to be perfect because there is no "right way" to be.

Verbal therapy often benefits when augmented by strategies that focus on accessing experiences and emotions stored in the body. Art, dance/movement, music therapy, and massage all access memory and tap into neural networks that are helpful in regulating affect. The great dancer and choreographer Martha Graham (1991) once said, "Movement never lies. It is a barometer telling the state of the soul's weather to all who can read it" (p. 8).

Meditation and mindfulness-based stress reduction have become almost commonplace in traditional medical settings for healing both physical and emotional illnesses. Researchers at Indiana State University discovered that mindfulness meditation in conjunction with eating meditations reduced binge eating in obese binge eaters from four times per week to two times per week (Kristeller & Hallet, 1999). Stress and anxiety, which are at the root of many physical problems, can be managed by meditation and, when meditation is taught to clients, it provides them with a sense of control over their own lives (Kabat-Zinn et al., 1992).

In a research project conducted by the Touch Research Institute of the University of Miami Medical School in conjunction with the Renfrew

Center, anorexic females received standard Swedish massage therapy twice weekly for 5 weeks. Results showed a reduction of anxiety and stress, increased dopamine and norepinephrine levels, decreased body dissatisfaction on the Eating Disorders Inventory, and lowered cortisol levels (Hart et al., 2001). Ancient healing rhythms and rituals for healing (such as chanting, drumming, and breath work) increase body awareness, regulate energy levels, promote states of relaxed alertness, strengthen impulse control, facilitate mindfulness, build self-esteem, and help integrate creative and logical thought processes important to wellness and recovery (Clohosey, 2003). For example, during a drumming workshop, a young woman with bulimia reflected, "This is the first time in 4 years that I didn't think about my eating disorder for 10 minutes."

Enhancing opportunities for spiritual development with positive rituals that honor one's humanity and aliveness can provide alternatives to replace the destructive rituals of the eating disorder (bingeing, purging, starving). Practitioners who recommend involvement in the healing arts that emphasize grounding and centering, such as yoga, karate, or pilates, find these resources to be helpful ways of engaging the body in a nonthreatening manner.

Accessing Stored Emotion

One way to access stored feeling is to listen for the "emotion" words in spoken language. Once an emotion word is identified (such as "I'm feeling angry," "She really made me sad," "I am too scared to change"), simply ask clients to relax their breath and then instruct them to move their nondominant hand to the part of their body where that emotion resides. This process helps clients notice sensations and begin efforts to integrate mind and body in a nonthreatening manner. "Tell me about your sadness," I might say when a client mentions that she has been "down" all week. "What does it feel like to carry it in your body? Is it stored deep inside of you or close to the surface? Is the feeling solid or elusive? Does it have a sense of heaviness or lightness?"

Questions like these lead to a rhythmic dance between client and healer in which each response draws the client closer and closer to moving into her body without really being aware of what is happening. The client is not *thinking* about her body, she is being *in* her body, without judgment or critique.

Asking clients to identify if the body part in which the emotion is stored has any special significance can also be helpful. One client reported that her anger was trapped in her stomach, which grew larger and larger as her anger stayed unexpressed. Another identified that her fear inhabited her legs, paralyzing her and keeping her stuck in place. Because many clients feel it is safer to externalize their feelings, they may feel more comfortable drawing their emotions rather than speaking about them. "Emotion" words, once identified, can be utilized in a creative arts manner, drawn, sculpted, or put into a collage.

These strategies that approach clients through body-focused means are usually not perceived as confrontational or "therapeutic," and as a result, clients feel less challenged or controlled. Through an exploration of emotions along these parameters, therapists and clients can enter into a mutual exchange that is attuned and authentic. The more respectful therapists are of a client's tempo and timing, the more likely it is that her protective "false self" will give way to genuine feelings stored deep within.

Therapists must always remember that clients are the real experts. They are the ones who bring experience and "knowing" to each session. I still remember how I learned this lesson years ago.

Margaret, a 36-year-old binge eater, entered treatment with an agenda that focused on how to deal with her husband's emotional abuse. When I asked Margaret to share her feelings about the abuse, she claimed to be angry, but her emotion did not match her words. Excitedly, I suggested that she use a "battaca" or padded bat to access her buried emotions. Over and over, she pounded the bat on pillows while I cheered her on. Margaret was unable to "feel anything" and seemed frustrated and stuck. A pleaser, Margaret profusely apologized for "not doing better." I began to realize that I was not respecting Margaret's timing and tempo but rather was on my own journey. I shifted gears to access her sense of the abuse experience stored in the body, trusting that she instinctively sensed how to identify and express her response to the events as they took place long ago. "What does your body need to do?" I asked Margaret. Without missing a beat, she immediately raised her voice, wrung her hands together, and replied, "I'd like to wring his neck!" Margaret's body had spoken. Our treatment sessions from that point on consisted of her wringing out wet towels while speaking of her abuse, allowing for a release of authentic emotion.

The Physicalization of Language

Emotions are, integrally, an experience of the body, interpreted and labeled by the mind. In *The Body Remembers*, Babette Rothschild (2000) explained that each emotion has a different bodily expression and is characterized by a discrete pattern of skeletal muscle contractions visible on the face and in body posture (somatic nervous system). How that emotion looks on the outside of the body communicates it to others. How each emotion feels to the individual internally, on the inside of the body, communicates it to the self. Because clients with eating disorders are so out of touch with their emotions, they benefit greatly from the experience of transferring cognitive concepts to their physical manifestations.

Helping clients identify specific words or phrases that serve as metaphors for sensations or feelings in the physical body can bring clarity to the meaning of their struggle with a new perspective: "I can't stand on my own two feet," "I'm coming apart at the seams," "It's too big a leap for me." These metaphors can take concrete form for clients. Grounding exercises can be taught to help clients experience being centered; wrapping shawls and blankets around clients can provide the feeling of safety; and practicing leaps through the air helps those who are fearful of risk taking. Imagery or physical enactment can express metaphors such as, "I feel like I'm always put on the back burner," "My progress is slow as molasses," "I'm simmering inside." The "back burner" can be guided through a journey in the kitchen, and the "simmerer" can go through some temperature adjustments as the therapist has her turn up the heat. Physicalizing the progress of the molasses can be very powerful by first having the client describe the feeling of trying to move through molasses and then actually attempting to reach a point in the room while handicapping herself in a manner that induces that feeling. She might wear heavy boots, have someone hold her feet, or wear a snowsuit.

The vignette next provides an example of how therapists might work with putting the identified word into its physicalized counterpart to help clients embody their struggle with passivity.

Case Example: Gail's Representation of Feeling Cornered

In an eating disorder treatment group, Gail, a 36-year-old architect, recounts her difficulty in speaking up for herself with individuals she perceives as authority figures. "I become immobilized and completely passive," she states. "I feel like a little girl, cornered by everyone bigger and more powerful than I am." I pick up on the word "cornered" and ask Gail to elaborate on the feeling. She shares her thoughts. "I just feel so stuck. The anger stays stuck inside of me, and I can't access it to make me take action. I'm completely at the mercy of everyone who is keeping me cornered." I ask Gail to draw her feeling of being cornered. Figure 10.1 illustrates the link between Gail's feeling of being physically cornered and the language she uses to *emotionally* express that concept.

After she talks about her picture, I wonder if she is willing to put herself in a corner of the room to heighten that experience. She reluctantly agrees and positions herself facing outward toward the group. When I ask her how she feels, she responds that she is feeling nothing because she does not feel at all trapped: "I can just walk right out of here." I suggest that she invite a few of the group members to represent the authority figures who

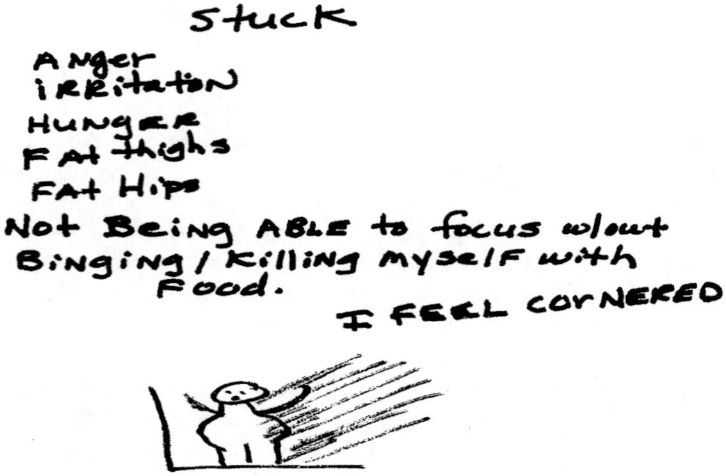

Figure 10.1

keep her stuck. Gail chooses three "actors" and takes her time positioning them looming over her with arms linked.

At the given signal, Gail takes her place in the corner, and the actors create the physical and emotional barriers that keep her there. Gail stands paralyzed for several moments and then makes a few ineffectual attempts to move from her space. The group keeps her trapped. "You have choices," I say. "You can stay in the corner, or you can take action. This time, do something different." Gail continues to make no move. "Breathe," I suggest. "Ground yourself and breathe through your fear." In a sudden swift motion, Gail drops to the floor, snakes out between the legs of her oppressors, and flees to the safety of the other group members. "I'm free," she exclaims. "I got myself out of the corner!"

Gail is able to identify the exact moment when her mind and body made the decision to move. "I suddenly found myself taking action," she declares. "I don't even remember thinking about it." Gail identifies the feeling that captures how she felt when she broke free as "exhilarating:" "I won't let my body forget how good I feel right now."

The following is a list of client words that can readily be transferred from the cognitive into physicalizations: trapped, stuck, struggling, in a bind, wound tight, enduring, collapsing, falling apart, smothering, cornered, struggling, above it all, stuffed, frantic, entombed, boxed in, shaky, drowning.

Once therapists identify an "action" or physical word, point it out and ask clients open-ended questions. "Tell me about being trapped? What does that feel like for you?" "Where is the trapped feeling in your body? How does it manifest itself?" "What kind of trapped is it?" Offer examples to lead clients. "Is it like being in a box? Being held back? Being stuck?" Once clients have a sense of "trapped," ask if they would like to explore "trapped" on a body level so that they can learn more about that feeling. They can set up a scenario, as Gail did, or even do an imagery exercise. Remember to respect the tempo and readiness of clients and let them set the boundaries.

From Body and Mind Problems to BodyMind Solutions

The body and mind cannot be treated separately; they operate as a unitary whole. Imprinted thoughts in the mind and their physical counterparts in the body are resistant to change and respond most effectively to therapeutic bodymind approaches. Clients' bodies become a mirror of their eating disorder. The rigid thinking of the individual with anorexia is reflected in her rigid, inflexible body. The bulimic's problems with containment and her shifting pattern of using food to alternately stuff and empty the body (taking it in and then ridding oneself of it) has its counterpart in methods for undoing the consequences of impulsive, often chaotic, thoughts and behavior. For binge eaters, their beliefs that they are not worthy or deserving enough to be selective lead to body boundaries that are wide open for taking in whatever food or relationship is available. The reciprocal relationships between body and mind, language and emotion, and client and healer create a pathway to body ownership and an acceptance of the authentic self. Reclaiming the forsaken body means a return to real feelings, which can be identified, experienced, and expressed. Only then is a whole and complete body image restored.

References

Benson, H. (2002). Interview entitled "Spirituality and healing in medicine." In M. Thomas (Ivanhoe president), *Ivanhoe's Medical Breakthroughs. Ivanhoe Broadcast News* (pp. 1–5). Retrieved on October 15, 2007, from http://www.ivanhoe.com

Benson, H. (2004). Timeless healing: The power and biology of belief. In J. Robison and K. Carrier (Eds.), *The spirit and science of holistic health* (pp. 85–101). Bloomington, IN: AuthorHouse.

Chopra, D. (1990). *The new physics of healing, a groundbreaking look at your body's life-changing power.* Boulder, CO: Sounds True Audio.

Church, D. (2007). *The genie in your genes.* Santa Rosa, CA: Elite Books Self-Healing Newsletter.

Clohosey, K. (2003). *Healing re-percussions.* Presented at Thirteenth Annual Renfrew Center Foundation Conference, The Changing Face of Eating Disorders. Philadelphia: Renfrew Center Foundation.

Damasio, A. R. (1994). *Descartes' error.* New York: Putnam.

Hart, S., Field, T., Hernandez-Reif, M., Nearing, G., Shaw, S., Shanberg, S., et al. (2001). Anorexia nervosa symptoms reduced by massage. *Eating Disorders: The Journal of Treatment and Prevention, 9,* 217–228.

Fisher, G., Fisher J., & Stark, R. (1990). Males with eating disorders. In A. Anderson (Ed.), *Eating disorders monograph series* (pp. 53–76). New York: Bruner/Mazel.

Forbes, B. (2007). Yoga and the emotional body. *Yoga Bulletin, 16*(4), 6.

Freud, S., & Breuer, J. (1893). *Studies in Hysteria.* London: Penguin Group.

Graham, M. (1991). *Blood Memory.* New York: Doubleday.

Kabat-Zinn, J., Massion, A., Kristeller, J., Peterson, L., Fletcher, K., Pbert, L., Lenderking, W., et al. (1992). Effectiveness of a meditation-stress reduction program in the treatment of anxiety disorders. *American Journal of Psychiatry, 149*(7), 936–943.

Kleinman, S., & Hall, T. (2006). Dance/movement therapy: A method for embodying emotions. In Renfrew Center Foundation, *Healing through relationship series: Contributions to eating disorder theory and treatment. Vol. 1: Fostering body-mind integration.* Philadelphia: Renfrew Center Foundation.

Kristeller, J., & Hallett, B. (1999). Effects of a meditation-based intervention in the treatment of binge eating, *Journal of Health Psychology, 4,* 357–363.

Krueger, D. W. (1989). *Body self and psychological self: A developmental and clinical integration of disorders of the self.* New York: Brunner-Routledge.

Lapides, F. (2007). *Clinical implications and applications of psychoneurology: Translating neuroscience to the consulting room.* Retrieved February 2007 from http://www.psybc.com/seminar.php

Lowen, A. (1967). *Betrayal of the body.* New York: Macmillan.

Marks, L., & Schultz, B. (2004). Handouts from Fourth International NICABM Conference on the Psychology of Health Immunity and Disease. Vol. B, December 1–12, 1992. In J. Robison & K. Carrier, *The spirit and science of holistic health* (pp. 67–84). Bloomington, IN: AuthorHouse. (Original work published 1992)

McGeeney, S. (1988). *Touching adult children of alcoholics. Massage Therapy Journal, 27,* 3.

Merriam-Webster. (1970). *Webster's Seventh New Collegiate Dictionary.* Springfield, MA: Author.

Montagu, A. (1971). *Touching: The human significance of the skin.* New York: Harper and Row.

Pert, C. B. (1997). *Molecules of emotion: The science behind mind-body medicine.* New York: Touchstone.

Ressler, A., & Kleinman, S. (2006). Reframing body image in the treatment of eating disorders. In The Renfrew Center Foundation, *Healing through relationship series: Contributions to eating disorder theory and treatment. Vol. 1: Fostering body-mind integration.* Philadelphia: Renfrew Center Foundation.

Rice, J. L., Hardenbergh, M., & Hornyak, L. (1989). Disturbed body image in anorexia nervosa: Dance/movement therapy interventions. In L. Hornyak & E. Baker (Eds.), *Experiential therapies for eating disorders through body metaphor* (pp. 252–278). New York: Guilford Press.

Rothschild, B. (2000). *The body remembers.* New York: Norton.

Terr, L. (1990). *Too scared to cry.* New York: Harper and Row.

Weil, A. (2007). Attitude is everything with aging. Andrew Weil's *Self-healing Newsletter*. In D. Church, *The genie in your genes* (pp. 49–73). Santa Rosa, CA: Elite Books. (Original work published 2006.)

Whitehouse, M. S. (1999). Physical movement and personality. In P. Pallaro (Ed.), *Authentic movement: Essays by Mary Starks Whitehouse, Janet Adler, Joan Chodrow* (pp. 51–57). London: Kingsley.

Woodman, M. (1997). *Addiction to perfection: The still unravished bride: A psychological study.* Toronto: Inner City Books.

section three

Effective Clinical Practices:
Special Themes

chapter eleven

Shame, Compassion, and the Journey Toward Health

Jane Shure and Beth Weinstock

Introduction

Shame is a mighty force. It can make one feel inherently flawed or defective, invalid as a human, and essentially unlovable. In its extreme form, it is experienced as an internal and ultimate truth about one's core being. Shame takes one prisoner, inhibiting spontaneity, draining life's energy, creating emotional paralysis, and triggering an impulse to disappear. Women with eating disorders are often consumed by their shame, living under its spell and tormented by its power.

Shame affects mind, body, and behavior. Physically, shame draws the body inward and manifests in symptoms like blushing, sweating, nausea, and a racing heart. Cognitively, shame appears as severe and constant self-criticism, causing the belief that one is never good enough, smart enough, nice enough, or thin enough. Behaviorally, shame is reflected in patterns of withdrawal, secrecy, avoidance, deception, and self-destruction. Shame acts like a thief, robbing one's spirit and injuring one's soul.

Despite its powerful and potentially crippling impact, shame was not a focal point in psychological literature until recent decades (Karen, 1992). Freud, for example, focused on guilt rather than shame. He saw shame as a cover for deeper emotions (Lewis, 1992), acknowledged it as self-evident, but did not attempt to explore its vicissitudes and dynamics (Karen, 1992).

Contemporary theorists, however, have begun to name shame as an important element in modern psychology. One author described shame as "fluid, diffuse, indeterminate, complex and evasive" (Edelson, 1988, p. 33), while another said that shame is like "a wound made from the inside out dividing us both from ourselves and from one another" (Kaufman, 1992, p. xx). Karen (1992) believed that shame is a major cause of emotional distress in our time, while Nathanson (1987) saw attention to shame as the missing factor for success in psychotherapy. The addictions recovery movement has educated people about the relationship between dysfunctional families and children who carry shame (Bradshaw, 1988; Fossum & Mason, 1986; Kaufman, 1992), and 12-step programs have consciously helped to diminish the shame related to addiction through acceptance and acknowledgment.

Confusion remains over the essential nature of shame as well as its etiology and primacy as an emotion. Some writers claim that there are healthy degrees of shame that contribute to the creation and maintenance of social norms (Scheff, 1988) and that a well-integrated person's self-reflection about recurrent shaming behaviors can spur personal growth and development (Lynd, 1958). There is also debate over the age at which shame develops (Lewis, 1971). Some theorists say that shame is a primary emotion that develops within the first 7 months of life, independent of interaction, introspection, or self-consciousness (Plutchik, 1962). Other theorists maintain that shame is a secondary emotion that only appears after a child observes herself in relation to how she is seen by others (Karen, 1992). Object relations theory points to shame as a result of deficits in patterns of interpersonal interaction (Kohut, 1971). Nathanson (1992) views shame as an innate biological mechanism, hardwired in the brain and genetically determined. Another perspective comes from existentialist writers, who speak of shame as a permanent and inescapable aspect of "being in the world" (Edelson, 1988).

There is no question but that shame has become an important point of interest in contemporary psychology. Although theorists differ about how to conceptualize and understand it, they agree that shame is a powerful, often-unconscious force with significant clinical and personal implications.

Origins of Shame

Women who struggle with an eating disorder inherently suffer from a shame disorder. Sometimes, this is based primarily on the deep shame that accompanies symptomatic behavior, but more often it is deeply rooted in developmental and cultural experience. A shame disorder is one in which the felt sense of shame becomes powerful enough to interfere with healthy growth and development.

Trauma-Based Shame

All forms of trauma can result in feelings of shame. Trauma involves the uncontrollable and often the unexpected, leaving one stunned and unable to comprehend a given sequence of events. This can be fertile ground for self-denigration. Feeling responsible for a fire, a car accident, or a sexual assault can leave one feeling not only "at fault" but also reprehensible for being at fault.

Culturally Induced Shame

Western culture is highly consumer based. It creates the illusion that we need more than we have, that our next purchase will make us both desirable and whole, and that to be happy we must achieve what is touted as the American ideal. The advertising industry is brilliant at selling American women an image of what they "should" look like, thereby creating an unrealistic standard against which women compare themselves. Of course, most women fall short, resulting in a sense of inadequacy. To bridge the gap between cultural ideals and one's own self-image, the media and the diet industry sell self-improvement in the form of diets and exercise regimens. Women are encouraged to be "good" by following diet plans, to be disciplined by avoiding "bad" foods, and to link deprivation with salvation. The unfortunate result of these cultural messages is that many women battle with their bodies, shame themselves for wanting to eat, and excoriate themselves for "being bad" when they actually eat. The myths under which Western women live are powerful: "You can never be too rich or too thin," "Thin is good and fat is bad," and "Only the thin are lovable." Even the most enlightened women can become vulnerable to harsh body criticism and a shame-based drive to improve their outward appearance.

Attachment Deficits and Shame

When shame emerges as a frequent emotion in early childhood, it has a seminal effect on ego development. Psychodynamic theory and observations of early mother-infant behavior teach the importance of early interactions between infant and caregiver in establishing a sense of self. Before the infant has language or cognition, she has touch, sight, and sound. These perceptions help shape the infant's sense of being in the world. The feeling tone with which a parent holds a daughter, gazes into her eyes, coos and makes nurturing sounds or strokes her cheeks to give comfort all contribute to a template that establishes a felt sense of being valued, worthwhile, lovable, and positively regarded. What we call "love" is established by these patterns of interaction.

When a child's needs for loving reflection are ignored or otherwise not met, her internal self-perception is that she is to blame, and that she is deficient. Children assume that the external world and their caregivers are benevolent and willing to give if they are worthy to receive. If a child is not fed when hungry, changed when wet, held when frightened, or comforted when sick, she will believe that her very wants and needs must be excessive or wrong. Most often, she will conclude that she is, in some way, "bad." This perception of internal basic "badness" is felt as shame.

Once internalized, shame has an impact on identity development and creates a fertile ground for ongoing self-criticism. Negative self-talk feeds a pattern of magnifying flaws and minimizing strengths, which in turn can lead to self-destructive behaviors and an ongoing cycle of self-hatred and shame.

Familial Shame

In the normal course of development, every child inevitably experiences moments of shame. At different points in the maturation process, she will feel inadequate to certain tasks, less capable than an older sibling, and frustrated in the mastery of new skills. At these times, she may feel inept, incompetent, and ashamed. Good parenting helps children struggle with and manage these difficult feelings by normalizing them and encouraging self-acceptance. Children learn to self-soothe and tolerate frustration when parents are compassionate. When parents are impatient and hold unrealistic expectations, their children may not develop sufficient skills for navigating shame and may become deficient at calming themselves.

In some families, blaming and critical parenting styles are the predominant tones of interaction with children. Parents in these shame-based families (Bradshaw, 1988) are habitually scolding, ignoring, accusing, and intimidating, thus creating excessive degrees of shame. Limited in their ability to convey appreciation and respect to their children, these parents create a climate of rejection that slowly erodes their children's self-worth.

Other families overtly abuse. When abuse occurs, children often feel at fault. They need to hold the belief that their parents or caretakers are competent, benevolent, and protective. The alternative, the truth that the very people they depend on are actually hurtful, is too painful so they blame themselves instead of their parents. This transference of blame maximizes feelings of safety and minimizes emotional pain, thus lending relief to anxiety that would otherwise emerge.

A child will internalize the harshness of her upbringing in the form of a strict "inner critic" (Shure & Weinstock, 2007) that tells her she is inadequate, unworthy, and bad. It tells her that she is falling short, that she did not do something well enough, that someone else could do it better, that her feelings are foolish, that she is making a big deal out of nothing, and that she is stupid and unlovable. With a harsh inner critic, a child has few healthy defenses for coping with emotional distress and feelings of shame. She is at risk for developing compensatory defenses, many of which may be self-destructive. In contemporary Western culture, when a girl develops unhealthy defenses, she is likely to demand perfection in her appearance, silence her own voice, act aggressively toward her body, attend to others' needs at the expense of her own, and dissociate from painful feelings and thoughts.

Shame, Dissociation, and Eating Disorders

Shame, as well as hurt, sadness, anger, fear, and powerlessness, gets under the skin and becomes incorporated in the body. The body becomes a container for negative thoughts, painful feelings, and distorted perceptions. When a child lives in an environment where she is not safe to express thoughts and feelings, she must find a way to cope with them by herself. Blocking the distress from awareness accomplishes this need.

But blocking these thoughts and feelings presents a conundrum for one's internal life. It is a problem for the psyche to not know what it knows, to not think what it thinks, to not feel what it feels, to dismiss rage and despair. Yet if these feelings and thoughts are expressed, the child risks precipitating punishment back from the parents they are dependant on and who are the source of their pain. This often leaves the child angry at herself for having her painful thoughts and feelings in the first place since they give rise to this predicament.

Dissociation provides a way to cope with this dilemma by compartmentalizing that which is unacceptable (Rothschild, 2000). Once forbidden thoughts and feelings are split off and placed out of awareness, dissociation allows the child to live as if the thoughts and feelings do not exist. Of course, they do exist, held in a disconnected part of the self (Goulding & Schwartz, 1995). Encoded in the body, these thoughts and feelings find expression in somatic distress and behavioral enactments.

In all their forms, eating disorders offer a creative form of adaptive dissociation. Eating disorder symptoms such as restricting, purging, overeating, excessive exercise, and always feeling too fat enable disconnection from, and denial of, one's original wounds, deep feelings of shame, current interpersonal stresses, and other painful realities. They also offer a false sense of feeling "in control" and function to numb pain. Once set in motion, eating disorders provide a self-shaming, circular reification of self-hate. The original motivation to protect parts of the self and provide them with "safe storage" ultimately leads to patterns of self-harm and to the reinforcement of a shame-based sense of self. In attempting to adapt to the various circumstances that have made them feel ashamed, women with eating disorders engage in behaviors that cause them to feel more ashamed, in turn leading to even more eating-disordered behavior and more shame.

The following sequence of thoughts illustrates the self-shaming cycle that maintains and reinforces symptoms while obscuring awareness of pain and conflict from original sources:

> If I am bulimic I wake up in the morning and prom-
> ise myself, "I'm going to be good and not purge
> today." I get through the morning, and I don't purge.
> "I'm good!" I get through the afternoon, and I don't
> purge. "I'm good!" I get through dinner still not
> purging. "Again, I'm good!" Then, when it's time to
> study, I suddenly head for the refrigerator—off on
> a binge, and then I purge. "I'm bad again! Actually,
> I'm worse! All I can do is be bad. I'm never going to
> be good." In bingeing and purging I prove how bad
> and disgusting I really am, just like I always thought.
> But there's always tomorrow. So, once again, I prom-
> ise myself "to be good tomorrow." When I wake
> up the next morning, I repeat my mantra that "I'm
> going to be good today." Sometimes I'm loud about
> this, sometimes I'm quiet, sometimes I plead with
> myself, but always I have less assurance. And the
> shame cycle deepens.

Metaphorically, a woman suffering with an eating disorder develops an internal "scale," using her symptoms to weigh her "goodness" and "bad-ness." Daily she tests herself, creating and re-creating shaming behaviors and shameful feelings, "proving" over and over again her most core nega-tive belief: that she is disgusting. She concludes that her "badness" is all her fault because she believes she could, and should, be disciplined and in control.

After years of living with dissociation as a defense and lifestyle, women often have no idea that their eating disorder is related to issues from early childhood experiences, shame-based historical patterns, or trauma. They believe that they are just bad for having an eating disorder. Feeling out of con-trol and overwhelmed, they experience a "monster-like" force inside them that insists they maintain their eating disorder (Shure & Weinstock, 2006).

Working With Shame in the Treatment of Eating Disorders

Working With the Monster

Women usually enter treatment tormented by a complex relationship with their self-hatred. They feel rage against this monster part of themselves, depleted by its force, and powerless to resist its tyranny, and yet they are protective of it. The monster acts much like a dictator who oppresses and frightens people to reign supreme. It threatens and bullies, undermines and taunts, overall creating a spell of fear and defeat. Eating-disordered clients come into therapy wanting to rid themselves of this monster and assume that life will then be normal. They expect that their therapist will agree that eliminating the monster is the goal of treatment.

Not so. Effective therapy is based on understanding that the monster is actually a defense, adopted and developed over time to protect against painful, difficult, and potentially overwhelming feelings, even in spite of the self-destructive behaviors and the self-defeating feelings it engenders. The monster has a function and a job description. It maintains the myth that "If I override hunger I can be in control" and that "When I am thin I can feel good about myself." The monster creates reasons to hide from others and avoid the inevitable anxieties that go with a full life. It relegates the eating-disordered person to the role of the identified patient, thus protecting the family's hidden dysfunction (Minuchin, 1974). It serves to punish parents by expressing rage and inducing their powerlessness and supports the belief that, once one is sick enough, parents will finally take responsibility for their transgressions. Finally, the monster functions to hold all awareness, focusing attention on the suffering caused by the eating disorder while displacing lifelong feelings of sadness, grief, rage, fear, loneliness, and abandonment. Once consumed by the monster, the original wounds from childhood are obscured.

The therapist's first task is to invite a joint venture into exploring the monster's role, including the conscious and unconscious motivations behind its self-protective yet self-destructive influence. The client must get to know her monster and give it a voice to promote a dialogue with other parts of the self in the healing process.

When women with eating disorders are helped to reframe their monster as a misguided attempt at self-care and as a creative form of adaptation, they have an opportunity to develop a more compassionate view of their struggle. As compassion and curiosity are reinforced in therapy, shame is challenged, and clients are freer to heal. Building an alliance among client, monster part, and therapist promotes the initial and essential trust for a therapy that can safely process shame. The eating disorder symptoms can then be talked about without the goodness/badness power struggle that so often ensues within families and inside the self. As the client experiences the counterforce to shame, being accepted and understood without judgment, she internalizes a greater sense of safety.

Working With Shame in the Therapeutic Relationship

Treatment involves psychoeducation about shame and the self-shaming cycle described above. Eating-disordered clients do not come into therapy thinking about the importance of shame. Yet, they tell of it in a multitude of ways as they describe their daily experiences, feeling deficient in comparison to others, uncomfortable with positive feedback, and guilty for having eaten too much or too little. Interestingly, as people become aware of shame, they often feel shame for carrying it. As recognition of shame is heightened and self-acceptance supported, fertile ground avails itself for therapeutic intervention to help dissolve shame's toxic effect.

Clients will inevitably feel shame in the course of treatment with their therapist. They will feel shame for being 5 minutes late, for asking a question, or for choosing not to ask a question. They may feel shame when their therapist answers their phone call or when they don't answer their phone call. Given clients' hypersensitivity to rejection and their feelings of inadequacy, therapists need to be cognizant of their language and tone of voice. While each and every one of these interactions will not become the subject for therapeutic conversation, the therapist needs to track them, to be mindful of shame's omnipotence, and to decide what to bring into conscious awareness and when to do so.

In the course of working with eating-disordered clients, therapists will encounter a heightened experience of, and consciousness of, their own shame triggers. It is common for therapists to feel incompetent given the tenacity of eating-disordered symptoms, to wonder if a different therapist would do a better job, and even to feel guilty for not suffering as the client does. Without attention to these countertransferential challenges, therapists may inadvertently act in ways that shame their clients. To prevent shaming and protect safety within the therapeutic relationship, it is imperative that therapists be aware of these complex dynamics.

Mindfulness and the Brain

Recent research (Siegel, 1999) demonstrates that the brain creates literal pathways, called *neural networks*, made up of thoughts and feelings that become associated over time. When early life experiences create feelings of helplessness, fear, pain, and shame, neural networks grow and increase the likelihood that distress and anxiety patterns will be hardwired in the brain. Most eating-disordered clients ruminate and dwell in negativity, self-criticism, and shame, thus reinforcing brain patterns that cause suffering. Their monster maintains the voice of an inner critic with repetitive and automatic negative self-talk that is often out of awareness. Luckily, while history can create deep trenches of negativity, the brain has plasticity and can generate new neural pathways that allow for growth and development (Scaer, 2005).

Mindfulness is a practice that can facilitate the observation and interruption of historical patterns, laying the groundwork for change. Mindfulness focuses awareness and attention to the present moment. Based on the belief that suffering increases as a result of judgment, avoidance, and lack of awareness, it involves noticing thoughts, feelings, and body sensations to identify patterns that contribute to suffering. The goal of mindfulness practice is to nonjudgmentally observe and accept thoughts, feelings, and body sensations without resistance.

In the process of developing mindfulness, eating-disordered women can learn that their thoughts and feelings do not necessarily reflect current reality but may reflect past patterning. They can create an inner witness to their shame and their self-destructive tendencies. Once observed without blame or judgment, negative patterns can more readily be replaced by new ones.

Compassion

Compassion is the antidote to shame. It is the willingness to be openhearted and accepting of our own pain and the suffering of others, with an intention to promote healing. It holds deep awareness that all living beings are ultimately connected and interdependent, bridging the suffering of one being to another. Successful therapy relies on compassion as the guide to creating a therapeutic holding environment in which clients can learn to experience and tolerate their difficult feelings, no longer needing to distract themselves away from them. Compassion "involves learning to relax and allow ourselves to move gently toward what scares us ... to stay with emotional distress without tightening into aversion, to let fear soften us rather than harden into resistance" (Chodron, 2002, p. 50).

Eating-disordered women live under the influence of a mind imprisoned by shame and suffering. They are ruled by self-loathing and have no compassion for their own struggle. This can change when therapists access the depths of their own compassion and offer it. In the face of life-threatening symptoms, with safety a primary concern, it is a mighty challenge for therapists to stay compassionate while managing their own anxiety, anger, or disappointment. The impulse is, often, to control symptoms to relieve the pain of both client and therapist. Moving too quickly toward this end and being overly invested in shifting behaviors can eclipse the greater therapeutic power that comes from being present, accepting suffering, and maintaining a stance of deep caring. Compassion is powerful, and as it is absorbed into the client's psyche, it will take root and grow.

Healing the Weight of Shame

The following clinical dialogues focus on interventions that work directly to heal shame. They model how to help clients distinguish past realities from present circumstances, identify when and how they inaccurately assume responsibility for others' actions, and explore how their patterns of self-harm originated in the service of self-protection. These clinical examples demonstrate the therapist's active participation, use of supportive and nonshaming language, and sensitivity about activating shame. The dialogues were taken from actual therapy sessions and modified from their transcripts.

Distinguishing Past From Present

Throughout Molly's early adolescence, she was physically and sexually abused by her uncle. Although Molly's mother knew, she did nothing to intervene and stop it. At age 29, after many hospitalizations for an eating disorder, Molly had her first healthy romantic relationship. The following dialogue is an example of supporting the client as she moves through fear toward healthier interpersonal connection.

Molly: It's not fair of me to be involved with him; he doesn't know what he's getting into.
Therapist: I know you're convinced that no one can really care for you.
Molly: It's my body; he will see the scars.
Therapist: From what you say, I'm sure he has his own scars.
Molly: What if he touches me and I freak out; I'd be so embarrassed.
Therapist: You keep telling me how good he is, how unusual. I can imagine he might just hold you, or ask what you need. You told me about a friend's boyfriend who keeps hanging in.
Molly: But that's not me.
Therapist: Maybe being cared for is more possible than you think.
Molly: Last night I didn't binge or purge when I got home from being with him.
Therapist: How come?
Molly: I just didn't want to.
Therapist: You mean you were full up on life?
Molly: I guess so. But that's one day. I can't give up my eating disorder; I'd be flooded, terrified.
Therapist: It's interesting that last night you just didn't want to.
Molly: My eating disorder has been what saved me. It's the only thing that has kept the terror at bay.
Therapist: When you were 10 and abandoned by your mother to an abuser, you had to manage a no-way-out situation. Your eating disorder made perfect sense then. It helped you to feel you were purging the unpurgeable and to dissociate from your body when you needed to.
Molly: And it's worked.

Therapist: It worked when you had nothing else to help you cope and nothing else to replace it with. You now have people and resources that treat you kindly and can help you feel safe.

Molly: I can't tell him … if he knew what I do at night, he would reject me. He hasn't seen the real me yet.

Therapist: Molly, you are so much more than your abuse and your eating disorder. Your intelligence, competencies, humor, are all real parts of you. I know this to be true.

Integrating the Private and Public Self

Jennifer was very successful in her professional world and suffered extreme guilt for her eating disorder, believing it nullified any of her positive qualities. The following dialogue is an example of helping the client to integrate different self-parts.

Jennifer: The eating disorder is a creative solution to unbearable problems. I can appear to be fully functional to the outside world. In private I throw my guts up, and in public I look like an upstanding citizen. It's a creative way to stay away from what I'd otherwise be present to.

Therapist: So it's functioned to have you not feel difficult feelings while also hiding the part of you that struggles?

Jennifer: Yes, and it works, but I feel so much shame about living a dual life. I tell myself that the public person is a phony, and I'm putting one over on everyone.

Therapist: If you would let yourself claim both parts, because we all have a public and private self, you might feel less shame.

Tracking the Client's Process Toward Resolution

A conflict with Pat's boss scared her and triggered old feelings of shame. An event at work reminded her of being ridiculed by her father, who would assume she "should know something" and then criticize her when she did not. This dynamic left Pat with chronic feelings of "uselessness, stupidity, and worthlessness." The following dialogue is an example of staying present with the client's process and holding the space until resolution evolves.

Pat: My boss sounded just like my father and the little girl in me retreated and disappeared deep inside myself. I caved. I was scared to death of my father because I never knew what to expect from him. The humiliating tone in my boss's voice took me by surprise and I caved.

Therapist: How did you cave?

Pat: I panicked. I went right into: What have I done, there's no way it can be undone. I became terrified and hid away from my terror just like I used to do with my father. When I do this, I end up feeling raw.

Therapist: What might comfort that raw feeling?

Pat: When I go inside, I end up scratching myself, and then I end up feeling that rawness, and I get mad at myself for doing this. I'd need to feel safe in order to come out—I need some kind of healing, but I don't know how to do it.

Therapist: What kind of healing would rawness need?

Pat: I'm not sure. I know that the rawness is a result of the little girl scratching from the inside out.

Therapist: When you were young and not safe, going inside was an attempt to protect yourself, to comfort yourself and help create a feeling of safety. Staying present probably felt overwhelming and way too frightening. Going inside gave you some relief because you felt less exposed, but you also experienced some other form of pain, represented by that sensation of rawness. You did not cause the pain, your parents did, and that's why you retreated. Your metaphor of scratching reminds me of a story told by the Buddhist teacher, Pema Chodron [2005]. The story, passed down to her by one of her teachers, says that we are all like children with a bad case of scabies. We feel the itch from our pain and discomfort, and we have an urge to scratch. Even though we are told that the scratching will make it worse, our instinct is to go for immediate relief. So we scratch, feel temporary relief, yet the scabies spreads and gets worse. If you think about the story, your positive intention was to help yourself feel better, and you wound up instead feeling raw and hurt.

Pat: While you were talking I had an image of my dog's gentle paws. When she wants something she approaches it, pats it, and gets her needs met. Maybe the little girl needs to seek assistance before she hides. I kind of admire that in my dog.

Therapist: If you followed your dog's lead, what would that look like?

Pat: I could try to approach situations at work without involving my boss. I can approach conflict by anticipating it and seeking input from others.

Therapist: What else might you do?

Pat: Well, then I could try and reassure the little girl within me and tell her that I'll take care of her and listen to her. I don't think that I've listened to her before.

Therapist: That's really great. I love that you're getting to recognize the power you have when you listen to that scared part of yourself.

Working With Shame in the Therapeutic Relationship

Sue came from a highly critical and accomplished family. In spite of her own competencies, she constantly worried about making mistakes or being inappropriate. The following dialogue is an example of processing feelings of shame when they occur between client and therapist.

Therapist: It seems you handled the work situation quite well and didn't get triggered.

Sue: Yeah, I was able to argue my case successfully; the decision went my way in the end.

Therapist: That's not what I meant. (Clients' face changed color, shoulders dropped, silence.) I'm wondering how you just heard what I said?

Sue: I don't know what you mean. ... I guess I missed something you were saying. I always do that.

Therapist: I'm wondering if my saying, "That's not what I meant," felt shaming?

Sue: I guess so.

Therapist: I'm not surprised. As I said it, I realized that I could have sounded shaming. I was thinking about your shame history and how you held your ground in this situation. I wanted to point that out, but now realize that I took the attention away from your triumph at work; I was more focused on feeling excited that you held your own and resisted feeling shamed by your boss. We were thinking about different aspects of your success.

Sue: Now I feel really stupid; I always feel like maybe I'm not understanding what I'm supposed to.

Therapist: Let's slow down and take a look at what's happening here between us. It's such a good example of how sneaky and ever-present shame can be. I was on one track, and you were on another, and you automatically assumed that you were at fault for something and then shamed yourself. What actually happened was that I wasn't doing a great job at communicating with you and confused you by my response. You didn't do anything wrong. When you assume that something is your fault, I can see how shame swallows you up, and that's so sad.

Sue: Yes, that's what happens. The shame pit is so hard to get out of. I'm glad I didn't go there at work this time. And I see what you mean about what happened here. I sure do go into shame and blame myself at the least opportunity.

Therapist: Actually if we look back, you're doing a good job of breaking this hard pattern ... you just did it at work.

Sue: That's true. Actually you were the one who brought up shame today.

Therapist: You're totally correct. It's so important that we can reflect together about this shame dragon when it shows up between us. This is hard stuff, and I really appreciate your hanging in with it. Next time I say something and you feel shame come up, I hope that you'll let me know so that we can process it like today.

Compassion: The Antidote to Shame

Women who suffer with eating disorders suffer with shame. Shame is woven into the fiber of their being, coloring mind, body, behavior, and spirit. The symptoms of their eating disorder serve as both metaphor and enactment of their shame. Lasting recovery requires an understanding of shame's ubiquitous and elusive nature, as well as a collaborative exploration of its origins and its expressions in self-destructive behaviors.

Shame exists like hidden land mines in the territory of treatment. Vigilance is required to recognize the different forms in which it may manifest in therapy. Many clients will perceive shame regardless of the therapist's careful intent. Therapists who acknowledge, respect, clarify, and accept their clients' feelings demonstrate compassion. As compassion is experienced in the therapeutic relationship, clients will internalize feelings of acceptance and slowly develop compassion for themselves.

Compassion is the antidote to shame. It helps us join with others and accept the inevitability of pain, disappointment, and vulnerability. Compassion provides connection, kindness, and understanding that helps sustain us through the struggle to be human.

References

Bradshaw, J. (1988). *Healing the shame that binds you*. Deerfield Beach, FL: Health Communications.

Chodron, P. (2002). *The places that scare you*. Boston: Shambhala.

Chodron, P. (2005). *Getting unstuck: Breaking habitual patterns and encountering naked reality*. Boulder, CO: Sounds True Audio.

Edelson, S. (1988). *Turning the gorgon: A meditation on shame*. Woodstock, CT: Spring.

Fossum, M. A., & Mason, M. J. (1986). *Facing shame: Families in recovery*. Deerfield Beach, FL: Health Communications.

Goulding, R., & Schwartz, R. (1995). *The mosaic mind*. New York: Norton.

Karen, R. (1992, February). Shame. *The Atlantic Monthly*, 369–378.

Kaufman, G. (1992). *Shame: The power of caring*. Rochester, VT: Schenkman Books.

Kohut, H. (1971). *The analysis of the self*. New York: International Universities Press.

Lewis, H. B. (1971). *Shame and guilt in neurosis*. New York: International Universities Press.

Lewis, M. (1992). *The exposed self*. New York: Free Press.

Lynd, H. M. (1958). *On shame and the search for identity*. New York: Harcourt, Brace.

Minuchin, S. (1974). *Families and family therapy*. Cambridge, MA: Harvard University Press.

Nathanson, D. (1987). *The many faces of shame*. New York: Guilford Press.

Nathanson, D. (1992). *Shame and pride: Affect, sex, and the birth of the self*. New York: Norton.

Plutchik, R. (1962). *The emotions: Facts, theories, and a new model*. New York: Random House.

Rothschild, B. (2000). *The body remembers: The physiology of trauma and trauma treatment*. New York: Norton.

Scaer, R. (2005). *The trauma spectrum: Hidden wounds and human resiliency*. New York: Norton.

Scheff, T. J. (1988). Shame and conformity: The deference-emotion system. *American Sociological Review, 53*, 395–406.

Shure, J., & Weinstock, B. (2006). The body as a shame container. In The Renfrew Center Foundation, *Healing through relationships series CD Vol. 1: Fostering body-mind integration*. Philadelphia: Renfrew Center Foundation.

Shure, J., & Weinstock, B. (2007). *Calming your inner critic*. Retrieved January 16, 2007, from http://www.selfmatters.org/html

Siegel, D. (1999). *The developing mind: Towards a neurobiology of interpersonal experience*. New York: Guilford Press.

chapter twelve

The Embodied Therapist
Perspectives on Treatment, Personal Growth, and Supervision Related to Body Image

Carolyn Costin

Introduction

Of the very serious and complex eating disorder symptoms, body image disturbance is one of the most challenging to treat and is known for being the last thing to remit in recovery. Given that body image disturbance significantly contributes to relapse, careful exploration and understanding of body image is critical to successful treatment. Clinicians working in this area need to have a grasp of this topic, not only from the perspective of their clients but also from their own. While the clinical literature validates that transference and countertransference issues are particularly powerful in the treatment of eating disorders, it generally neglects exploration of these issues specific to body image.

Regardless of well-grounded theoretical and clinical training, female professionals who work with eating disorders commonly experience something similar to the following:

> "Lately, I have begun to go home at night and think about my body. I feel fatter now than when I started working with eating disorder clients. I feel like I am beginning to scrutinize the food I eat and even feel myself wanting to not eat desserts. I hear the clients in my head talking about how fattening these foods are and how weak they feel when they eat this type of food, and then I start to feel fat and weak, too."

Daily exposure to the distress eating-disordered women experience as they complain about their eating, size, or body fat can be challenging, especially since contemporary culture constantly promotes thinness, dieting, and the virtues of abstaining from "fattening" foods. Male therapists undoubtedly have to deal with the body image issues of their eating-disordered clients, but they are, generally, not challenged in the same way as female therapists. For the most part, males are not subjected to the same kind of scrutiny and competition from female clients regarding size, shape, and weight. Having grown up with fewer sociocultural pressures regarding appearance and weight, male therapists identify less with the embodied experiences of their female clients. The dynamics may change with a male client and male therapist. As most clients with eating disorders and their therapists are female, this chapter explores the interplay between female clients and clinicians in the area of body image.

This chapter includes examples, observations, and suggestions gleaned from three decades of experience as an eating disorder therapist and clinical supervisor. It will help clinicians to explore, understand, and process three separate but overlapping issues related to treating body image and their subsequent transference and countertransference issues: the clinician's relationship to her own weight, eating patterns, and body image; clients' tendencies to scrutinize and comment about the clinician's body; and self-disclosure and authenticity in the therapeutic relationship.

The Embodied Self

Through our bodies we come to know and experience ourselves as distinct, separate entities in the world. According to Freud (1923/1961), bodily experiences are the center around which the ego is developed. We are embodied beings, using our bodies for everything from basic survival to interpersonal communication. Cultural messages and structures shape the experience and meaning ascribed to the body, and in today's Western culture, the female body is a commodity, a unique form of currency and power. Females can attract mates, earn more, and garner attention and status based on how closely their body matches the currently accepted, idealized standard.

Based completely on subjective perception, body image is a complex product of the imagination. According to Hutchinson (1994), it is "the psychological space where body, mind, and culture come together—the space that encompasses our thoughts, feelings, perceptions, attitudes, values and judgments about the bodies we have" (p. 153). Kearney-Cook (1989), a pioneer in this area, wrote that body image forms in childhood, but the ongoing social and somatic experiences of adolescence are superimposed on this image. Body image is always a work in progress, richly affected by the normal events of psychosocial development, as well as by trauma.

Individuals with eating disorders are commonly unable to see themselves realistically and are dissatisfied with, disgusted by, and even full of hatred toward their bodies. Those with anorexia are most known for extreme body image disturbance, not seeing how emaciated they really are, and not wanting to gain weight or "get fat" even when at extreme and dangerously low weights. Those with bulimia and eating disorders not otherwise specified (EDNOS) may also suffer body image distortion. Regardless of actual distortion, clients with eating disorders are obsessed with body image concerns and resort to unhealthy and destructive food patterns and weight-related behaviors, often posing serious health consequences.

While body image disturbance is central to the diagnoses of eating disorders, it also is a normative experience for women today (Levine & Smolak, 1998; Maine & Kelly, 2005). Whether in the clinician's or the client's chair, all women are affected by contemporary culture's disparaging treatment of the female body and the cultivation of impossible standards for beauty.

Incorporating body image as a focus for treatment raises many questions regarding how female therapists deal with their own body-related issues: how much, if any, disclosure in this area is appropriate; how to stay honest and authentic, yet not disclose inappropriate personal body image struggles; what personal body image struggles are appropriate to share; how to avoid getting triggered by clients; how to protect yourself, care for your body, accept, and, even love, your own body in the midst of working with others who suffer from severe body dissatisfaction to the point of a mental illness. It is easy to see how issues of *transference* (the process in psychotherapy by which the client unconsciously redirects feelings, fears, desires, emotions, and ways of relating with important people in their past onto the therapist) and *countertransference* (when the therapist unconsciously reacts to the transference of the client along with general ways that the therapist's own emotional issues can be stimulated) arise around body image conflicts, whether acknowledged or not.

Body image countertransference issues can critically affect the success of the therapy, even causing personal consequences to some therapists. Professionals with no previous history of eating or body image problems can be triggered to scrutinize themselves and think critically about their own body, weight, and eating habits. Recovered clinicians might be better prepared to deal with these issues, having previously conquered such demons, but they are vulnerable to being triggered into relapse. All clinicians will be better prepared to deal with their eating-disordered clients if they understand the potentials and pitfalls that can arise in dealing with body image issues.

Therapists treating eating and body image disorders have to navigate their clients' complicated relationships to their bodies while keeping themselves in check and balance. Clinical training rarely prepares therapists for the various kinds of personal challenges that arise. The following are real scenarios that eating disorder therapists will most likely face:

- How do you help a client turn her focus off of weight loss concerns if you are engaged in dieting behaviors?
- How do you deal with a client who hates her legs for being grossly fat when yours are twice as big?
- How do you get a client to stop weighing herself daily when you also do so?
- How do you help clients cultivate inner beauty when you are dieting or injecting Botox for those annoying wrinkles?
- How do you respond to a young woman who claims that she definitely does not want to look like you?
- Where can you safely discuss these issues to improve your insight, skills, and comfort level with such deeply personal material?

As a clinical director and supervisor, I have witnessed professionals confront, change, or justify their own body image dissatisfaction and eating habits as a result of working with eating-disordered clients. Having suffered from an eating disorder in the past may be useful or particularly challenging. Those with a previous history of an eating disorder should be recovered for at least 2 years prior to engaging in this work and should engage in ongoing professional supervision to help navigate these issues. All female clinicians working with eating disorders must address their own body-related issues. *Embodiment*, our psychological experience of our physical selves, is an ongoing process that can enrich us personally and professionally; understanding it is essential to effective treatment.

The Clinician's Relationship to Her Own Weight, Eating, and Body Image

Ideally, female therapists can serve as positive, healthy role models for their eating-disordered clients by demonstrating self-acceptance, care, and love for their own bodies. It is healing for clients to see females who are comfortable with their own bodies, living a life free from restrictive dieting or other disordered behaviors, thoughts, and desires. Acceptance does not mean that the therapist always loves what she sees in the mirror, can never have a negative thought about her own body, or can never engage in any behavior to improve it; rather, it means that she knows how to navigate these feelings and behaviors without being destructive to herself.

One way I help clients navigate body image issues is by using some of my own experiences that helped me recover from anorexia and exercise addiction. Early in treatment, I help clients separate their perception, attitude, and behavior toward their bodies. Perception is what the person sees, whether distorted or not. For example, the eating-disordered woman will say and believe: "My stomach sticks out and is fat." Attitude is the meaning she makes of what she sees: "Therefore, I am unworthy and unattractive." Behavior is what she does about it: "I will vomit my food." All three (perception, attitude, and behavior) are important to explore. Despite being a difficult and long-term task, it is important to help clients gain a more realistic body image. Trying to talk a client out of her own perception or out of feeling fat is a useless endeavor.

One way I work with clients on attitude is to instill the notion of "so what." When I suffered from anorexia, I struggled to keep my stomach flat and not weigh over a certain amount but ultimately had to face that it was getting me nowhere. I came to the realization that I could perhaps spend the rest of my life pursuing these goals, but so what, achieving them would not get me what I really wanted: happiness, love, joy. When I felt fat or unworthy because my stomach stuck out or had any similar "anorexic thought," I started to ask myself: "So what?" So what if someone's stomach sticks out, or she has big thighs? What, if anything, does a stick-out-stomach or big thighs interfere with? I ask clients to think about the people they like, love, and respect the most and question if these people are the thinnest people they know. Invariably the answer is, "No." I then ask clients to think about who likes them and why. I also ask them to consider what price they would have to pay for getting thinner thighs and if that price is really worth it. The intensity of these ideas diminishes with the use of so what, while the clients are helped to understand and cope with the underlying feelings, no longer hating or hurting themselves. So-what does not mean that the client's feelings do not matter; empathy and understanding are essential.

The so-what technique only works when therapists have practiced this themselves and have come to terms with their own bodies. We can perceive and feel certain things about our bodies, but it is our behavior, and what we actually do about it, that will or will not get us into trouble. Therapists can sometimes help by sharing that they too have "bad body image days," occasionally wish clothes fit better, or that they looked thinner. The art of so-what is to notice these things and let them go, not put too much emphasis on them, or act on them destructively. This is the art of self-acceptance.

Mindfulness and distress tolerance practices such as those taught in dialectical behavioral therapy (Linehan, 2005) are useful tools to address body image obsessions and promote self-acceptance. These techniques help clients to observe without judgment, take the emphasis off appearance, explore what really matters, and make peace with their natural size; they build these skills in the therapist as well. In fact, over the years, many therapists have confided that they healed their own unrecognized body image issues by helping clients make peace with theirs.

Sharing details of my own history is one way I have used my embodied experience to help clients. To be truly authentic, therapists have to learn how to best use their experiences therapeutically, based on their own clinical theory, perspective, and comfort zone. This requires careful reflection to decipher if a specific personal experience is being shared for the sake of the therapist or the benefit of the client. I often will ask myself and those that I supervise: "How are you hoping that this will help the client? How might you want to share this to relieve yourself or to take care of your own emotional needs?"

Recovered from an eating disorder several years before becoming a therapist, Rena Roberts, an eating disorder therapist I supervise in California, knows severe body image struggles firsthand. Through disciplined self-awareness, integrating her personal and professional growth, she has learned what to share with clients, what to do with her own feelings, and how best to help her clients in their body image struggles. In her words (personal communication, 2007):

> If I am going to help a client improve her body image, it is important that my body image is solid. I need to have explored, processed, and accepted my own flaws in order to help another accept hers.
>
> Although I have been recovered for many years, my own body image has needed continual work. As I go through different life phases, I need to continue to process feelings about my body and come to a place of acceptance again. For example, I could not ignore the feelings brought on by body changes due to pregnancy. As I age, it seems like every few years some new hormonal changes are also changing my body a little this way and a little that. Each step of the way, a decision is made about how I will respond to these changes and accompanying feelings. I call this body image maintenance.
>
> For the first time in my life, I have been considering a tummy tuck because of the damage to my skin

on my stomach during my pregnancies. I have terrible discoloration and stretch marks. Just considering this plastic surgery has made me feel guilty and indulgent and perhaps even hypocritical; on the other hand, it has helped me to understand and accept my clients with less judgment.

I have a client who has had various dermatological and plastic surgery procedures, and she continues to desire more of this type of work. Previously, I felt judgmental regarding her behavior. With my experience, training, and ongoing supervision, I have contained that judgment and remained helpful to her. Since pondering my own tummy tuck, I have grown in compassion and humility with this client and aging women in general. The real question is how to deal with body image transference in an effective way. If we simplify client questions/concerns about our bodies as being about their eating disorder, we miss an opportunity to entertain deeper discussions where topics such as the body of the therapist might be included. Clients walk around all day comparing themselves to others, constantly worried that they don't measure up. When we directly address their concerns about us and our bodies, we dispel the power that their assumptions might have.

Scrutiny and Comments From Clients Regarding the Clinician's Body

As a supervisor, I explore body image transference and countertransference and try to cultivate a healing professional dialogue when it is safe to talk about these issues. I still remember when an 85-pound teen with anorexia looked at me and said, "Uh, I don't want to be that fat." I responded by laughing and saying, "Well, good thing I love my body and am comfortable with it at this size, but we will have to see what size your body needs to be." I went on to tell her that I was not comfortable with my weight gain in the beginning, and that it gets easier and easier as time goes on. I told her, "Your mind eventually catches up to your body." Later, I discussed this exchange in supervision, and others shared similar experiences. We were all able to laugh together. Laughter is good medicine, for client and clinician.

Unfortunately, many therapists do not process countertransference feelings for fear of seeming inadequate, unprofessional, or "not recovered." These challenging scenarios are not personal failures but rather opportunities to grow professionally. Those clinicians who work in a treatment program but do not feel comfortable bringing issues up in supervision should find an outside therapist or supervisor to help. The worst thing is to ignore it and hope it all goes away.

During her supervision over the years, Rena worked through several of these discomforting body image challenges. At this point, Rena is an accomplished and seasoned therapist, but she recognizes that body image challenges always come up (personal communication, 2007):

> Once a client said to me, "I don't want to hurt you. No offense, I don't think you're fat, but I wouldn't want to look like you." It didn't feel all that great. Part of me thought, "Why not? I look pretty darn good. I definitely look better than your anorexic self. Wow, she's really sick." I even felt insecure that perhaps she had seen my tummy hang out sometime. I thought I should be more careful in how I dress and even that maybe it's my complexion, and she associates that with eating. All of these things went through my mind instantly. But I knew it was hard for her to say, and that she was looking to gain something from the comment.
>
> First, I reassured her that I always wanted her to tell me what was on her mind even if it seemed rude or wrong in some way. I reassured her that she was very sensitive in her delivery of the comment, and I knew there was no ill will in the comment. I wanted her to know that she could have an open honest relationship with another human being. When we talked about the content of her comment, my client was able to tell me some important things. She wanted to get better, but she didn't feel able to have a "normal" body. She still felt a great need to be thinner than everyone else. "OK," I said, "I knew that, but why did you start that topic with a comment about my body?" Then the underlying feelings surfaced. She felt sad and ashamed of her inability to recover more fully because she had been in therapy so long and had been to multiple treatment centers. She felt guilty because I had worked so long and so

hard with her that she wished she could do it for me. She was very tearful as she explained how grateful she was for our work and how she thought she must be such a disappointment to me. She feared that I would not want to accept her and support her if she were to maintain a weight that was too thin. She stated, "I'm still waiting for you to give me the boot and tell me I'm a hopeless case."

All of this came from a discussion that started with my body! At this point I understood the transference and why it presented that way.

Self-Disclosure and Authenticity

Therapists working with eating-disordered clients must consider how to respond to questions about their own body, weight, and food. This brings self-disclosure front and center, an issue for which there is a wide spectrum of beliefs, theories, and practices. What is best for the client must always be the main guide. Whether a therapist chooses to disclose anything personal is a matter of choice and therapeutic style. In any case, it is important to be able to deliver an authentic therapeutic response.

Before sharing personal information, clinicians need to be trained in how to avoid inappropriate self-disclosure, becoming overly involved with a client, sharing too much detail, or overly personalizing material. Therapists need to acquire skills in how to respond authentically, while holding back personal information that would not be in the client's best interest.

A great example of the risks and art of self-disclosure occurred during group therapy when an intern's stomach was growling. The client sitting next to her interrupted the group by asking the intern if she had eaten breakfast. The intern responded by saying: "No, as a matter of fact I haven't." Everyone could then feel the tension in the room. All of the clients were in residential treatment, all had to eat breakfast every morning, and we stressed the importance of this meal. Several questions arise with this scenario: How should the intern have responded? Should she tell the truth; if not, isn't that lying? How should I, as the main group facilitator, have responded? As her supervisor, what should I say to the intern later?

Of course, there are a variety of responses to these questions. What I did was to immediately respond by asking the client if the growling stomach made her uncomfortable and why. I then let all the clients discuss the situation and how they felt about the intern not having breakfast. I used the current situation to discuss how the clients get affected, or "triggered" as they often call it, by others. I pointed out to the clients that they were going to routinely run into people who engage in behaviors, such as skipping breakfast or a snack, that to a normal person might not mean much, but to someone recovering from an eating disorder could be inappropriate and potentially dangerous. We also were able to explore what being "triggered" really means and where personal responsibility enters the picture. The discussion was helpful to the clients, but it took some work getting the focus off the intern and her lack of breakfast.

What did the intern need to learn from the breakfast incident situation? In supervision, I told her that I understood her dilemma, but that telling the clients she had not eaten breakfast was inappropriate. This kind of personal disclosure could cause all kinds of conflicts for clients, as well as cause them to worry that she is not a good role model. Her disclosure could give clients an excuse not to eat breakfast or to mistrust her. The intern admitted that she was confused about what to do when she was put on the spot. Not knowing how to respond, she thought it was best to tell the truth. I explained kindly that the whole truth is not always the right answer. In this situation, the best response to "Did you eat breakfast" would be not to lie but rather to reply with something that brings the issue back to the client, such as the following:

- "Oh I see that my stomach growling bothers you. Why is that?"
- "My stomach growls when I eat and when I don't. How is it affecting you?"
- "Well, I guess my stomach is still hungry. Does that bother you?"
- "That's a personal question, but what would it mean to you if I did or didn't eat?"

Eating and food questions come up in individual therapy sessions routinely. I have been asked if I ate, when I ate last, and what I ate, all in the same day by different clients. Most of the time I can just answer truthfully and tell the client, "Yes, I ate … " and fill in the details. I do this if I think the answer is either useful for the client to hear or, at the very least, not problematic and will end the topic quickly so we can move on. Other times, answering is not so simple and could be triggering, for example, if I have not yet eaten lunch, and it is late. I try to think more of the process of the questions, or the deeper meaning, rather than the content. Sometimes, the therapist needs to answer indirectly, as I suggested regarding the breakfast incident: not to lie but also not to feel trapped by the content of the question and instead to address potential clinical meanings. There is a balance here. It is important not always to evade giving a direct answer; otherwise, the eating-disordered client will feel put off and avoided. These clients are very sensitive, so answering their questions is important. The key is to know when to answer with content and when to answer with a process comment.

Self-disclosure can be helpful sometimes, while other times, it can be problematic or damaging. If unsure, err on the side of an authentic, honest but nondisclosing response as in the breakfast examples I provided and do not disclose anything that makes you feel uncomfortable. This will only cause tension that the client may misinterpret. It is even appropriate to say that you are not comfortable discussing the details of what has been asked. Everyone has a right to privacy and boundaries. Understanding why they may want to know more about you and what you can comfortably share takes time and experience. Self-disclosure and authenticity are important issues to discuss with colleagues and supervisors on an ongoing basis.

It can also be quite useful when therapists disclose some of their own healing and recovery in the area of body image. For example, I might discuss how difficult it was to gain weight, and how I kicked and screamed through every pound. I let clients with anorexia know that they cannot wait to be "ready" to gain weight, and that no one is ever really ready. When appropriate, I share a few mantras that I used to say over and over to myself, such as, "Full is not the same thing as fat," or "You cannot be the judge of your own body." I tell my clients that I had to find someone I trusted more than I trusted the eating disorder. All of these ideas sprang from my own struggle and recovery from anorexia and my own body image problems. Therapists can draw on many types of experiences in their own lives to help clients understand the process of letting go, giving up old habits, and managing fear.

When therapists disclose personal information about overcoming a problem, they must avoid assuming that the client will need the same things or respond in the same way. What works for the therapist may not work for the client. Talking about the details of one's problem or illness should always be avoided. It is the process of getting through something, not the specific details of the problem, from which clients can benefit. Rather than discussing how many laxatives one took or weight one lost, a more appropriate form of self-disclosure for a recovered therapist would be discussing how the therapist was able to conquer problems such as laxative abuse, accept a more realistic body weight, or any methods or strategies used to stop engaging in eating-disordered behaviors. Rena described an interesting self-disclosure experience (personal communication, 2007):

> Due to adult acne, I once decided to try a recommended alternative treatment that involved a diet. As a result, I lost about 5 pounds. One of the natural laws of treating eating disorders is that eating disorder clients will notice any changes in their thera-

pist's weight. One client began the session by saying she was worried about me, and that she wasn't sure how to bring it up. "Are you OK?" she said. "I can see you have lost weight. I am sorry to put you on the spot, but it's bothering me."

In the first instant, I was annoyed. I am recovered and have worked in this field for over 10 years. I don't want to discuss my acne or medical choices with my clients. It was hard enough to stick to this diet. I wanted sugar and caffeine, damn it! I wasn't in the mood to help her with her body comparison issues. I then felt bad. But the truth is, it is hard to have my body under constant scrutiny from clients or colleagues. Because I specialize in eating disorder treatment, I have found that people watch my eating and scrutinize my body and question my recovery. I tried the best I could to just listen to the client, tell her I was OK and hide my feelings. After the session, I vented these feelings to my mentor, Carolyn Costin. She reminded me that this kind of reaction from a client goes with the territory and helped me understand my feelings.

I helped Rena not to take the client's comments personally. Our processing helped Rena to understand her own reactions so they would not interfere with the therapy. To process before responding is helpful. If a therapist becomes upset by something in a session and can control it enough so it does not show, she should move past the issue as best she can and process it later. If she cannot hide her feelings, it is best to acknowledge them briefly, breathe deeply to become calm and centered, and ask to come back to the issue at a later time. This gives the therapist time to work things through before further discussion of it.

Rena continued (personal communication, 2007):

During the next session, I asked her what her observation about my body had brought up for her. We discussed a few issues, but things still seemed tense. Then, I decided to disclose the truth to her. She was right that I had lost weight, so I validated her observation. I told her that I was on a special diet to treat adult acne. I did not give her specifics about the diet. I told her there was initial weight loss that had stopped, that I was being monitored by a

doctor, and that we had discussed the weight loss
and were doing things to address this. Instantly,
she relaxed. Relieved at the explanation, her interest
switched to how it was for me as a recovered person
to experience weight loss. She wondered if it triggered me or worried me. Now, she was comparing
our levels of recovery rather than our bodies. She
began discussing how she feels when her pants fit
a little looser. She talked of her desire to someday
be fully recovered so that if she needed a "special
diet" for some kind of health reason she could do it
without being triggered to relapse. Her worry that
I may be relapsing completely flipped to her trying
to glean from me what it takes to be fully recovered.
Maybe more importantly, she began to talk about
being fully recovered one day.

Rena was able to turn a precarious situation regarding her own body
into a therapeutic conversation. Another skilled therapist who is substan-
tially overweight often brings up her own body shape, asking if the client
wants to talk about it. The important thing is to be comfortable in one's
own embodied self.

Embodied Awareness: A Tool for Recovery

Eating disorder and body image treatment is difficult, challenging, but
rewarding work. Helping clients heal the wounds that underlie their mistrust, dissatisfaction, and hatred of their bodies takes tremendous empathy, skill, expertise, and finesse. The work requires therapists to be aware
of their embodied experience and of the constant cultural pulls toward
body dissatisfaction.

All clinicians grapple with the ideas expressed in this chapter as they
weave their way through their clients' recovery and their shared experiences regarding eating, weight, and shape in a society struggling with
these issues. Even those therapists who are grounded and balanced in
regard to self and body acceptance will need to explore these issues and
practice self-care. Caring for one's self physically, reading and staying
connected to feminist and spiritual ideas, and engaging in soul-nourish-
ing activities will all help to keep one's head and heart in the right place
when dealing with our own and our clients' bodies and souls. Each therapist needs to find her own way to connect to what is truly important in
life to be a conduit for that connection to take place in clients. Carefully
tended and appropriately nourished, the therapist's embodied experience

can be one of personal joy as well as a useful tool in the efforts to help clients navigate recovery.

References

Freud, S. (1961) The ego and the id. In J. Strachey (Ed. and Trans.), *The standard edition of the complete psychological works of Sigmund Freud* (Vol. 19, pp. 3–66). London: Hogarth Press. (Original work published in 1923.)

Hutchinson, M. G. (1994). Imagining ourselves whole: A feminist approach to treating body image disorders. In P. Fallon, M. A. Katzman, & S. Wooley (Eds.), *Feminist perspectives on eating disorders* (pp. 152–170). New York: Guilford Press.

Kearney-Cook, A. (1989). Reclaiming the body: Using guided imagery in the treatment of body image disturbances among bulimic women. In L. M. Hornyak & E. Baker (Eds.), *Experiential therapies for eating disorders* (pp. 11–33). New York: Guilford Press.

Levine, M. P., & Smolak, L. (1998). The mass media and disordered eating: Implications for primary prevention. In W. Vandereycken & G. Noordenbos (Eds.), *The prevention of eating disorders* (pp. 23–56). New York: New York University Press.

Linehan, M. (2005). *Cognitive behavioral treatment of borderline personality.* New York: Guilford Press.

Maine, M., & Kelly, J. (2005). *The body myth: Adult women and the pressure to be perfect.* New York: John Wiley & Sons.

Recommended Resources

Borysenko, J. (2006). *Fire in the soul.* New York: Warner Books.

Gilbert, E. (2007). *Eat, pray, love.* New York: Penguin USA.

Johnston, A. (2000). *Eating in the light of the moon: How women can transform their relationships with food through myths, metaphors, and storytelling.* Carlsbad, CA: Gurze Books.

Kornfield, J. (1993). *A path with heart.* New York: Bantam Books.

Moore, T. (1992). *Care of the soul.* New York: Harper Collins.

Tolle, E. (1999). *The power of now.* Novato, CA: New World Library.

chapter thirteen

Connecting Through Difference
Therapeutic Use of Self to Promote Eating Disorder Recovery

Cynthia Whitehead-LaBoo

Introduction

Many factors collude to result in clinical eating disorders. In an era of conformity and strict and unreasonable standards for appearance, weight, and desired image, feeling different from the norm can lead to a profound lack of self-worth (Seid, 1994; Wilhelm, 2006), fertile ground in which an eating disorder may take hold and grow. A deep sense of deficiency and disconnection grows deeper, leading to isolation, hopelessness, and increased immersion in the eating disorder, putting emotional, spiritual, mental, and physical health at grave risk (Zerbe, 1993).

As an African American woman of size, I know the pain and risks of being different firsthand, and I have used this knowledge and experience to help many clients recover from eating disorders. I must admit that it feels very powerful to walk into a room wearing self-acceptance on my sleeve. I am an enigma in a cultural climate in which fat people are not supposed to exude confidence and experience emotional and physical well-being. My empowered stance might take some clients aback because my presence and degree of energy in the room do not fit with how most expect a fat woman to act.

This chapter explores how I have used my experiences of difference, self-acceptance, and empowerment clinically to contribute to the recovery process of those struggling with the sense of difference and deficiency underlying their eating disorders. My personal empowerment, therapeutic use of self, and commitment to authenticity and health are critical tools in this work.

My Journey

As an African American woman of size, I have spent a good bit of my life being impacted by difference and have worked hard to embrace who I am as I am. My journey has truly been a process that involved dismissing the personal and societal standards that I allowed to define me in my youth, accepting the love of others who valued me as I am, and taking ownership of the fact that I have a host of wonderful personal attributes that have nothing to do with my size.

During my early adolescence, I became increasingly aware of my size and perceived that my body was not what it ought to be. Despite the fact that I was not actually fat, I *felt fat* and felt deeply pained by this belief; thus, I know firsthand how a distorted and negative body image can create a paralyzing degree of disempowerment. Concerns about my physical appearance left me feeling diminished and rarely confident during my vulnerable teenaged experience. It has taken years to come full circle and return to a place at which thoughts about size, food, and weight do not take up so much time and energy and to feel whole and empowered again.

Early in my work as a clinical psychologist, I realized that I could not work with clients all day focusing on how to foster emotional health, balance, and well-being in them without taking a close look at whether I was living an emotionally healthy, self-accepting, balanced life. My insights from years ago help me to frequently ask myself how I am doing with these very same issues. This willingness to take a hard look at myself has helped me to work through many painful experiences of difference and to embrace self-acceptance. In turn, I am well equipped to help my clients on their journey. I know firsthand that placing an inordinate amount of emphasis on the size of their bodies detracts people from acknowledging their other positive attributes and strengths (Zerbe, 1993). Moreover, I know firsthand that, to recover, clients must change core negative beliefs into core positive beliefs and embrace all of their positive attributes rather than focusing on negatively perceived attributes (Wilhelm, 2006). Having worked through my painful experiences of difference and my disconnection from my body and from my true beauty, I am a therapist who walks the walk of embracing my differences and loving myself unconditionally.

I realized that I had come into full acceptance of myself as a fat person while attending an eating disorders workshop many years ago. The facilitator of the guided imagery exercise asked, "How would you feel if you were larger?" I felt uncomfortable imagining myself as a larger person because I was already fat. As a woman of size, I have encountered seating

arrangements in the past that I have jokingly referred to as "big hip challenged," so the thought of having hips that are bigger than mine were
at that point was not a pleasant one. She asked, "How would you feel if
you remained the same size?" I felt comfortable with imagining myself
as I am. When she asked, "How would you feel if you were smaller," I
was astonished to discover that I felt confused, uncomfortable, and disempowered. I remembered that I did not feel confident or powerful or
have self-esteem when I was much younger and relatively thin compared
to my present size. I was not truly accepting of myself on the inside, so
being thin on the outside was not enough. In this transformative moment,
I realized I had grown into my size and was comfortable as a plus size,
fat woman. My journey to become self-accepting was facilitated by many
experiences, such as attending feminist conferences on eating disorders,
and becoming familiar with authors who have written about health at
every size (Gaesser, 2002) and about the power of self-acceptance as large
women (Burgard & Lyons, 1994; Goodman, 1995).

To facilitate effective psychotherapy, all psychotherapists need to be
self-aware and grounded in the knowledge of who they are as individuals
despite whatever differences or personal challenges they have overcome.
Jourard (1971) suggested that this awareness, and the resulting feelings of
self-confidence and self-esteem, give the therapist an aura that is compelling to the client. Clients have a sixth sense about their therapist's authenticity and, consciously or not, will decide to engage in a deep trusting
relationship based on this perception. Thus, facing my painful experiences of difference relative to my size and skin color have enhanced my
work as a psychotherapist.

Acknowledging Difference to Enhance Connection

As an African American woman and as a fat person, I am not inherently
powerful in our current Western culture (Jones & Shorter-Gooden, 2003).
Quite simply, I am not privileged with regard to race or size. There will
always be individuals who view me as an "N" despite the fact that I am
Dr. Whitehead-LaBoo. In addition, there will always be individuals who
view my size negatively even if I am accepting of it. I had to fight for my
empowerment by finding a voice with several significant individuals in
my life, and I share this with clients who may benefit from hearing my
story. Finding my voice helped me to resist the voices of others and to
move from the disempowerment of difference to true empowerment and
genuine positive self-definition.

As I work primarily with Caucasian clients, I carefully consider whether
to speak about my lack of privilege as an African American and the challenges that I have had to face and overcome. Each interaction that I have

with a Caucasian client is a multicultural experience, but I only bring up differences in race or my lack of privilege if the issue of cultural differences appears to be pertinent to the work. For example, when a client is from an area where she is less likely to have had experiences with people of color, I am likely to bring our racial differences into the room. When speaking with clients about the lack of privilege associated with not fitting into the current beauty ideal, I may process what it is like to experience and negotiate the lack of privilege associated with being an African American woman. In discussing these issues of privilege, I empower my clients to consider that they do not have to let their lack of privilege define them, just as I do not allow it to define me.

Being a part of a minority culture implies that I will very likely know more about the majority culture than the majority culture will know about my culture. When my Caucasian clients discuss various issues with me, I usually understand what they are trying to communicate because the majority-driven media informs me daily about the lives of Caucasian people. Thus, I am versed both in my culture and in the culture of the majority of my clients. For this reason, I have generally not encountered difficulty working as an African American therapist with predominantly white clients. In addition, I work in a city that has a large African American professional population, so encountering an African American professional on my campus is less likely to feel unusual. If I worked in a different type of community with less racial diversity and integration, I might encounter more difficulty in working with Caucasian clients and be compelled to bring issues of race into the room more consistently.

Given that many individuals who are from the majority culture know little to nothing about minority cultures and that many therapists who are considered minorities are not familiar with other minority cultures, all therapists must be sensitive to issues of difference and diversity. Cross-cultural counseling occurs whenever the therapist and client are different with regard to race and ethnicity (Sue & Sue, 1999) but can also include differences based on sex, sexual orientation, socioeconomic status, and age (Atkinson, Sue, & Morten, 1993). Factors such as religion can also create division, misunderstanding, and even prejudice. Therapists should openly process these and other differences with clients and explore how such differences resonate in treatment as well as in the client's everyday experience. As understanding our clients is an essential element in effective psychotherapy, a therapist should never be afraid to ask questions or seek clarification. It is more damaging to pretend that you understand when you do not than to ask your client to help you to understand her experience. For example, acknowledging and exploring cultural differences that occur when Caucasian therapists treat minority clients are associated with safety in the therapeutic relationship (Chin, 1994).

No matter what stage of their career, therapists should pursue opportunities to learn about working effectively across cultures and other differences by attending workshops, taking classes, reading, discussing these issues with peers and in supervision, and keeping an open mind about the possible impact of differences in therapeutic encounters. Through such consciousness raising, therapists can begin to trust their clinical instincts and to process differences to foster greater therapeutic connection. I suggest simple statements such as: "I am aware that we are different in some ways, and I want to process how you are feeling about our differences and our work thus far." Or, "What is it like for you to be working with someone who is ... " (name the difference). Rich therapeutic material may emerge when therapists risk being open and honest about differences with eating disordered clients.

Sizing Each Other Up

Although appearance concerns, body shame, and weight preoccupation are central themes for people suffering from eating disorders, clients are not likely to bring up issues of difference related to size on their own. Thus, during the first session with eating-disordered clients, I ask what it is like for them to be sitting with someone who is fat by society's standards and actively engage in a discussion about how I am different with regard to size. I usually speak about how I have reclaimed the word *fat* and how I do not allow the word to define me. I do not challenge my clients to take on my beliefs; I simply present them as my truths and invite my clients to express their honest thoughts and feelings as well.

This often involves explicitly informing my clients that using the term *fat* does not offend me, that I can accept this aspect of myself and still understand their painful perception of themselves as fat, regardless of what size they actually are. In my work with clients who have eating disorders, it has been more important for me to bring up my size than my race because appearance, weight, shape, and body image have become sources of great pain to them. Clients may initially feel misunderstood if I do not invite an open discussion about differences in size and various issues related to body esteem. In addition, I inform my clients that I exercise regularly and eat in a healthy, balanced manner. This self-disclosure provides a model of self-care and plants the seed that health, balance, and physical activity are important regardless of one's size. Self-disclosure and honesty with regard to our own body type demonstrates the therapist's own process of self-acceptance and helps clients to believe that we may understand the lack of privilege they feel, whether fat, thin, or average in size.

When I asked a client what my size meant to her early in our work, she replied that she perceived me as genuinely accepting of myself as soon as she sat down in my office. She did admit, however, that openly discussing my size and my use of the word *fat* helped her to be sure that her perception was accurate. If I had used the word *large* or *big* rather than fat, she would have wondered if I really accepted being fat. This particular client had also attended an eating disorders group that I co-led in the past with a very petite therapist. She had speculated about whether this therapist had body or food issues because we never openly discussed size differences in the group.

A Caucasian client who was heavy responded to the same question with these revealing words: "I am so glad that you are heavy, and I am glad you are black. I was afraid that you were going to be a skinny white woman." As we processed our similarities and differences, I was aware that this client might not have ever spoken about her competitive urges and fears if I were white and thin. These were important issues for her to explore and understand in her recovery process. Had I glossed over this sensitive issue, her treatment would have been compromised.

When working with large therapists, clients need to get a sense of their degree of self-acceptance in order to believe the therapist can help them. When working with petite therapists, clients might feel judged regarding their size. Thin therapists need to acknowledge that thinness is a privilege in our current culture, but that size is only one aspect of self-definition. Although it is sometimes difficult to bring these issues up, what goes unsaid may negatively affect the process and outcome of psychotherapy (Teyber, 1992). I have learned a great deal about my clients through these discussions; more important, they have learned about themselves and engaged in open, trusting dialogues about very sensitive issues. Quite simply, as Jourard (1971) posited many years ago, for therapists to inspire honesty in clients, therapists themselves must be honest. Such open exploration always reaps new insights and healing.

Self-Acceptance: From Clinician to Client

As an African American woman and as a fat person, I have had to fight to see myself through my own positive and accepting lens rather than the negative lens of others who tried to discount me because I was African American or fat. For me, authenticity involves being open about my self-acceptance journey and my experience as an African American woman of size. All therapists must weave their personal experiences of difference and self-doubt and their journey to self-acceptance and self-worth into their professional work.

Self-acceptance implies the ability to embrace and feel good about yourself as a whole, including those qualities that you and others may judge harshly. When practicing self-acceptance, one is less likely to be self-chastising and is more likely to have the energy to work on making appropriate changes in one's life. In short, self-acceptance is the capacity to feel great about what and who you are and not devastated by what and who you are not. When speaking with clients, I call this the capacity to "just be," and I encourage them to risk defining themselves by their standards rather than the negative standards of others. Just being also implies a positive acceptance of the ways in which you are different from others.

My work with Nancy shows how I helped her to just be. Nancy was a graduate student who had suffered with binge eating disorder since childhood, had major self-esteem issues, and described herself as "walking around in self-hatred." Seeing herself as "disgusting," she hated her body because she was not thin. Nancy spoke at length about the trauma she endured as a child, being both verbally and emotionally abused by peers and some family members. In school, she endured teasing for being fat and as the favorite student of her teachers. At home, she felt completely misunderstood because her intellectual skills made her different from her family. Believing she was not worthy of anything good, she tended to surround herself with people who were happy to take advantage of her and abuse her. The self-abuse of her daily binge episodes functioned as punishment for being fat.

Like many clients who develop binge eating disorder, food became her friend, solace, and reliable companion. Nancy would eat in front of the TV, watching soap operas, reading fashion magazines, and fantasizing about how life would be for her when she looked like the thin female images that she saw. She wanted desperately to be thin as she had been when younger because, like most eating-disordered clients, she believed that this would solve all of her problems.

Nancy talked at length about feeling so different from the cultural ideal and feeling judged by society. She went through a phase during our work when she felt that her determination to continue bingeing and never be thin was a big "F you" to society. I stated my belief that the best way to get back at society was to dare not to agree that she was less of a person because of her size but instead to accept her differences.

I spoke about how I probably would not have become Dr. Whitehead-LaBoo if I had agreed with society's idea of what an African American woman should be and how I facilitated my success by daring to be different from the culture's expectations and to define myself by my own standards. I often brought myself into the work with this client because we were both large women. I shared that I felt better about myself now than when I was smaller because I was no longer feeling diminished.

Nancy often spoke about the differences she perceived in size acceptance between white and black communities, and I agreed that the African American community generally enjoys a wider range of size acceptance.

I explained that, due to the long-standing history of racism in America, African Americans have never been able to define their worth based on appearance alone. Historically, it did not matter how beautiful you were if, in the eyes of society, you were a black person and therefore less privileged and acceptable (Comas-Diaz & Greene, 1994; Jones & Shorter-Gooden, 2003). My willingness to acknowledge the differences between our cultures with regard to size acceptance helped Nancy to feel that I understood that our experiences as fat women were also different. Processing our racial differences provided both helpful insights and a deeper sense of connection between us.

As we discussed Nancy's past and current feelings, traumas, and relationships, I cared for her unconditionally and encouraged her to engage in self-care behaviors and to make healthy choices with regard to how she lived her life and the people she allowed to be in it. Stressing that one did not have to fit into an ideal to be worthy of love and respect, I modeled and promoted emotional and physical health and disclosed some of the struggles I had faced and overcome during my own self-acceptance journey. Although Nancy and I were different in many ways, Nancy could relate to my struggles and could appreciate that the process of recovery involves taking steps forward and steps back over time.

My authentic, forgiving, accepting, patient, and loving stance with this client helped her to heal old wounds and grow in ways that I had not anticipated. I was aware as we ended that our open and honest processing of both our similarities and our differences helped her to take important steps on her journey of self-healing. During our final session, she read a letter indicating how much she had learned, changed, and grown during our time together. In summary, Nancy expressed thanks for my teaching her that diets do not work, and that being thin would not alter the way that she felt if she did not address her deeper feelings. She also expressed appreciation for my helping her to find her worth and not allow others to define it for her or take advantage of her. She expressed that she was working on trying to be self-accepting, that the work was hard, but that it was the only way to move toward recovery. At the end of the letter, she acknowledged that my consistent, positive affirmation of her and my own self-acceptance had helped her to change.

I was quite emotional as Nancy read the letter and humbled by it. I had been so busy thinking about her ongoing symptoms that I did not realize how powerful a dynamic our relationship had been in her life. Our therapeutic connection gave Nancy hope that she would continue recovering even if she was still struggling with symptoms at times. This case exemplifies the healing power of an authentic and honest relationship and how the therapist's modeling of self-acceptance can bridge the gap of difference and despair.

Self-Acceptance Through Empowerment

Clients benefit from working with therapists who have learned to empower themselves regardless of negative personal and societal influences that affect them. When therapists are not grounded in their own emotional health and personal power, they may sometimes fool themselves, but they will rarely fool their clients.

Outside negative forces impinge on us at every turn; women have to fight especially hard to have self-worth (Goodman, 1995). This ongoing battle is much easier when we are walking in self-acceptance rather than in self-hatred (Wilhelm, 2006). Eating disorders are truly disempowering, so clients need much support to reclaim their self-worth, inner strength, and confidence. As clients find these resources and begin to manifest them through words and deeds, they often experience a decrease in symptoms (Johnston, 1996). Asserting their right to establish and maintain boundaries gradually moves them to a place of empowerment. This case illustration highlights the importance of modeling wellness and promoting self-acceptance and empowerment in clients.

I worked with Elaine over the course of 3 years. A graduate student who alternated between extreme dieting and binge eating disorder for years, Elaine had never considered that this cycle might be harmful. Because of lifelong critical messages about appearance from her mother, she believed that she needed to look a certain way to be acceptable. Elaine was a large woman and therefore felt a deep sense of shame about her body and about her very existence. With her diminished esteem and sense of inferiority based on her size, she had a tendency to put much of her energy into taking care of and pleasing others rather than taking care of herself. Elaine believed that if she made herself indispensable to others, she would not be alone.

The struggle to engage in self-care was an ongoing theme during the years we worked together. Early on, I disclosed that I used to diet, and that I know now that restriction and self-criticism are self-punishment and not self-care. Elaine believed that she was not worthy of self-care because she no longer looked and felt as she did when she was younger. She grieved her lost youth and the fact that her body would never again be able to do the things it could do in the past. She brought in pictures of herself when she was very thin and fit and spoke about all of the physical activities she engaged in at that time. Refusing to accept her current body, she realized that she was holding on to the possibility of recapturing her young adult experience.

Elaine found my self-disclosure regarding my own journey helpful. I shared that I would quickly turn down the opportunity to go back to the smaller size that I was during my late high school and early college years if I had to feel as insecure as I did at that time. I expressed my awareness, based on both personal and professional experiences, that feeling good was not completely dependent on the size or youth of one's body. I also suggested that letting go of the past and living in the moment would very likely give Elaine more energy to focus on being emotionally and physically healthy in the present. In response, Elaine stated that I was one of only a few women she knew who seemed to be relatively self-accepting with regard to physical appearance. She further noted that the other individuals in her social sphere who were self-accepting were also older African American women. We processed our awareness of cultural and racial differences with regard to size acceptance in an effort to promote a mutual understanding of one another as therapist and client. I was honest about the fact that I have to fight hard to take care of myself each day, and that self-acceptance is an active ongoing process.

As therapy progressed and Elaine began to sit in positive self-acceptance, she was much less likely to use food to cope when difficult situations arose. When we ended our work, she spoke without judgment about having gained 25 pounds since beginning graduate school and was proud of the fact that her weight had been stable for a year and a half. No longer focused on fitting into clothes that she had worn in her younger years, she was deciding what to give away. As for many women with eating disorders, the process of ridding oneself of what no longer fits can represent a very important step toward self-acceptance, self-definition, and empowerment. While clothing is a concrete example of this, recovery also requires ridding oneself of demands, relationships, and behaviors that diminish self-esteem.

Elaine decided to adopt the mantra "just as I am" to help her engage more fully in doing things in the present rather than waiting until some point in the future when her body was different. She conveyed that one of her biggest turning points during our work was when she began to contemplate no longer dieting. As we terminated, she thanked me for accepting my differences, speaking openly about them, and helping her to embrace her own differences. Connecting through the many differences between us and speaking about my journey to empowered self-acceptance as a fat, African American, middle-aged woman were central to the progress Elaine made. She could now embrace her differences, accept who she was, and no longer try to meet unhealthy cultural ideals.

Final Thoughts: From the Danger of Difference to the Value of Connection

Our current societal climate does not promote well-being or self-acceptance in individuals who do not fit into the stereotyped thin ideal. Women are pressured to pursue an unhealthy and unnatural body type (Bordo, 2003; McFarland, 1995; Thompson, 1994) to avoid being considered unattractive, sloppy, lazy, damaged, and weak (Gaesser, 2002; Goodman, 1995; Seid, 1994). Focusing on what is wrong with them robs women of self-confidence and of the ability to recognize their positive attributes, leaving them disempowered and empty. Feeling different, and not readily validated by society based on appearance, can lead to dark and dangerous places, including life-threatening eating disorders.

I am both personally and professionally aware that the pain of difference can be associated with the size of one's body and the color of one's skin. The previous clinical vignettes exemplify how eating disorders thrive when people feel different, unaccepted, and not validated by others. Just as I did on my personal journey, these clients learned that embracing their differences helped them to find wisdom, self-acceptance, and peace. The cases also highlight the importance of modeling wellness and promoting empowerment in our clients and the degree to which acceptance of oneself and of one's differences, through authentic and honest therapeutic relationships, can promote health, well-being, and recovery in psychotherapy with clients who have eating disorders.

References

Atkinson, D. R., Sue, D. W., & Morten, G. (1993). *Counseling American minorities: A cross cultural perspective*. Madison, WI: Brown and Benchmark.

Bordo, S. (2003). *Unbearable weight: Feminism, western culture, and the body*. Berkeley: University of California Press.

Burgard, D., and Lyons, P. (1994). Alternatives in obesity treatment: Focusing on health for fat women. In Fallon, P., Katzman, M. A., & Wooley, S. C. (Eds.), *Feminist perspectives on eating disorders* (pp. 212–230). New York: Guilford Press.

Chin, J. L. (1994). Psychodynamic approaches. In Comas-Diaz, L., & Green, B. (Eds.), *Women of color: Integrating ethnic and gender identities in psychotherapy* (pp. 194–222). New York: Guilford Press.

Comas-Diaz, L., & Greene, B. (1994). An ethnocultural mosaic. In Comas-Diaz, L., & Greene, B. (Eds.), *Women of color: Integrating ethnic and gender identities in psychotherapy* (pp. 3–9). New York: Guilford Press.

Gaesser, G. (2002). *Big fat lies: The truth about your weight and your health*. Carlsbad, CA: Gurze Books.

Goodman, C. W. (1995). *The invisible woman: Confronting weight prejudice in America*. Carlsbad, CA: Gurze Books.

Johnston, A. (1996). *Eating in the light of the moon: How women can transform their relationships with food through myths, metaphors and storytelling*. Carlsbad, CA: Gurze Books.

Jones, C., & Shorter-Gooden, K. (2003). *Shifting: The double lives of black women in America*. New York: HarperCollins.

Jourard, S. M. (1971). *The transparent self*. New York: Van Nostrand Reinhold.

McFarland, B. (1995). *Brief therapy and eating disorders: A practical guide to solution-focused work with clients.* San Francisco: Jossey-Bass.

Seid, R. P. (1994). Too close to the bone: The historical context for women's obsession with slenderness. In Fallon, P., Katzman, M. A., & Wooley, S. C. (Eds.), *Feminist perspectives on eating disorders* (pp. 3–16). New York: Guilford Press.

Sue, D. W., & Sue, D. (1999). *Counseling the culturally different: Theory and practice.* New York: John Wiley & Sons.

Teyber, E. (1992). *Interpersonal process in psychotherapy: A guide for clinical training.* Pacific Grove, CA: Brooks/Cole.

Thompson, B. (1994). Food, bodies, and growing up female: Childhood lessons about culture, race and class. In Fallon, P., Katzman, M. A., & Wooley, S. C. (Eds.), *Feminist perspectives on eating disorders* (pp. 355–378). New York: Guilford Press.

Wilhelm, S. (2006). *Feeling good about the way you look: A program for overcoming body image problems.* New York: Guilford Press.

Zerbe, K. J. (1993). *The body betrayed: A deeper understanding of women, eating disorders and treatment.* Carlsbad, CA: Gurze Books.

chapter fourteen

Therapy Redux
The Evolution of a Treatment Relationship

Stephen Zimmer

> All other doubts, by time let them be clear'd:
> Fortune brings in some boats that are not steer'd.

William Shakespeare (1609)

Introduction

Graduate school and clinical internships never really prepared me for the challenge of being an eating disorder therapist. When a client's symptoms do not improve regardless of what one does and when, after years of effort, the client's condition gets worse, not better, how does one maintain hope and remain persistent? Often, the client and the experience gleaned during the therapeutic engagement are our best teachers. For me, the lessons to be learned from the psychotherapy I describe are simple but profound. Recovery is a process that demands patience (Palazzoli, 1978) and is more complex than can be fathomed at any given moment. Tolerating the limitations of one's knowledge and abilities and acting in response to the client's best interest rather than one's own anxiety are crucial.

From my first days in practice, I endeavored to create valuable, enduring therapeutic relationships with clients. But, how much did I understand about "enduring" early in my career? I did not fully appreciate that it would be normal to see clients episodically throughout their lives (and mine) and at different points in the recovery process (Johnson & Connors, 1987). Indeed, recovery from an eating disorder can follow a circuitous and, at times, surprising path that includes well-planned interventions as well as random events and clearly illustrates the fact there is rarely a straightforward relationship between the start of treatment and the beginning of healing.

*   *   *

On a Tuesday afternoon in June 2004, a voice on the answering machine announced her return.

> "Hi, this is Carla Knefler. I haven't been doing that great. Could I come in to see you?"

It had been 15 years since I had last heard from Carla. Immediately, 6 exhausting years of therapy came to mind. When she had arrived in my office initially, as a sophomore in college, she actually seemed to be doing quite well with her anorexia. But after 3 years of therapy with me, an eating disorder specialist, and at that time, the co-clinical director of the Center for the Study of Anorexia and Bulimia in New York City, her anorexia returned in force, and I could do absolutely nothing about it. Over the rest of our time together, I used everything I ever learned, to no avail. We both became utterly demoralized, I even more than she. Nevertheless, I had liked her quite a lot, and after so long, I was curious about why she decided to come back. During the first session I began to hear why:

> "I've been getting ready to call you for a long time. A couple of years ago I made friends with a girl named Kristin. I hadn't had fun like that since college. Seeing the way she was living, I started to wonder what was wrong with me all over again."

I made a quick study of her body: She looked healthier than she had, which was a relief; but she was still underweight. Her pants draped oddly over her meager thighs. When she sat back, her running shoes barely reached the floor. Her delicate good looks had survived the passage of time, and only the fine lines emanating from the corners of her eyes hinted that she was no longer 25. I would ask for the name of her doctor and call later in the week to get a current assessment of her medical status.

> "When Kristin got transferred to a new store, Todd, a guy who worked in Human Resources, must have noticed I lost my lunch partner. He kept asking me out, and I was so lonely I started saying yes. Once we took a weekend trip to Montreal. We were eating dinner in a restaurant, and I could tell he was in a funk. Finally he said, 'Carla, I just want to be close to you.' I felt so bad. I really cared a lot for him but not in the right way. I don't think I can love anybody

the right way. I'm 40 years old. If something doesn't
change, I'm going to miss my whole life."

Extraordinary words coming from a chronic anorexic. She had, for the
duration of her illness, denied wanting anything beyond being the thinnest. Now, something had shifted. She wanted, it seemed, to take some of
the focus off her own body and try to focus on someone else.

> "Todd wanted more of a sexual relationship while
> I avoided it as much as I could. I knew that meant
> there was something wrong with me. I went off the
> Prozac just to see if it could be suppressing sexual
> feelings. But it made no difference and right away
> the depression was back."

I was surprised to hear that Carla had been taking Prozac.

> "Originally, it was you who wanted me to go on
> antidepressants, but the psychiatrist you had sent
> me to said they [tricyclics and monoamine oxidase
> inhibitors] could lower blood pressure, which is bad
> when you're 69 pounds. Eventually, she changed
> her mind. If I gained 5 pounds she would put me
> on Deseril. I lost 3 pounds. That's just me. Even
> when I was little, whenever I got pushed too much,
> I resisted with all my might."

Carla and I have this in common. We suffer from a similar unwill-
ingness to be pushed. The first time we worked together, for example, I
could not tolerate the relentless rigidity of her symptoms, part of what
undermined the treatment. In her second course of therapy, this common
trait we have would help me anticipate her resistance and intuit when to
ask her to do more. Above all, when Carla returned to my office, she was
ready for a push.

When asked to contribute to this book, it occurred to me that the story of
Carla's two therapies, spanning as it did the majority of my work as an eating disorder therapist, would illustrate the changes in my approach over
time and the unusual way an apparently chronic patient "recovered" from
anorexia. During the summer of 2007, as her second course of therapy was
winding down, I invited Carla to work with me on formulating this chapter, thinking her perspective, in her own words, would be of particular
interest to the reader as well as reflective of the collaborative nature of our
work. So, for a dozen hours that summer, we reminded each other of what

had happened when, what went wrong, what worked, and why. Neither of us imagined how important it would be to both of us to document our work. Understanding more clearly what we had done together solidified our gains. Incidentally, the details of Carla's life have been changed to ensure confidentiality, and Carla (a pseudonym) has reviewed this chapter and has given written permission that it be published.

Carla had quit therapy in 1988. I was sure she left over an ill-considered ultimatum: hospital or termination. I had capitulated to the conventional wisdom: Starving patients are often inaccessible to psychotherapy and belong in a hospital. In fact, Carla had been right to resist hospitalization. She had not been ready to give up her eating disorder. Of even more critical importance, I was not willing to risk continuing to fail with her and used the ultimatum as my escape. If I could have endured her paralysis without losing hope, perhaps she could have as well.

Carla did not remember it quite the same way:

> "You never gave me an ultimatum. Maybe I never gave you the chance. You had been my therapist for so long, and I was getting worse. It was very demoralizing for you and me both, so I just quit."

The fact remained: She chose to leave because the treatment had stalemated. Since 1988, I have come to appreciate a concept John Keats, the Romantic poet, described as negative capability: "When man is capable of being in uncertainties, mysteries, doubts without any irritable reaching after fact and reason" (Rollins, 1972, p. 193). In therapy, this means tolerating apparently insoluble situations without feeling forced to draw conclusions or to take premature actions. In our first course of therapy, I sometimes offered interpretations or suggestions, not because I knew what Carla "really meant" or because I knew what she should do, but because not knowing was too uncomfortable. In that first course of therapy, she had needed me to tolerate her self-starvation while remaining curious about who she was and who she might or might not become. If I could not do that, how could she?

> "The night after my first session back, I couldn't get to sleep; I was so happy. You were glad to see me, you were listening, and you could still make me laugh. But, I woke up the next day really anxious. Talking to you made me realize I was feeling even worse than I had thought. I was afraid I might not be able to function at work, so I called and asked for another session."

In the second session, I asked if we could begin to talk about her past. I wanted to learn what had happened to her these last 15 years; also, I wondered if we could go much further back and, different from our last try, find ways to reimagine her family history and help her see old resentments in new ways.

> "Three years after college, I was still living at home when I took a job selling women's suits at Bergdorf Goodman. The weight had started to come off again. I got so boney it hurt to take a bath. That's when I quit therapy with you. At that point, my mother got very depressed. She had been relieved to see me semi-okay when I was at college and then had to watch me fall apart again. My mother's best friend had recently begun taking Prozac and couldn't remember ever feeling so good, so she convinced my mother to go see her doctor. My mother told him about my being anorexic for 14 years and how nobody would give me an antidepressant because of the blood pressure stuff. The doctor told her she should send me in.
>
> "As soon as I went on the Prozac, I started sleeping again. After a while, people said I seemed like a different person. That was late October 1989. I still had a lot of anxiety, but the Prozac was definitely helping. I met Kristin and Todd after I began on Prozac, and I started eating chicken again."

Antidepressants, selective serotonin reuptake inhibitors (SSRIs) included, are not always effective with emaciated anorexics, but they helped Carla. On her return to therapy, I noticed something had shifted. It was impossible to know if Prozac was responsible, but without it Carla might not have made it back to my office.

*   *   *

The first time Carla was in therapy with me, her suppressed rage toward her parents made her feel too guilty to talk about them. This left her rage intact. Now, we would take a new approach, a way she could better accept. We collected her family stories like amateur anthropologists, making small discoveries, hoping they would help us better understand the world into which she was born.

"When my mother went into labor with their first child, my father wasn't with her. Something went really wrong, and the baby was stillborn. His name was Raymond. The doctor asked my mother if she wanted to bury the baby or should they dispose of it. She said dispose of it. That was just her, wanting a bad thing to be over as quickly as possible. When my father got to the hospital, the baby was gone. This drove a huge wedge between them.

"Coming after Raymond, somehow I knew they needed me to be good—but I was good from the start. As soon as I could walk, if you told me not to touch something, I wouldn't. I could keep busy for hours taking care of my dolls. Not my baby sister Lora; she was always in trouble and wound up getting a lot more of the attention."

Being good was bad for Carla. The family took pride in her self-sufficiency, not noticing she was becoming increasingly detached and alone. Her elementary school experience made matters worse.

"I absorbed such weird things from Catholic school, like you have to put all your energy into not giving in to the fact that you're basically bad. Getting mad at your parents, questioning authority, expressing opinions, was bad. Discipline was good."

And Carla told me, in more detail, how difficult puberty was for her:

"I thought I looked disgusting. The boys acted like idiots around me, and the girls said the boys only liked me because of my chest. The Irish girls were all so skinny, and their mothers told them about everything. Meanwhile, my body was doing all this stuff, and my mother ignored the whole thing. I got so mad that I turned off to my mother without even knowing it."

*   *   *

On a Sunday morning in November 2005, about a year and a half into Carla's second course of therapy, I was in the grand ballroom of Philadelphia's Marriott Hotel attending the Renfrew Center's Eating Disorders Conference. Craig Johnson, director of the Eating Disorders Program at

Laureate Psychiatric Hospital in Tulsa, Oklahoma, stood at a far corner of the stage, near a huge screen on which the frames of his PowerPoint presentation were clicking by.

It sounded like Johnson was saying eating disorders could be inherited. He talked about "turtles" and "hares" and described patients with serious eating disorders as exhibiting one of two clusters of personality traits: The turtles were shy, harm avoidant, restrained, and had low self-esteem. In addition, they were introverted, compliant, obsessive, anxious, concrete, orderly, inflexible, perfectionistic, and prone to emotional flooding. The hares were dramatic, erratic, novelty seeking, easily bored, histrionic, argumentative, and drawn to and then overwhelmed by complexity. He was not suggesting an "anorexia gene" but the existence of inheritable personality traits that could presage an eating disorder (Johnson, 2005). Immediately, I thought of Carla. She had the entire turtle cluster, every single item.

After Johnson's presentation, I caught up with him in the hotel lobby to talk with him about Carla. I mentioned that she had gotten a lot of help from antidepressants while she was out of psychotherapy, had gained some weight, and seemed motivated in a new way. Johnson's eyes lit up. He said:

> "She probably had a comorbid anxiety or depressive disorder that was helped by the SSRI. The majority of anorexics have one or the other. I'm totally intrigued by people like Carla who manage to develop new skill sets fairly late in life. I think kids with 'turtle' temperaments may have developmental delays regarding their ability to tolerate stress and complexity. If the therapist hangs in with them, in long-term supportive psychotherapy, they can do things in their 30s and 40s that they couldn't dream of doing 10 years earlier." (C. Johnson, personal communication, November 10, 2005)

In our next session, I mentioned to Carla what I had learned. The genetic hypothesis fine-tuned our approach to her family history. Although there were unfortunate circumstances in Carla's story, there were no culprits.

As early as first grade and throughout her school years, Carla remembers being timid, obsessive, perfectionistic, fearful, and easily overwhelmed. Then, she had been unprepared for an early menarche and received far too much attention for her developing body. When she focused on her eating, she felt a little more in control.

> "Stuyvesant High School was pretty overwhelm-
> ing. It was huge, and when classes changed the kids
> swarmed in the hallways. There were all kinds of
> kids: hippies, Asians, kids in crazy outfits, kids with
> really long hair, druggies."

If Carla could have gone to a small, carefully structured high school
with excellent psychological services, while her parents began a successful couple's therapy, perhaps her predisposition would not have developed into a full-fledged eating disorder. As it was, the multiple stresses
she encountered on entering high school combined to cause a blow to her
psyche that she and I, in retrospect, considered the "precipitating event."

> "Right away they put me in this brutal honors math
> class. Three kids who later became valedictorian and
> salutatorians of my year were in that class. Here I
> was, just trying to do well, and these kids were miles
> beyond me. That first semester was a huge struggle.
>
> "And then at the first team meeting for gymnas-
> tics, the coach said everyone could stand to lose 5 or
> 10 pounds. That's when I started dieting. Eventu-
> ally, my mother made me quit gymnastics because
> I was so skinny. By senior year, I was 69 pounds.
> My parents made me go to therapy, but it didn't do
> anything."

Before long, Carla finished high school, a gifted student, but in retreat
from family and friends. Starvation had become her refuge.

> "Toward the end of senior year, I went on a weekend
> for interested students at Marymount College. The
> first night there was a barbeque, and nobody made
> a big deal about me eating, which was a pleasant
> change. Going to a school that wasn't too competi-
> tive and where the people were very 'live and let
> live' seemed like the right thing."

Her intuition was correct. At Marymount, Carla would gain strength
and feel more comfortable than at any other time she could remember.
Typical of the "turtles" described by Johnson, her academic performance
was extraordinary.

"When I started Marymount, if I didn't feel smart at least I felt ahead of the other kids. I found that very relaxing. I made friends with a few girls in my dorm, and we stayed friends the whole 4 years. By senior year I'd gained 20 pounds, but I never wanted to. The big thing was that I wasn't paying so much attention to it. I started therapy with you at the beginning of my sophomore year. That was 1982. Nobody pushed me to go. I looked at my friends going to parties and dating, and it was obvious that I should be having a lot more fun than I was."

During Carla's first course of therapy, my approach had been influenced by my family therapy training. I believed that whenever possible, one should go back to one's family and engage in a dialogue to resolve conflicts. To the extent Carla knew this, it probably inhibited her. I no longer thought she had to resolve anything directly with her parents. Instead, I only hoped she would be able to tolerate an awareness of what had happened and how she had been trapped and to tolerate it without any "irritable reaching," which might deny her the possibility of a fresh perspective.

"When I moved back home after college it wasn't any better for me than when I was a kid. My parents didn't communicate well, so they antagonized each other a lot. There was constant tension in the house. My anxiety went way up.

"My parents' issues come right out of their childhoods. My mother couldn't have things she wanted, and she had to go to City College because there was no money for anything more. So, it was hard for her to make sacrifices to give me what nobody ever gave her. She had very good reasons to be messed up by her childhood experience; it had been a lot worse than mine.

"My father's father didn't provide for his family, and he was an alcoholic, so my father thought that being gentle, having a secure job, and being a good provider was what his role should be. He never thought being emotionally supportive was a father's role because his father wasn't like that."

As we sifted through episodes in her family's life, Carla became more comfortable feeling angry at her parents and at other things as well. Instead of the long silences, she would be quiet only at the beginning of the session, as though she needed time to shift gears. Then, the words flowed.

> "After college I worked as an aide in an adolescent unit of a psychiatric hospital. There I learned I would not become a psychologist, mostly because of my eating disorder. In the fall of 1988, I got hired at Bergdorf Goodman's. I knew they liked me, but I also knew they didn't see me as having management potential. I was too preoccupied with my eating disorder to care. You were freaking out about how skinny I was getting, and I knew you were going to try to make me go to a hospital, so I quit therapy."

*   *   *

Since Carla returned to therapy, every detail we unearthed was discussed, debated, and reinterpreted; as that process went on, her anger diminished, and her resentments eased. But, she had come back to therapy because she did not want to be alone anymore. She was 40 years old, was terribly shy, had never been in love, and had never felt sexual pleasure in her adult life. I thought the problem required a practical approach, but everything I could imagine seemed risky.

> "First you loaned me a book of short stories called *The Gates of Paradise*. I was glad I didn't have to go to a store and buy it. You said to underline the places I liked and tell you about them. It was a miracle I did any of that. Then you told me the parts you liked. That made me realize we were living on the same planet.
>
> "After reading a bunch of those stories, you suggested I go to Barnes and Noble and look for a book I might find 'erotic,' which was crazy because I had never found anything erotic. Weirdly enough, though, there was a book that seemed, well, promising. Once I began reading, I noticed I was having physical sensations. They came automatically. That was important because it meant the feelings were real, and I wasn't trying to talk myself into anything.
>
> "I still had a book you asked me to buy 20 years before, called *For Yourself*, by Lonnie Barbach (1975). I hadn't told you, but I reread some of it not too long before I called. If I couldn't touch myself, how would

> I ever stand to be touched? Rereading that book, I
> remembered something I had buried for a long time.
> When I was 7 or 8, I used to touch myself—and I
> liked it. But when Lora was 3, my father caught her
> doing it in the living room. He got very upset at her.
> My mother was gentler and explained you only did
> that in private. For me though, the curtain came
> down on the whole thing."

I had forgotten I had ever recommended *For Yourself* to Carla. As we
discussed her rediscovery of the book, we hit on the word "homework" to
describe the suggestions Barbach made to help women understand their
bodies and become more comfortable touching them.

> "You would ask, 'What's happening with your
> homework?' It wasn't as annoying as it sounds. In
> fact, it was kind of funny. I thought I was getting
> somewhere, but only so far. I was okay when things
> happened automatically, but it was really hard to
> actually fantasize. Maybe fantasizing was wanting,
> and I still associated wanting anything sexual with
> being a bad person. I started to think the homework
> wasn't really going anywhere."

When she began avoiding it, I stopped asking Carla about her homework. Pressuring her probably would have increased her frustration,
causing her to resist. After a couple of months, I gingerly raised the subject. After all, I suggested, doing the homework had not been unpleasant.
And, sometimes just hanging around, staying in the vicinity, even when it
seems like there is nowhere to go can be helpful. So, she started doing her
homework again and was a little less goal oriented about it.

> "A couple of times, the idea of using a vibrator came
> up. You suggested I try it. I didn't tell you that I did,
> but I did. It was a little one. I got it the same time
> I got a much sexier 'how to' book. Then it wasn't
> 'homework' anymore. I could start to see, to feel
> really, what the fuss was about. It was my own
> private thing and what the hell. One evening I felt
> something new, and I remember coming to the next
> session pretty speechless. Luckily, you figured out
> what had happened because I never could have said

> it. I think I blushed, then you said congratulations, and we laughed."

After the excitement died down and sexual enjoyment became a normal part of Carla's life, I asked her if it was time to take this show on the road. She knew I meant men. But how would she do this? She did not drink and had no one to go with to bars. None of her friends knew any single men. We considered courses she could take that might attract single men, but her shyness made that another unlikely bet. The only viable alternative, though horrifying to Carla, seemed to be computer dating.

> "I promised to sign up for Match.com and eHarmony, but I forgot about it as soon as I left your office. Then you started bugging me, so I went to their Web sites and read the introductory material. I couldn't picture doing any of it. Match.com reminded me of a gross fraternity party, and eHarmony wanted like a master's thesis before you could go out on a date. Eventually, I tried to sign up with eHarmony, but I had a problem with the computer stuff. That was when you took out your laptop. You said your mother applied to colleges for you when you refused to do it, why shouldn't you sign up with eHarmony for me? I gave you my credit card and dictated my information.
>
> "There was one guy who I spoke on the phone with three times. The last time was on his birthday when he called me drunk from a bar. That was it with that guy as far as I was concerned, and I decided I wanted to quit the whole computer dating thing. Then you got mad. You said that I had promised to really give this a try, and that maybe it wasn't worth it to stay in therapy if I couldn't push myself to take these kinds of risks."

As Carla might say, "Life is weird." The last time I gave her an ultimatum (or thought I had), I did not see her again for 15 years. Then, if I had had more "negative capability" or, as Craig Johnson had said, if I had just stayed the course and been supportive, maybe our second therapy would never have been necessary. I had promised myself to give no more ultimatums, yet I'd done it again. I had no idea whether she would stay or go.

"I agreed to try the eHarmony thing again because I didn't want to lose therapy. I didn't think anything would happen, but I did need the practice. I took it slow. Very slow! At eHarmony, they have an elaborate series of structured question-and-answer sessions that I have to say were pretty good for me."

She was different from the young woman I knew in 1988. She no longer wanted to be alone, and for the time being, I was the alternative. I think she endured my pushing because she wanted to stay with me.

"That was how I met Bill. First, we wrote back and forth, following eHarmony's ridiculous instructions. At least he seemed to have a sense of humor. He said right away that he was looking for a wife. I guess a lot of people would have loved that, but it didn't excite me. I went out with Bill because I promised you I would."

I knew immediately this was romance. I saw it in her eyes. I could even sense each step toward Bill was a step away from me. Carla had discovered a way to be in the world despite her anorexia. She would have to develop her own romantic sensibility. She had pointed us in a new direction.

"On our first date, he seemed surprised I could carry on a conversation, so he was all excited, which was not exactly mutual, but it wasn't bad either. Without thinking about it, I gave him this big hug goodnight.
"On our second or third date I took the train to Sheepshead Bay, where he lives, to see a concert with him. The trains were all messed up, and I was very late. I was afraid he would be mad, but he wasn't, not at all. I think it meant something to him that I came out to the far end of Brooklyn to see him. He said it was too late for the concert; let's go out to eat instead. I was fine about changing plans, which is not typical for me.
"That night we started kissing. I was thinking—good practice. The next week, we went ice skating in Bryant Park. After skating, he wanted to drive me home. I said fine because it was better than taking the train. When we got to my apartment, he wanted to see where I lived. I got worried the house might not

> be clean, but said ok. I made coffee, and we started kissing again. I guess I should have expected that. I wasn't feeling much, but he was excited, which was nice. There was one moment that stuck out in my mind: I'm embarrassed to say, but when he was trying to undo my bra, I helped him. I didn't hesitate. Naturally, he wanted to keep going, but I said let's wait, which he was fine with. After he left, I kept thinking it was really very strange I helped him like that. You would say my unconscious liked this boy.
>
> "I don't remember the first time we had sex very well at all. I can't even remember where it happened. Probably his place. It wasn't a disaster, but it wasn't great either. He could tell I was very nervous. He seemed focused on not freaking me out. He didn't make it too serious or too big a deal. He was sweet about it."

Something I find both frustrating and fantastic is how the most extraordinary changes quickly become commonplace. In no time, Carla got used to being in love, having sex, and sharing her life with someone else. Not that she was blissfully happy. She had a new, albeit less dire, set of issues to deal with. She soon cut her therapy sessions to once a week; she and Bill were saving for a trip.

> "Stuff came up about spending our lives together for two reasons: traveling back and forth to Sheepshead Bay was a big pain in the butt. And like I said, Bill had wanted to get married from the beginning. He was sort of on a mission about that. So, we had these theoretical conversations about weddings, children, where to live, which furniture we'd keep, which would go (his), and things like that. Then, one evening out of the blue, he proposed to me.
>
> "I couldn't talk, so I just kept hugging him; so he asked me again, and I still couldn't talk, so I nodded, and he asked me, is that a yes? And I managed to say, yes. I don't know why. It was still only March. We had been going out for 5 months. I hadn't spent any time in Sheepshead Bay, and I had no idea if I could stand it. My heart said yes."

When Carla told me the news, I was thrilled. I kept saying "Oh my god," and I am not a religious person.

* * *

"Bill is very gung ho about having kids but I told him it might not work with me. I thought I probably had screwed up my body being so skinny all that time and not getting my period for so many years. Even if I did get pregnant, I wasn't sure I'd be a very good mother. I'm so nervous, and chaos is very uncomfortable for me. But I wouldn't say I wasn't interested either. He wanted to know if I would adopt if we couldn't have our own, and I said that would probably be all right. I want him to be happy, too.

"My eating disorder hasn't changed too much since I got married, but my body image is better. When I was in college, I was in better shape, and my body was better looking, but I couldn't appreciate it. I still don't appreciate it really, but Bill does. All and all, I feel like I got really lucky."

* * *

So much that occurs is random, and almost everything is out of our control: This can make living terrifying and being a psychotherapist daunting. During our first therapeutic engagement, neither SSRIs nor computer dating existed. There was no genetic hypothesis to assist understanding eating disorders, Carla had no use at all for body/sexual literature, and as her condition deteriorated, I could not bear her continuing to "fail."

Fifteen years later, things were different. By the time of the second therapy, SSRIs and eHarmony were widely available, although Carla never took medication to gain weight or join eHarmony to get married. Eating disorder researchers were spreading the word about the influence of genetics, Carla had realized she did not want to miss her life, and I learned more about tolerating uncertainties and doubts and when to push or not push.

According to Keats (1817), Shakespeare possessed enormous negative capability. His vast capacity to be aware of our world as it really is, with all its contradictions, mysteries, and doubts, enabled him to capture the essence of who we are. Without sufficient negative capability, we run for cover, desperate to allay anxiety ("irritable reaching"). This is the way addictions and compulsions such as anorexia begin. That had been Carla's story until she realized she did not want to miss the fundamental human experience of loving another and returned to therapy. We worked together to create a narrative that might open a way for new possibilities. To do this, we had to extend ourselves into one uncomfortable place after the other. And, she continues to extend herself. Carla became pregnant a year after she married Bill. The fetus did not develop normally, and they chose to abort the pregnancy. They are considering adoption but are not sure about it. She continues to struggle some with her body, and work has not changed very much, but her relationship with Bill has made things a little easier and a lot more fun. It seems, at least for the moment, that Carla is not missing her life after all.

Salvador Minuchin, a pioneer of family therapy with anorexic patients, once said, "Anorexia, this is a Greek word. This is Greek to me!" (2005), intimating that anorexia was not really a disease per se but only a cluster of unusual symptoms that meant something a little different for each sufferer. When Carla resumed her anorexic symptoms in the middle of her first therapy, I took the tack of focusing on her "cure" and in the process lost my curiosity about the meaning of her anorexia as well as my capacity to tolerate her ongoing self-starvation. When she came back, I still wanted to cure her (my rescue instinct still intact), but in the intervening years, I had learned to harness that instinct by employing more finely honed tools of the trade: listening carefully; using my imagination; asking unlikely questions; taking the time to think before reacting; being willing to be afraid, to take risks, to stay curious, to invite criticism, and to accept help, above all, from the patient herself.

References

Barbach, L. (1975). *For yourself.* New York: Anchor Books.

Johnson, C. (2005, November 7–10). *Something new, something old.* Paper presented at the Fifteenth Annual Renfrew Center Foundation Conference, Philadelphia.

Johnson, C., & Connors, M. E. (1987). *The etiology and treatment of bulimia nervosa.* New York: Basic Books.

Minuchin, S. (2005). *Inviting the family dance* [audiotape]. New York: Minuchin Center for the Family.

Palazzoli, M. P. (1978). *Self starvation.* New York: Aronson.

Shakespeare, W. (1609). *Cymbeline,* Act IV, Scene III.

Rollins, H. E. (Ed.). (1972). *The Letters of John Keats, 1814–1821* (Vols. 1 and 2). Cambridge, MA: Harvard University Press.

chapter fifteen

Working With People Who Live Dangerously
Perspectives on Managing Negative Countertransference During the Treatment of Eating Disorders

Andrea Bloomgarden

Introduction

Countertransference, broadly defined, refers to therapists' personal feelings and reactions to clients. Historically, psychoanalytic writers interpreting the works of Freud believed it was the analyst's responsibility to avoid countertransference to prevent interference with the therapeutic process. To be emotionally detached, hence objective, was the ideal therapeutic stance. For example, in 1912 Freud stated:

> I cannot recommend my colleagues emphatically enough to take as a model in psychoanalytic treatment the surgeon who puts aside all his feelings, including that of human sympathy, and concentrate his mind on one single purpose, that of performing the operation as skillfully as possible. (Freud, 1912/1963, p. 121)

More recently, many contemporary analysts and psychotherapists have taken the position that attempting to eradicate the human element is by no means the best way to conduct psychotherapy. A number of authors, including Maroda (2004), Orange, Atwood, and Stolorow (1997), and Aron (1996), advocated thoughtfully navigating the treatment relationship and embracing the fact that the therapist is human, and therefore will have emotional reactions to each therapeutic encounter. From this perspective, since countertransference is inevitably part of treatment, the therapist's job is not to avoid personal reactions but to "use" them in a manner that will be beneficial to the therapeutic process.

In fact, recent psychotherapy research suggests that different kinds of therapist reactions and behaviors contribute to the development of different kinds of treatment relationships, with dramatically different effects on treatment outcomes. A psychotherapy relationship characterized by therapist empathy, support, hopefulness, warmth, responsiveness, and judicious self-disclosure is associated with a positive therapeutic alliance that enhances effective psychotherapy (Brown, 1994; Horvath & Bedi, 2002; Linehan, 1993; Miller & Stiver, 1997; Norcross, 2002; Walker, 2002; Yalom, 2002). On the other hand, too much of a take charge attitude, characterized by coldness, irritability, and premature interpretations, generally leads to a negative therapeutic relationship and poorer treatment outcomes (Horvath & Bedi, 2002).

Negative countertranference, or negative personal reactions therapists have toward clients, has the potential to promote a negative therapeutic relationship, leading to therapeutic impasse or failure. From the contemporary perspective, negative countertransference should not, perhaps cannot, be eliminated but ought to be managed skillfully enough to make a productive contribution to treatment (Gabbard & Wilkenson, 2000; Gelso & Hayes, 2002; Kahn, 1997; Linehan, 1993; Maroda, 2004).

Regarding eating disorders treatment, therapist behaviors and attitudes that are helpful to the development of a positive therapeutic alliance are similar to those that are useful with other clients. Garner, Vitousek, and Pike (1997) emphasized the importance of "appropriate warmth, sensitivity, compassion, genuineness, honesty, flexibility, engagement, acceptance and positive regard" (p. 99). Yet, therapists who strive to embody these qualities with eating disorders clients can instead find themselves flooded with uncomfortable feelings and triggered into behaviors that produce difficult, conflicted therapy relationships. This chapter aims to explore some of the most common sources of negative countertransference during eating disorder treatment and illustrate ways to deal with it effectively. Therapist self-care and therapist self-disclosure are singled out for special discussion in relation to negative countertransference reactions.

Sources of Negative Countertransference

While any countertransference response is possible given a therapist's history and personality, certain reactions during the treatment of eating disorders are relatively common and expectable. Eating-disordered clients pose challenging treatment issues due to their attitudes toward therapy. Although often at risk for their lives and suffering intensely, both emotionally and physically, it can take years before they are willing to follow a treatment protocol.

The readiness-to-change literature provides a useful model to understand the extraordinary reluctance to change that characterizes eating-disordered clients. According to Prochaska and Norcross (2002), people pass through a sequence of stages when they make a change in their lives. Eating-disordered clients are most likely to comply with treatment recommendations when they are in the "action" stage of change. However, three stages precede action: precontemplation, contemplation, and preparation. During precontemplation, regardless of overt eating disorder symptoms and related difficulties, the client may not believe that there is even a problem warranting therapy. In contemplation, there is some recognition that a problem exists, coupled with a great deal of ambivalence about any real need to change. In the preparation stage, the client demonstrates the beginnings of change but not necessarily a commitment to follow through on behaving differently. Eating disorder treatment often starts with the client in precontemplation or contemplation, meaning therapists must view treatment in terms of motivating a desire for change rather than an effort to actually resolve symptoms (Garner et al., 1997; Miller & Rollnick, 1991).

During precontemplation and contemplation, eating disorder clients are not only disinterested in change, but also not willing to take care of themselves. As a result, they persistently engage in dangerous symptomatic behaviors, including self-starvation, vomiting, laxative abuse, excessive overexercising, self-mutilation, and substance abuse, in spite of the risk of medical complications and even death. Moreover, during these stages, clients are frequently dishonest, either by commission or omission. To maintain the status quo, they lie about their readiness to change or about their symptom severity to prevent therapists from making additional treatment recommendations.

When therapists attempt to treat clients who are not ready to work on changing, they are seldom able to have an impact on symptoms; yet, at the same time they are accountable for their clients' lives. Thus, eating disorder therapists can find themselves in the uncomfortable position of being responsible for helping someone who is strenuously resisting treatment and acting self-destructively. In these circumstances, it is not unusual for therapists to struggle with some or all of the following negative countertransference reactions: sadness, disappointment, fear, panic, shame, feelings of incompetence and inadequacy, anger, frustration, disillusionment, hopelessness, and impotence. It is extremely important for therapists to figure out what to do with these feelings. Left unattended, they can damage the treatment relationship and threaten therapeutic outcome.

In addition to what the client is doing or not doing in therapy, therapists bring their own personal history to the treatment relationship. Since therapists are human, they also have a set of insecurities, traumas, wounds, losses, and current problems. Therapists' personal issues can be stimulated by the therapeutic dialogue or brought into the treatment relationship independent of ongoing interaction. In either case, it is possible that such issues will provoke negative countertransference reactions that are detrimental to treatment outcome. Maroda (2004) crafted the term *"countertransference dominance"* (p. 49) to refer to times when a therapist unconsciously steers the therapy in a direction that is more about the therapist's unconscious needs than about the needs of clients.

For example, suppose a therapist has a strong desire, based on early experiences with siblings and peers, to appear competent in the eyes of her colleagues. During one session, she starts to feel very angry about her client's lack of progress. As a result, she says, "You're not really trying hard enough!" The therapist believes that this is an appropriate intervention since she is "just being honest"; besides, it is time for her to confront the resistance. She tells herself this will finally begin to motivate her client. However, it is also true that prior to this session the therapist had heard about her sister's recent promotion, making her feel competitive and insecure. Furthermore, she is due to present her work to her supervision group and feels a good deal of anxiety about how the members will respond to this client's current condition, worrying that her client's lack of progress will reflect badly on her. While in some cases encouraging a client to try harder might be a helpful intervention, in this example, the therapist most likely reacted in the way she did because she was threatened by feelings of inadequacy. In other words, the intervention was driven by countertransference dominance aimed primarily at solving the therapist's need.

Finally, in the field of eating disorders, it is not uncommon for therapists to have a personal history that includes some kind of difficulty with weight, eating, or body image (Bloomgarden, Gerstein, & Moss, 2003). To be effective, these therapists must have a reasonable command of their own issues. When therapists are still actively struggling with eating-related problems, they are at risk for intense countertransference reactions, potentially leading to urges to behave symptomatically and to confusion about how to guide a client toward recovery. This is not to say that therapists must be entirely clear of any concerns about eating, food, or body image. Indeed, from a contemporary perspective, therapists need not be, and probably cannot be, wholly rid of all their "issues." Thus, the goal is to be alert for, and have a means to deal with, the inevitable influence of personal issues instead of trying to erase them entirely.

Management of Negative Transference

Ideally, a therapist is prepared for negative countertransference experiences and is able to recognize and deal with them as they develop during the course of treatment. In general, it is the therapist's self-awareness that protects the client from thoughtless or unconscious reactions to determined treatment resistance or the influence of personal issues.

Therapists have three options for working effectively with their negative countertransference. They can make an effort to understand why they are experiencing these particular kinds of feelings so that the insight gained will help to transform their ongoing reactions into something more conducive to a positive therapeutic relationship. They can work on changing their own relationship to their negative countertransference such that their experience and expression of these reactions is transformed into something that preserves a positive therapeutic relationship. Or, they can strive to express, or self-disclose, their feelings honestly, in a sensitive and caring manner, in an attempt to "use" the reaction to help clients understand the impact of their eating-disordered attitudes and behavior. These three options are not mutually exclusive and are best accomplished with the support of colleagues, supervisors, or a treatment team, with whom therapists can share feelings in an open, nondefensive way. In particular, when therapists are able to talk openly about the interface of their personal history with the particular issues with which the client is struggling, there is a better chance of achieving an informed, balanced perspective and less likelihood that countertransference dominance will drive the treatment.

Therapist Self-Care and Managing Countertransference

Since working with eating-disordered clients can be extremely taxing, therapists need their own emotional support to prevent burnout and reduce undue, nontherapeutic, negative countertransference reactions. Therapists who do not "nourish" themselves in this way are much more likely to feel increasingly overwhelmed, burdened, exhausted, drained, and annoyed by their eating disorders work. Frequently, these kinds of feelings cause therapists to behave in ways that are insensitive, nonempathic, and damaging to the therapeutic relationship.

As one aspect of self-care, it is essential for therapists to find and make ongoing use of a supervisor, a peer supervision group, or a consultation team. Linehan (1993) stressed that one purpose of the DBT (dialectical behavioral therapy) consultation team is to prevent therapist burnout, and Koerner (2007) discussed how the team functions to treat the therapist, improve therapist emotion regulation, and decrease therapists' counterproductive behaviors. Comtois et al. (2007) believed that the consultation team is necessary even for outpatient therapists working in private practice because it helps to keep therapists on task and prevents negative countertransference reactions from harming the therapeutic relationship. Similar to clients with borderline personality disorder, for which DBT was developed, eating-disordered clients have chronic, sustained, and long-standing problems that need a great deal of attention and require the therapist to be emotionally strong, grounded, clear thinking, and consistently centered. Maintaining this kind of therapeutic stance is highly unlikely unless an eating disorders clinician has sufficient collegial, team, or supervisory support (Gavazzi, 2005; Jordan, 2006; Kottler, 1999).

In addition, therapists need to practice self-care in their personal lives. Doing so helps to prevent burnout as well as excessive or dysfunctional negative countertransference reactions. Also, neglecting self-care introduces a significant element of hypocrisy into the therapeutic relationship. In other words, if one subtext for eating disorder therapy is the promotion of better client self-care, therapists who are not taking good care of themselves are less likely to convincingly model the importance of this treatment goal. Thus, therapists serve themselves and their therapy relationships well by attending to areas in their lives that require care and attention. As used here, the meaning of self-care is very broadly defined. So, for example, a therapist could need medical attention, a supervision group, friendships, an intimate relationship, more physical activity, a vacation, hobbies, massage, psychotherapy, time with children, time to read, intellectual stimulation, or any number of other things to practice more effective and satisfying self-care (Gavazzi, 2005; Kottler, 1993, 1999).

Therapist Self-Disclosure and Managing Countertransference

In *Self-Disclosure in the Therapeutic Relationship* (Stricker & Fisher, 1990), Stricker writes that self-disclosure "can be defined, somewhat tautologically as the process by which the self is revealed" (p. 277). That is, from the aesthetic choices therapists make in what they wear, to the objects and pictures in their offices, to the cars they drive to work, to the wedding band they either wear or do not wear, self-revelatory information is inevitably disclosed to clients. Even if therapists attempt to be conservative regarding what they say about themselves during sessions, now clients can "google" their therapist and gather available online information. In some sense, then, the old ideal of withholding as much personal information as possible is an anachronism.

On the other hand, and in part arising from the recognition that the traditional "blank screen" is not possible, well-chosen, intentionally delivered self-disclosures have become an important strategy for actively managing, or using, specific countertransference reactions to create therapeutic benefit. For example, Hill and Knox (2002) referred to "disclosures of immediacy" (p. 255) to describe times when a therapist shares a feeling in the moment about a reaction to a client, such as "I feel sad hearing that," or, "I feel concerned about your health." In their review of the literature, Hill and Knox concluded that self-disclosure interventions are potentially therapeutic when they are thoughtfully planned, attuned to the needs of the client, and compassionately and judiciously delivered.

Before deciding to make such an intervention, the therapist should hypothesize what the intended beneficial effect would be and plan on making some assessment regarding whether it was actually helpful. A therapist could, for example, choose to disclose a personal reaction to something the client said to model a normal human reaction and demonstrate what would typically be felt by other people in her life. So, the therapist might remark: "I feel sad and frightened when I hear you say that you don't care if your eating disorder kills you." After hearing the client's response, the therapist could inquire about the impact of the disclosure by asking: "What was it like to hear me say that?" Even though the disclosure is in the moment, in real time, with the therapist's real feelings about the current situation, it is delivered professionally and thoughtfully, with some idea about its therapeutic effect and some effort to explore its influence. On the contrary, berating a client for not making progress, by saying something like, "I'm really disappointed in you," or bursting into tears and expressing terror that the client will die, is not likely to have a positive therapeutic effect. Such statements are also disclosures of immediacy, but they are not attuned to the client's needs; it is rarely helpful for a therapist to overwhelm a client with excessive affect. Moreover, clients have a right to expect that treatment interventions have a therapeutic purpose and will be delivered in a professional manner. Uncontrolled bursts of emotion do not qualify as attuned self-disclosures, strategically employed to achieve a treatment benefit. Further information about the art of using self-disclosure in a constructive and positive manner is available in the work of Hill and Knox (2002), Linehan (1993), Maroda (2004), and Baldwin (2000).

Managing Negative Countertransference in Clinical Practice

The following case examples are composites of real events and actual therapeutic interventions, modified and combined to protect confidentiality. They were created to illustrate elements of treatment that occur with regularity in eating disorder work and to discuss in some detail my own countertransference reactions to challenging clinical situations.

Case Example: On the Cutting Edge

"It takes 1 minute to pass out unconscious and 2 minutes to die." My client, Kara, who had cut her wrist a week ago, had missed an artery by a millimeter. She was telling me what would have happened had she hit the artery.

This was not a suicide attempt. The fact is, Kara screamed with both fear and surprise when she cut through seven layers of skin, saw her arm open up to reveal tendon and bone, and watched a rush of blood cascade out of her body. Luckily, her brother knew how to temporarily control the bleeding while rushing to the emergency room. This incident was actually a particularly pernicious side effect of being a "cutter," that is, a person who cuts herself when she is distressed. She was in an argument with her mother when it happened. Without thinking, she grabbed a new knife that was much sharper than she realized. Kara never thought of cutting as a potentially lethal coping mechanism, although everyone in her life, including me, as her therapist, had expressed concern about this symptom many times over. From her point of view, cutting was like her other symptom, purging, just a coping mechanism that therapists and parents insist on calling "dangerous."

I was really distraught, shocked, and surprised, when I learned about how Kara had hurt herself. I had worked with her for many years, while she improved markedly, stepped away from the revolving door of inpatient treatment, and attained a high level of functioning. I would have been heartbroken had she died, and it shook me deeply to encounter such a close call. Immediately, I felt stupid and incompetent: Why didn't I see this coming? But then, after much reflection, I realized that I was just trying to regain a feeling of control, to believe I could have seen this coming. In truth, I could not. There really were not any warning signs. She had not been cutting for many years. In fact, she was just as surprised as every one of her friends and family members that she was still capable of being that impulsive and self-harming.

It helped me to remember that I could talk to my peer supervision group about Kara's behavior and my countertransference reactions. In the group, we begin with a mindfulness exercise and then go around the room offering each member the opportunity to share thoughts and feelings about ongoing work (Linehan, 1993). When someone talks, the team is very accepting; in particular, we practice being kind to one another when someone begins to "vent" in a negative way. We recognize that being negative and blaming the client is usually a way of expressing anger instead of becoming open to underlying feelings. Our goal is to transform and deepen feelings rather than join in an accusation of the client and, by so doing, offer members the opportunity to explore therapeutic strategies in an honest, supportive context.

When I began to present my work with Kara, I started by saying, "I can't believe Kara cut herself! How could she do this to me? I'm so pissed." My colleagues listened quietly, looked at me with compassion, and then gently reflected how much I seemed to be personalizing the situation. As I explored the whole situation further, I became more and more aware of my fear. "I'm really scared, and I hate being in this position—I'm terrified because I care a lot about Kara, and she acted so recklessly about her own life. It doesn't seem fair."

Over the course of the meeting, group members validated my feelings and gave me as much space as I needed to honestly review my reactions to Kara's cutting. Just as for my own clients, it was incredibly replenishing to have permission to say exactly what I felt and have my colleagues understand and empathize with my feelings in a totally nonjudgmental way. In addition, they reminded me that I can never be entirely in control of therapy or expected to know everything that Kara is doing or thinking, and that shocking events like Kara's cutting herself are the natural perils of working with eating-disordered clients. Little by little, my balanced perspective began to return. I realized once again that the joy and meaning I derive from my work far outweigh the risks and emotional distress it sometimes causes me. As my colleagues heard me out, letting me say whatever, however it came out, and then helped me to reclaim the best version of myself, I felt a sense of calm and a readiness to go back to work.

After I met with my group, I was able to figure out how to talk with Kara. I decided to tell her, to self-disclose, that I was distressed about what she had done and felt really sad to think about what would have happened if she died. As I talked with her, she could read the look of seriousness on my face. Whereas I'm often quite playful during sessions and love to use humor, it was clear I was definitely not in a joking mood. I was careful not to be admonishing, but I wanted her to know that this had really affected me. I learned she experienced a similar reaction from many of her friends and family, and this time, it seemed she had really taken it to heart. I believe it was a testament to all of our work that Kara was truly grappling with the full meaning of mutuality in relationships. Finally, she was accepting the fact that she had a real and actual responsibility to think of and care about everyone, including friends, family, and therapist, who cared so much about her. As a result, she had an obligation, regardless of the stress in any particular life situation, to try her best not to hurt everyone else by hurting herself.

In the past, Kara had not felt that level of empathy for her loved ones. Selfishly, she would say: "If I want to die, let me go." But this time was different. She acknowledged she did not want to die. In short, Kara was powerfully affected by realizing that she did not want to upset her family, friends, and therapist. I believe I contributed to Kara's realization because I was able to contain my intense negative countertransference when the cutting first occurred and then, with the help of my consultation group, find a genuine and modulated way to communicate the distressing impact of her behavior.

Case Example: Worrying on the Sidelines

In early September, a beautiful, bright, college girl told her parents that she was bulimic. They were completely shocked. Angela seemed the perfect child, the one who had it all together, who never had any serious problems, let alone an eating disorder. When she came to her first therapy appointment, the first thing she told me was that she regretted having told her parents because she did not want to give up the symptoms. "What's wrong with it?" she said. "It works for me. And the doctor said I'm fine." After she told her parents about being bulimic, they took her to a physician who asked her to undergo a series of intrusive medical examinations, all of which suggested she was medically healthy. As a result, she regretted revealing her problem, and the original impulse for help seemed to be gone.

Based on her parents' description of her, my initial treatment plan was to refer Angela to a nutritionist, start her on maintaining food logs, explore her eating and purging patterns in detail, and set some goals for reducing symptom frequency. All this presumed she was in the action stage of readiness for change. However, as I listened, it became clear I needed a "plan B." Angela was thinking and feeling much more like someone in the contemplation stage and therefore was very unlikely to be interested in all that I had planned to do. Among other things, I decided to look for ways to engage her in the process of therapy by gently challenging the way she typically conducted herself. When I asked about her symptoms to gather basic history, I noticed she wandered off topic repeatedly, never answering my questions directly. Sweet as pie, Angela talked all about school and relationships, expertly managing to lead the session along a noninformative, circuitous route. At some point midway in the session, I chose to tell her that I was on to what she was doing, cleverly avoiding a discussion of anything that pertained to her problems. Although this was a risk, I wanted to find some kind of connection, something that would catch her attention.

It turned out that she knew she was doing her "avoidance thing." Angela was good at not being forthcoming about what she was doing. For example, she had been bulimic at home for at least 5 years, and her parents never knew. She had cast herself as the perfect daughter in the family. Given her older sister's cerebral palsy and her younger brother's attention deficit hyperactivity disorder (ADHD), she took on the role of the child who would not need anything, the "best little girl in the world" (Levenkron, 1978). When the family went out to dinner, her parents always had to make a plan for her sister's physical limitations and the potential disruptions caused by her brother's outlandish behavior but never needed to be concerned about Angela, who was always polite, courteous, and properly helpful should any difficulties arise. Almost from the beginning, she took it for granted that she was fine and without any real needs, so they were never known to her. Angela's friends became her role models and provided guidance in her life. And somewhere in there, she learned to be bulimic.

My countertransference was mixed. On the one hand, I felt a lot of empathy for her. Angela was a really smart person, and I admired many of the excellent personal qualities she embodied. On the other hand, because I felt responsible for her well-being, I was dreading the long road ahead. Motivating her to move from her current state of resistance would likely be an arduous task. I was disappointed that this was going to be a harder case than I thought. Also, getting her some good medical monitoring was going to be a chore. I was appalled by the patronizing and counterproductive medical care she had received, and now I had the additional job of undoing that bad experience.

Fortunately, I liked her, and this helped me to feel motivated. I planned to focus on my positive countertransference to build a good working alliance and to influence her to do the right things for herself. I hoped the impact of my caring and respect would help her to review and reclaim the importance of her own needs, moving her toward better self-care and a new kind of courage, based not on fulfilling others' needs but on pursuing her own. The negative side of my countertransference really could be reduced to fear. "What if she drops dead on me," I thought. "She's an athlete, so running around on a hot field, not eating, purging, or being dehydrated, how do I know that while I'm working on getting her to see another doctor, and developing some motivation to change, she won't drop dead at track practice?"

I wondered if I should self-disclose about my fear as a clinical intervention, to reflect back the serious danger of this illness. After some thought, I decided not to do this, at least not right away. I felt it might be perceived as overly dramatic since she was so far off from recognizing the dangers. Also, I thought the relationship was too new, and she was too young: I just sensed it would seem inappropriate. Instead, I gave her some reading about the medical complications of eating disorders and encouraged her to talk about it with me. In this way, perhaps we would have the opportunity to discuss the many ways in which bulimia can undermine health.

This case stimulated powerful negative countertransference reactions, including erratic, panicky fears that Angela would suddenly die and selfish anxieties that her parents would sue me for incompetence, and I would lose my career. Managing my negative countertransference required recognizing that, if I am going to treat eating disorders, I have to accept that considerable medical risk is a normal part of the job. It is one of the few downsides of this profession. As one of my trusted colleagues has always said, "Stuff like this wouldn't be an issue if we worked in a bank." An unadulterated expression of my fears about bulimia and sudden death would not constitute a therapeutic self-disclosure. This was my problem entirely, and to deal with it effectively, I spent a good deal of time talking with my consultation team.

So, with my countertransference in full awareness but decidedly contained, I worked patiently to build a solid treatment relationship and develop a genuine readiness to change in this truly wonderful young woman. Over the course of 6 months, I wove the message into our therapy about the importance of seeing a good doctor, one Angela would enjoy seeing and who would be much more considerate than her previous physician. Eventually, the appointment was made and medical monitoring finally commenced. Angela gradually reduced her symptoms and began to understand the importance of self-care, the value of recognizing her own needs, and the good feelings that come from satisfying them. After about a year, she got to the action phase and made changes sooner than I had expected, in part I believe, because I managed not to inject my fears into our therapeutic relationship.

The Gift and Challenge of Change

Psychotherapy is a mutual process in which therapists attempt to positively influence clients, and clients also affect their therapists, challenging them to develop new coping skills, take better care of themselves, and learn new things about themselves, life, and psychotherapy. Therapists working with eating-disordered clients will naturally have negative countertransference reactions that may be difficult to manage. Yet, at the same time, through these meaningful and challenging encounters, we receive a rare gift: an opportunity to become stronger, wiser, and more compassionate individuals.

References

Aron, L. (1996). *A meeting of minds: Mutuality in psychoanalysis*. Hillsdale, NJ: Analytic Press.

Baldwin, M. (Ed.). (2000). *The use of self in therapy*. New York: Haworth Press.

Bloomgarden, A., Gerstein, F., & Moss, C. (2003). The last word: A "recovered enough" therapist. *Eating Disorders: The Journal of Treatment and Prevention, 3*, 163–167.

Brown, L. (1994). *Subversive dialogues: Theory in feminist therapy*. New York: Basic Books.

Comtois, K. A., Koons, C. R., Kim, S. A., Manning, S. Y., Bellos, E., & Dimeff, L. A., (2007). Implementing standard dialectical behavior therapy in an outpatient setting. In L. A. Dimeff & K. Koerner (Eds.), *Dialectical behavior therapy in clinical practice* (pp. 37–68). New York: Guilford Press.

Freud, S. (1963). Recommendations for physicians on the psychoanalytic method of treatment. In Freud, S., *Therapy and Technique: Essays on Dream Interpretation, Hypnosis, Transference, Free Association and Other Techniques of Psychoanalysis*. New York: Macmillan. (Original work published in 1912.)

Gabbard, G. O., & Wilkenson, S. M. (2000). *Management of countertransference with borderline patients*. New York: Aronson.

Garner, D. M., Vitousek, K., & Pike, K. (1997). Cognitive-behavioral therapy for anorexia nervosa. In D. M. Garner & P. E. Garfinkel (Eds.), *Handbook of treatment for eating disorders* (pp. 94–144). New York: Guilford Press.

Gavazzi, J. D. (2005). Self-care as positive ethics: Developing a plan. *The Pennsylvania Psychologist Quarterly, 3*, 2–5.

Gelso, C. J., & Hayes, J. A. (2002). The management of countertransference. In J. C. Norcross (Ed.), *Psychotherapy relationships that work: Therapist contributions and responsiveness to patients* (pp. 267–283). New York: Oxford University Press.

Hill, C. E., & Knox, S. (2002). Self-disclosure. In J. C. Norcross (Ed.), *Psychotherapy relationships that work: Therapist contributions and responsiveness to patients* (pp. 255–266). New York: Oxford University Press.

Horvath, A. O., & Bedi, R. P. (2002). The alliance. In J. C. Norcross (Ed.), *Psychotherapy relationships that work: Therapist contributions and responsiveness to patients* (pp. 37–70). New York: Oxford University Press.

Jordan, J. V. (2006). Relational learning in psychotherapy consultation and supervision. In M. Walker & W. B. Rosen (Eds.), *How connections heal* (pp. 22–30). New York: Guilford Press.

Kahn, M. (1997). *Between therapist and client: The new relationship* (rev. ed.). New York: Freeman and Company.

Koerner, K. (2007, November). *Practicing DBT in Your Consultation Team*. Paper presented at the Twelfth Annual ISITDBT Conference, Philadelphia.

Kottler, J. A. (1993). *On being a therapist*. San Francisco: Jossey-Bass.

Kottler, J. A. (1999). *The therapist's workbook: Self-assessment, self-care, and self-improvement exercises for mental health professionals*. San Francisco: Jossey-Bass.

Levenkron, S. (1978). *The best little girl in the world.* New York: Warner Books.

Linehan, M. (1993). *Cognitive-behavioral treatment of borderline personality disorder.* New York: Guilford Press.

Maroda, K. (2004). *The power of counter-transference.* Hillsdale, NJ: Analytic Press.

Miller, J. B., & Stiver, I. P. (1997). *The healing connection.* Boston: Beacon Press.

Miller, W. R., & Rollnick, S. (1991). *Motivational interviewing: preparing people to change addictive behavior.* New York: Guilford Press.

Norcross, J. C. (2002). Empirically supported therapy relationships. In J. C. Norcross (Ed.), *Psychotherapy relationships that work: Therapist contributions and responsiveness to patients* (pp. 3–16). New York: Oxford University Press.

Orange, D. M., Atwood, G. E., & Stolorow, R. D. (1997). *Working intersubjectively: Contextualism in psychoanalytic practice.* Hillsdale, NJ: Analytic Press.

Prochaska, J. O., & Norcross, J. C. (2002). Stages of change. In J. C. Norcross, (Ed.), *Psychotherapy relationships that work: Therapist contributions and responsiveness to patients* (pp. 303–313). New York: Oxford University Press.

Stricker, G. (1990). Self-disclosure and psychotherapy. In G. Stricker & M. Fisher (Eds.), *Self-disclosure in the therapeutic relationship* (pp. 277–289). New York: Plenum.

Stricker, G., & Fisher, M. (Eds.). (1990). *Self-disclosure in the therapeutic relationship.* New York: Plenum.

Walker, M. (2002). How relationships heal. In M. Walker & W. Rosen (Eds.), *How connections heal* (pp. 3–21). New York: Guilford Press.

Yalom, I. D. (2002). *The gift of therapy: An open letter to a new generation of therapists and their patients.* New York: Harper Collins.

chapter sixteen

Forgiveness
The Final Frontier in Recovery From an Eating Disorder

Robin Sesan

Introduction

Women who struggle with eating disorders have closed themselves off to life in order to protect themselves from suffering. Peters and Fallon (1994) described bulimia as a disorder of denial, disconnection, and disempowerment. When interviewed, recovered women reported that what helped them was becoming more accepting of their "imperfect" bodies despite the ever-present images of perfection, talking about abuse histories to others who honored their pain and anger, moving beyond a victim stance, and shifting from the isolation caused by shame to connection with others. Recovery from an eating disorder is about opening up to life, the good and the bad, and living with a more open heart. It is through the practice of forgiveness, and the accompanying skills, that clients learn to transform anger and shame into compassion and love for themselves and others. Forgiveness is an essential component for lasting recovery from an eating disorder.

Many eating-disordered clients are fearful of opening themselves up to life. Their symptoms have developed as a defense against vulnerability resulting from interpersonal betrayals, abandonment, and humiliation. They generalize from these experiences and learn to distrust. They perceive that their bodies have betrayed them, and they do not trust themselves. They cling to the power accompanying anger as a way to shield themselves, believing that forgiveness will leave them weak and defenseless.

Mental health professionals have raised reservations about the value of forgiveness interventions, warning that such interventions may further invalidate clients' feelings and prevent them from learning the skills needed to manage affect. They fear that promoting forgiveness of others may take precedence over clients being able to forgive themselves. These concerns are particularly valid in the treatment of women who have been seriously neglected, victimized, or abused. Feminist therapists in particular are concerned that forgiveness therapy may exploit traditional gender role patterns by reinforcing the notion that a "good woman" does not get angry and must forgive to "make peace." The concern is that forgiveness interventions may prematurely encourage a woman to let go of healthy anger, effectively silencing her (Lamb & Murphy, 2002). In a feminist analysis of forgiveness therapy, McKay, Hill, Freedman, and Enright (2007) concluded that "forgiveness and feminist models of therapy are highly compatible" (p. 27). The flexibility inherent in forgiveness therapy allows therapists to address issues related to women's socialization to repair relationships at all costs, suppress anger, and avoid conflict before engaging in a process of forgiveness. Therapists' awareness and experience with their own willingness or resistance to be self-forgiving or forgiving toward people in their own lives will highly influence the treatment relationship with regard to moving clients in the direction of forgiveness.

Therapeutic focus on themes of forgiveness grows out of the positive psychology movement and integration of the teachings of Eastern philosophy with Western therapeutic practice (Germer, Siegel, & Fulton, 2005; Seligman, 2002). Developing skills in mindfulness and radical acceptance can help expand the world of an eating-disordered client (Kristellar, Baer, & Quillan-Wolever, 2006). *Mindfulness* is the practice of focusing one's attention on "what is" in the present moment, observing it without judgment or attachment to the way it should or should not be (Kabat-Zinn, 1994). *Radical acceptance* is the practice of relating to one's present life circumstances and feelings ("what is") with compassion (Brach, 2003). These practices pave the way to forgiveness, providing clients with tools that enable them to transcend the narrow focus on self and symptoms that prevent connection with others. The practice of forgiveness makes it possible to move beyond the constraints of an eating disorder and open up to life.

What Is Forgiveness?

Misunderstandings about forgiveness abound. Defining forgiveness may be as difficult as defining recovery itself. Forgiveness is not weak or naïve. It takes great courage and clarity to forgive because by its very nature it requires openness. It is easier to hold on to grievances and blame than it is to accept realities, manage pain, and move forward. Furthermore, there can be no forgiveness without remembering. It is important to remember past hurts and traumas, while working on letting go of those feelings that increase suffering in the present. Remembering the hurt allows clients to protect themselves from further harm. In addition, forgiveness is not condoning a behavior. It is recognizing that what happened was wrong, and that holding on to anger and resentment from the past creates suffering in the present. Forgiveness does not deny or minimize pain. In fact, to forgive requires experiencing the pain to learn how to use these feelings more wisely.

If forgiveness is none of the above, then what is it? Forgiveness is an approach to life that cannot be forced; it is something learned over time. Buddhism teaches that there is suffering in life, and that it is how we relate to our suffering that either causes great pain or freedom (Hanh, 1999). Forgiveness is learning to be less judgmental and live with a more compassionate heart, releasing the burden of negativity, and allowing for the possibility of greater happiness (Dalai Lama & Cutler, 1998).

In his pioneering work on forgiveness, Luskin (2002) brought together groups of women whose sons were murdered in the Northern Ireland conflict. He taught them a process of forgiveness that included a heart-focused meditation, in which they were taught to visualize loved ones or places in nature that were beautiful and awe inspiring whenever they felt anger associated with their senseless losses. He also had them focus on feelings of gratitude. Through this process, the women were able to find compassion in their hearts for themselves, for what they had suffered, and for others, including their sons' murderers. Their hearts expanded from a contracted position based in fear, and many who were bitter and depressed were able to join with one another, not only in their grief, but in their willingness and desire to move forward.

Forgiveness involves letting go of hope for a better past and making a commitment to live in the present (Luskin, 2002). To forgive, it is necessary to accept that others can and will disappoint us, and that we can and will disappoint others. Forgiveness is about accepting imperfection in ourselves and others. When we have mastered the ability to live in the present, accept things as they are, and tolerate imperfection, we can then forgive and feel more grateful for the life in front of us. Teaching clients to manage all the feelings that are a part of living gives them strength to transform beyond their pain.

There are many paths to releasing anger and granting forgiveness. Enright and Fitzgibbons (2000) described four phases of forgiveness. In the *uncovering phase*, the client explores how the injustice has had an impact on their life. In the *decision phase*, they learn about forgiveness and make a cognitive commitment to forgive. The *work phase* involves understanding the offender and gradually coming to view the offender as a person with human limitations. As anger diminishes and compassion grows, the client moves into a *deepening phase*, during which they broaden their view of forgiveness, become more self-forgiving, and search for some meaning in what they have endured.

Luskin (2002) presented a forgiveness model in which an individual is first taught to refocus on positive emotions. They then identify what they hoped for and in the process begin to explore their *unenforceable rules* (defined as expectations one carries about how something should or should not be or how someone should or should not behave without having the power to control the outcome). The final step in resolving a grievance is to affirm a positive intention of what they wanted, allowing the focus to shift from hurt to hopes and dreams.

Buddhist teachers are not as linear in their approach to forgiveness, but rather incorporate forgiveness practice into daily life through mindful living, acceptance, and loving-kindness (Chodron, 2001; Kornfield, 1993). Helping clients transcend their anger requires that they remain open not only to their own pain but also to the suffering of others. The path to forgiveness, no matter which model one chooses, teaches clients to transform their anger into compassion, liberating them from the need to use their eating disorder symptoms as a defense against painful feelings.

Eating Disorders as a Metaphor for Not Forgiving

The cost of not forgiving, and not being forgiven, is evident in many of the symptoms eating-disordered clients experience. In her work on healing, Caroline Myss (1996) asserts that the inability to forgive is a poison to the human spirit. Women with eating disorders come to us with a broken spirit. They are so consumed with eating, not eating, exercising, weighing themselves, counting calories, throwing up, buying diet pills, taking laxatives, lying, and hiding that they have lost themselves and their way. In the presence of unprocessed emotional hurt, pain stays trapped in the body, which can be numbed by an eating disorder. The unbearable "weight" of past hurts leads to depression, feelings of powerlessness, deficiencies in self-care, and self-destructive behaviors. The body does not know that the images playing over and over in the mind are memories, so the body continues to live in the painful experiences and the body aches (Dayton, 2003). Making peace with past hurts frees the body from pain and alleviates the need to numb oneself through controlling the body.

The practice of forgiveness includes an awareness and acceptance that things do not always work out the way we hoped. Each client has a story to tell and each client has a grievance story for no one gets through life without hurt and wounding. The grievance story is the story we tell about our wounding. There are often many perspectives to the same story, and the way in which the story is told determines how it is remembered and how it colors one's life. If we listen carefully to the grievance stories told by eating-disordered women, we hear about their unenforceable rules as they relate to relational disappointments, failure, negative feelings, and the war with their bodies. The thought processes of eating-disordered clients tend to be concrete, rigid, and critical, giving rise to feelings of anger, bitterness, guilt, and shame. Typical unenforceable rules for these women include "I should be liked and approved of by everyone," "I should always put others' needs before my own," "No one should ever leave me," "I should always do what is expected," and "When I am thin enough, I will be loved."

Sometimes, the families of women with eating disorders reinforce these unenforceable rules. Typically, although not universally, anorexic families tend to strive for perfection, set high standards for achievement, believe they are better than other families, and present a façade of happiness that belies the pain within the family (Minuchin, Rosman, & Baker, 2004). Families such as these teach children to be judging of others and themselves and promote a need to please, gain acceptance, and be loved through perfection. There is no room in these families for being fallible or being human. Such values are internalized by children, and the pressure to perform and please sets in place the need to look perfect, be thin and fit, and rigidly control one's feelings, needs, and appetites. Anorexic clients defend against their anger at such extreme standards through conformity, judgments, and the drive to be better than others.

While bulimic families share some of these same characteristics, they tend to be more chaotic in nature, thus the wounding to the child is more related to neglect than overinvolvement (Root, Fallon, & Friedrich, 1986). Children in these families can become parentified, leading to the development of pseudomaturity. Parentified children do not learn to self-soothe; instead they become caretakers to defend against the pain of neglect. They also have very high expectations for themselves, judge themselves harshly, and feel inadequate as a result of being expected to behave more maturely than their age. Many, but not all, anorexic and bulimic families are limited in their ability to teach children compassion, kindness, and forgiveness.

Case Example: Internalizing Perfection

Tara, an anorexic client, carries a grievance story about the pressures her father put on her to be perfect. Whatever she did was not quite good enough. If she brought home an A minus, there was no praise, only questions about why it was not an A. If she did not get the lead in the school play, he did not hide his disappointment. She internalized his standards and strove to be the "perfect" anorexic. Her grievance story is based on two unenforceable rules: "My father should love and accept me as I am," and "I should be able to perfect my body." Feeling victimized by her father's demands has prevented her from experiencing anger and interfered with her ability to take responsibility for her self-destructive behaviors. In therapy, we are working on countering her beliefs about the way things should be, accepting that neither she nor her father are perfect, and helping her move from the position of victim to that of heroine.

Encouraging eating-disordered clients to examine their unenforceable rules helps them understand that their suffering in life is made more difficult by clinging to a set of beliefs about the way things should have been or should be in the present. Buddhism refers to this notion of clinging as "attachment" and posits that when we "detach" from expectations, shoulds, and wants, we relieve ourselves of pain and suffering and become more able to appreciate what there is in our life, moment to moment (Chodron, 2001). The concept of working with attachments is core to Buddhist practice and can serve eating-disordered clients well in helping them manage troubling belief systems that often center on their own inadequacy and disappointment in others. It is through the process of letting go of unenforceable rules or attachments that a client's story can change from one that focuses on what they did not get to one that focuses on what they wanted and their disappointment about things not turning out as they hoped. As clients free themselves from attachments, they become more aware of what they already have and open to considering how to get what they want and need through healthier means. Luskin (2002) described this process as one of finding positive intention. Helping clients focus on their larger goal (rather than the hurt caused by not getting what they wanted) shifts their focus from loss to hope. When they transcend their grievance, clients can then move from victim to hero, directing their own life.

Case Example: Accepting Imperfection

So, what was it that Tara wanted? She longed for her father's love and acceptance and felt deficient because he did not accept her limitations. Therapy focused on her anger and grief about not being loved unconditionally, recognizing that very few of us are loved unconditionally, and learning to better accept herself so she would not need so much reassurance from others. She came to understand that her eating disorder was in part driven by anger and resentment about not getting what she wanted, and that her grievance story increased suffering and prevented her from having love in her life. As we worked on accepting her father's limitations as a parent, she could see him in a new light, as someone tormented by his own drive for perfection and isolated from others by his narcissism. Tara did not want that to become her life story.

We practiced loving-kindness meditations (Kornfield, 1993), which are prayers of care for oneself such as:

> May I accept myself as I am.
> May I know love.
> May I feel peace.

And, for her father we included:

> May you be safe from inner and outer dangers.
> May you know the peace of self-acceptance.
> May you know love.

Through these meditations and the practice of accepting "what is," Tara became more compassionate toward herself and her father. She was able to feel increasingly comfortable in her body and opened her heart to a new love relationship.

Themes Amenable to Forgiveness Interventions

There are central themes that emerge in the therapeutic work with eating-disordered women that lend themselves particularly well to integrating forgiveness practice into the therapy. This work with clients is best incorporated into the later stages of treatment, although the attitude of forgiveness, compassion, and mindfulness need to be present throughout the course of therapy. Clients are generally not ready or open to forgiveness until their underlying traumas, betrayals, and hurts have been affectively processed and they have developed new skills in affect management and self-soothing.

Perfectionism

Women with eating disorders experience tremendous shame about their bodies, their place in the world, and personal and cultural histories of victimization. The striving for perfection, which often underlies an eating disorder, is an unconscious attempt to create an antidote to their sense of inadequacy. Brach (2003) described the "trance of unworthiness" as the feeling that there is something wrong with us, often originating from childhood experiences, which leads to depression, anxiety, or the drive for perfection as a defense against shame. The inner voices of our clients are mean, often calling themselves such derogatory names as: "fat pig," "loser," and "lazy bitch." Clients suffer under this harsh inner critic and the self-loathing driven by perfectionism. This is when forgiveness and loving-kindness can be valuable.

When the trance of unworthiness appears in the therapy session, it is helpful to have the client pause and observe in the moment. By asking a client to close her eyes, settle into her breath and focus attention on what she feels in her body when thoughts and feelings of inadequacy arise, we teach her to experience the feeling, observe it without judgment, and stay with it. At the same time, we ask her to bring compassion to herself, to touch her heart gently as she experiences the suffering associated with self-loathing. She can then offer herself a message of acceptance or forgiveness, such as "May I accept myself as I am," or "I forgive myself for the suffering I cause."

As therapists, we need to model acceptance, kindness, and compassion in the face of clients' self-disparagement. Careful self-disclosure about ways in which we are not perfect, mistakes we have made, and how we have developed compassion for our own imperfections gives our clients permission not to be perfect and to forgive themselves as well. Clients may resist becoming more compassionate toward themselves, but experiencing loving-kindness in the therapy helps motivate them to move in this direction, planting the seed for eventual forgiveness. The willingness to forgive is the beginning; over time, and with practice, one's heart will soften.

Relational Disappointments

Issues related to abandonment, attachment, and the attending difficulties of managing relational disappointments are common among this population. The onset of an eating disorder often coincides with a relationship loss and the lack of skills to manage the ensuing emotions. These clients seem to have greater difficulty than others with self-soothing following a relationship disruption. They turn to food for comfort, restrictive eating for safety, or overexercising as a way to distract themselves or discharge anxiety. They express their anger at the way things "should" be, highlighting unenforceable rules in the form of "I was so good to him. Why did he leave me?" or "If only I was thinner, this would not have happened." In helping clients learn about the inevitability of loss, opportunities exist to teach forgiveness and the practice of gratitude as a way of coping with difficult feelings. It is as easy for clients to become stuck in grief and anger associated with loss as it is for them to remain stuck in self-attack and self-blame. Many people close off after a loss, perceiving themselves as too fragile or unworthy to try again. Anorexic clients try to shrink themselves and metaphorically attempt to disappear. Those who binge eat isolate themselves from others and use food rather than relationships for comfort. Bulimic clients try to take in again but cannot allow themselves to keep that which they desire.

Case Example: Mindfulness Practice as a Path Through Loss

Maria, a 32-year-old woman, has struggled with binge eating disorder since her father abandoned the family when she was a child. She never thought she would have an intimate relationship as she did not trust others easily and did not feel worthy of someone's love and acceptance. In therapy, we worked on her self-esteem, anger about being abandoned, and understanding how she used her weight as a barrier between herself and others. During her first year of graduate school, Maria became involved in a romantic relationship. Despite many warning signs to the contrary, she trusted and began to hope for a long-term relationship, children, and the "normal" life she had always wanted. After a year, her boyfriend disappeared without warning. Maria became very symptomatic, depressed, and suicidal. This loss triggered fears of being alone and painful feelings of abandonment and unworthiness.

Through a series of mindfulness meditation practices, Maria learned to observe her loneliness and her longing for security without judging herself. When flooded by fear, she returned to her breath, focusing on the rhythm of her breathing, learning to calm and soothe herself. As she was more able to manage painful feelings through mindfulness practice, we worked on holding these feelings with gentleness, and her heart began to soften to herself. But, she remained very angry with her now ex-boyfriend, wanting to hurt him and seek revenge, thus causing another kind of suffering. After validating her anger, we searched for the positive intention in her grievance story. Maria wanted a loving relationship and a family. She became aware that her boyfriend had opened up a world to her that she did not believe was hers to have. Maria was able to feel some gratitude for what he had given her but remained clear that she would not let him back into her life. She forgave herself for being "naïve," recognized new strengths, and reclaimed her sense of worth.

Managing Anger

Anorexic clients tend to deny their anger, direct it toward themselves, or act in passive-aggressive ways (Enright & Fitzgibbons, 2000). Bulimic clients are generally more open with their anger, fear that their anger is out of control, and use bingeing as a means to stuff anger down, only to get rid of it through purging. Binge-eating clients display a more passive acceptance of their anger, swallowing it with food rather than expressing it to those who have hurt them. Helping clients learn to deal more effectively with anger is an essential part of therapy. Clients can all too often become trapped in their anger, learning how to feel it, express it, but not how to release it as they continue to blame others for their suffering. Forgiveness practice goes beyond the realm of coping with anger, teaching clients how to live differently in the world.

Blame defends against shame and loss (Karen, 2001). It is safer for clients, already bathed in shame, to blame another, as opposed to facing their pain or responsibility. When eating-disordered clients blame others for their suffering, they stay connected to hurtful past relationships through painful memories, resentments, and all-consuming negative affect. As a result, the person who hurt them (even if they are no longer in their life) continues to hurt them, holding power over their emotions in the present and challenging their sense of control. It is empowering for a client to reclaim control through letting go of resentments. By doing so, they are living in the present and not letting past hurts color their moment-to-moment experience. Remaining stuck in anger and blame limits one's ability to pursue relationships that might bring happiness and joy. Moving beyond blame is an important step in granting forgiveness to another or oneself.

Guilt, Self-Hatred, and Entitlement

Guilt and self-hatred are intense within this client group. Eating-disordered women talk about feeling "bad" about letting others down, lying, pretending, and hiding. They feel guilty about betraying others and hate themselves for *"not being good enough,"* let alone perfect. Brach (2003) noted that "every time we betray ourselves by not seeing our goodness, we break our heart" (p. 258). Women with eating disorders break their hearts over and over again. If one's heart is broken, the ability to find compassion for oneself or others is limited at best. Cognitive therapy makes just a dent into this intense self-directed hate. Self-forgiveness is a far more effective way of going deeper. Through this process, clients are asked to identify aspects of themselves that feel unforgivable. They direct anger and hatred toward themselves for failing at life's important tasks, hurting others, being self-destructive, not achieving enough, being selfish, not having a perfect body, gaining weight, and so on. Once unforgiveable aspects of the self are revealed, clients can be helped to understand that what drives their judgments and self-harming behaviors are fears, wants, unmet needs, and the pursuit of safety. Opening to the fear beneath the judgments frees the client from self-judgment as it is replaced by empathy, self-compassion, and loving-kindness. *Loving-kindness* is the tenderness and love we experience when we see goodness in ourselves, others, or the world. It can be cultivated through a focus on the way our heart feels when we reflect on someone we love and wish them happiness. Over time and with practice, clients can begin to direct loving-kindness to themselves.

Once a client has developed skills in self-forgiveness, it is possible to address the more sensitive issue of entitlement, often masked by self-hatred, shame, and guilt. Feelings of entitlement seem to surface around a demanding nature of how the world "should" be, anger about how they have been mistreated, and believing that they are the only one who has been harmed, betrayed, or rejected. Asking clients about the ways in which they have suffered opens up a dialogue about their perceptions and the realities of their suffering. Expanding this dialogue to include people they have hurt puts the suffering into a more mutual context and draws the client out of self-absorption. Helping a client acknowledge that her behavior has caused fear in loved ones, guilt about their responsibility for her illness, financial hardship from paying for expensive treatment, and benign neglect of other children in the family begins the process of placing the eating disorder into a context that reaches far wider than the client.

Eating-disordered clients are ever vigilant for potential criticism. Therefore, an intervention around their complicitness in causing suffering to others requires a very delicate balance of support and challenge. Without such support and a very solid therapeutic alliance, a client could easily feel judged and shamed, driving the protective defense of self-attack, which would take the focus away from the issue at hand. Exploring the client's role in hurting others from a place of compassionate acceptance, acknowledging that everyone suffers and causes suffering, can help an eating-disordered client shift from isolation to connection. By placing suffering into a wider context and teaching about suffering as a part of the human condition, clients are more able to transform narcissistic absorption and entitlement into appreciation and gratitude.

Case Example: Developing Compassion for Self and Others

Sara, a 24-year-old eating-disordered client, suffers because of her long-standing sense of entitlement. Sara did not have it easy growing up. Her father was an active alcoholic, and her mother was cold and distant, having not been mothered well herself. Money was an issue in her family, with her parents claiming financial hardship yet spending freely on themselves. Sara did not feel wanted, loved, or valued. She came to therapy angry, bitter, and resentful. After addressing feelings of hurt and the layers of grief associated with emotional neglect, we began working toward acceptance of "what is." Begrudgingly, Sara allowed me to teach her mindfulness meditation, and she agreed to practice daily. We explored her suffering in the context of expecting and not getting. She began to see that the entitlement rage beneath her eating disorder kept her "small" and disengaged from the possibility of having her needs met in healthier relationships. I modeled compassion and acceptance, hoping Sara would become more accepting of herself. She became aware that her feelings of victimization, entitlement, and judgment of others kept her alone and separate. Sara realized that her mother and father also felt like victims, which limited their ability to give to her. She wanted to live more generously. As Sara became gentler with herself and others and detached from the expectation that her parents should take care of her, she began feeding herself.

Forgiveness on the Road to Recovery

Women with eating disorders suffer tremendously and bring suffering to others, especially to those they love. They have withdrawn from life and, as a result, deny themselves the very love, acceptance, care, and connection for which they long. The road to recovery from an eating disorder is long, with many hills, valleys, twists, and turns along the way. There is a deeply spiritual side to this journey that must be addressed. We do a disservice to our clients and their families by ignoring issues of forgiveness in the recovery process. This truth became apparent to me when I had the opportunity to work with two couples side by side with similar stories but very different outcomes.

Case Example: Forgiveness as a Window to Love

I received a phone call from David, who was concerned about his wife Paula. They had been married for 20 years, and she had been bulimic throughout their marriage. David, at 50, was struggling with midlife issues and no longer wanted to live with the limitations placed on their relationship by Paula's eating disorder. He insisted that Paula seek treatment, or he would end the marriage. Paula, at 42, was bingeing and purging several times a day. She and David never talked about her eating disorder. Also unaddressed was David's anger control problem. They lived with an unspoken agreement: "I won't talk about your eating disorder if you don't talk about my anger."

Paula entered therapy fearful but open and motivated to get well. As her symptoms decreased, she began feeling. A well of grief emerged for all the years she had lost, guilt about how she had neglected and hurt David and her son, and shame about how narrow her life had become. She also began accessing hurt and anger related to emotional abuse she experienced as a result of David's anger. She challenged David to gain control of his anger, and he became angrier, unleashing his feelings about the ways in which Paula's bulimia had cost him many years of his life.

Paula and I began the work of forgiveness, addressing her guilt about how she had harmed herself and those she loved. We began building self-compassion for the ways in which she had failed herself. Paula accepted that she had emotionally abandoned David. From a place of deep remorse, she offered David a sincere apology. But, she appropriately continued to hold David responsible for his hurtful expression of anger. He agreed to learn to better manage his anger, and in brief couple's therapy they worked on acceptance and forgiveness. Both of them needed to accept the past, make peace with their losses, recognize what was good and strong in their connection, and forgive each other for years of unavailability. This work strengthened their relationship.

The outcome for Carey and John was different. Married 16 years, Carey and John presented for couples therapy following Carey's inpatient treatment for chronic anorexia, the onset of which began after she was married. During her inpatient stay, Carey addressed underlying issues related to her anorexia and gradual closing off to life. She disclosed years of abuse in her marriage. As a way of coping, Carey slowly stopped eating and, day after day, went through the motions of mothering her three children and attending to John until her weight became critically low, and she had to be hospitalized.

During inpatient treatment Carey restored her weight, normalized her eating, worked on body image distortions, and learned to listen to her own voice. On discharge, her greatest challenge was to repair her marriage. Through individual therapy, Carey developed compassion for herself and John, forgiving him for his humanness, and stopped blaming him for her anorexia. John was unable to move forward. He remained angry, verbally abusive, and unforgiving. Following many months of couples and individual therapy, Carey and John separated. In the end, John's inability to accept responsibility for his behavior, let go of his resentment from the past, and open his heart to Carey as an equal cost him his marriage.

Paula, David, Carey, and John each had a choice to make in moving forward. Each one could have let their grievance story become an orientation to life, or each one could have transcended the grievance and opened up to the possibility of there being a new and better story by which to live. Had the issue of forgiveness not been an integral part of the treatment, the losses to each of them would have been much greater.

Forgiveness: The Promising Path to Peace

Forgiveness therapy offers women with eating disorders a clear path out of suffering. They learn how to be mindful, nonjudgmental, accepting, and compassionate and are able to use their "wise mind" as they negotiate life's hurdles (Linehan, 1993). Not only do they become more trusting of others, but also they learn to trust themselves as they more effectively manage very difficult feelings. It is through the process of accepting what is, experiencing pain and fear, and letting it touch our hearts that we develop compassion and hardiness for life. The practice of forgiveness offers us the peace we seek and the peace we wish for our clients.

References

Brach, T. (2003). *Radical acceptance*. New York: Bantam Dell.

Chodron, P. (2001). *The places that scare you: A guide to fearless living in difficult times*. Boston: Shambhala.

Dalai Lama & Cutler, H. C. (1998). *The art of happiness*. New York: Riverhead Books.

Dayton, T. (2003). *The magic of forgiveness*. Deerfield Beach, FL: Health Communications.

Enright, R. D., & Fitzgibbons, R. P. (2000). *Helping clients forgive*. Washington, DC: American Psychological Association.

Germer, C. K., Siegel, R. D., & Fulton, P. R. (Eds.). (2005). *Mindfulness and psychotherapy*. New York: Guilford Press.

Hanh, T. N. (1999). *The heart of the buddha's teaching*. New York: Broadway Books.

Kabat-Zinn, J. (1994). *Wherever you go, there you are*. New York: Hyperion.

Karen, R. (2001). *The forgiving self*. New York: Anchor Books.

Kornfield, J. (1993). *A path with heart*. New York: Bantam Books.

Kristellar, J. L., Baer, R. A., & Quillan-Wolever, R. (2006). Mindfulness-based approaches to eating disorders. In R. Baer (Ed.), *Mindfulness and acceptance-based interventions: Conceptualization, application and empirical support* (pp. 75–89). San Diego, CA: Elsevier.

Lamb, S., & Murphy, J. G. (Eds.). (2002). *Before forgiving: Contemporary views of forgiveness in psychotherapy*. New York: Oxford University Press.

Linehan, M. (1993). *Cognitive-behavioral treatment of borderline personality disorder*. New York: Guilford Press.

Luskin, F. (2002). *Forgive for good*. New York: HarperCollins.

McKay, K. M., Hill, M. S., Freedman, S. R., & Enright, R. D. (2007). Towards a feminist empowerment model of forgiveness psychotherapy. *Psychotherapy: Theory, Research, Practice, Training, 44*, 14–29.

Minuchin, S., Rosman, B., & Baker, L. (2004). *Psychosomatic families: Anorexia nervosa in context*. Cambridge, MA: Harvard University Press.

Myss, C. (1996). *The anatomy of spirit: The seven stages of power and healing*. New York: Three Rivers Press.

Peters, L., & Fallon, P. (1994). The journey of recovery: Dimensions of change. In P. Fallon, M. A. Katzman, & S. C. Wooley (Eds.), *Feminist perspectives on eating disorders* (pp. 339–354). New York: Guilford Press.

Root, M., Fallon, P., & Friedrich, W. (1986). *Bulimia: A systems approach to treatment*. New York: Norton.

Seligman, M. P. (2002). *Authentic happiness*. New York: Free Press.

Index

A

Abuse
addressing in family context, 105
emotional, 246–247
within family, 99
physicalization exercise example, 154
Academy for Eating Disorders, xiii
Acceptance
installation in group therapy, 114
of therapist's body image, 182–183
Action stage, 223
Acupuncture, 67
Addictions
within family, 99
and research on shame, 163–164
Adolescents, feminist-oriented group
therapy for, 111, 116–117
Adrenaline, reduction through yoga
practice, 70
African-American women of size, 193,
194–195
range of size acceptance for, 199–200
Alienation, from body and disowned self,
146
Altruism, installation in group therapy,
114, 123
Ambivalence, towards recovery, 85
American Holistic Integrative Medical
Association (AHIMA), 64
American Psychiatric Association's
Practice Guidelines, 9–10
and importance of therapeutic
relationship, 82
Amino acids, 71

Amplification, through guided imagery,
135
Anesthetization, through eating disorders,
26
Anger
in couples therapy, 246–247
as defense against shame, 244
difficulties in releasing, 243
effects on breathing, 133
managing with forgiveness, 243–244
and premature forgiveness, 236
transforming to compassion and self-
acceptance, 235, 238
Anorexia nervosa, 3
attempts to disappear in, 242
body image in, 181
case example, 247
chronicity of, 7
denial of anger in, 243
distrust of therapists in, 82
dread of fatness in, 36
and feelings of inadequacy, 87
healing power of love in, 73–74
heritability of, 211
high mortality rates with, 83
importance of accurate diagnosis, 72
individual psychotherapy for, 35–36
individualized meaning of, 220
as maladaptive effort at self-protection,
37
perfectionism in, 239–240
perfectionist families in, 239
pursuit of thinness in, 36
rigid thinking and body in, 157
unenforceable rules in, 239–240

Eye movement desensitization and
    reprocessing (EMDR), 65

F

Faith
    and identity, 22
    sowing seeds of, 32
Family dynamics, 7, 213
    in anorexic, bulimic, and binging
        families, 239
    case example, 209–212
    in eating disorders, 98–99
    and identified patient role, 169
    and origins of shame, 163–164, 166–167
Family resistance, as indicator of systemic
        dysfunction, 98
Family therapy
    as adjunct to individual treatment, 98
    beginning treatment stages, 99–103
    client's fear of, 101
    communication rules in, 101
    and communication styles, 101
    denial issues, 98
    with eating disorders, 95–96
    and family dynamics, 98–99
    historical view, 96–97
    Maudsley method, 97
    and mealtime battlegrounds, 96
    Milan method, 97
    multifamily therapy and support
        groups, 106–107
    partner issues, 105–106
    as potential allies, 107–108
    secret rules perpetuating malfunction,
        97
    separation-individuation issues,
        103–104
    therapeutic issues, 103–105
    unspoken expectations in, 98
Father-daughter sessions, 102
Father hunger, in adolescent girls, 104
Fathers
    obsession with taking control, 95
    withdrawal during female adolescence,
        104
Fatness
    authenticity and, 198
    dread of, 36
    embracing, 194–195
    as feminizing for gay men, 50

self-acceptance in, 197
    as symbol of negative feminine
        archetype, 50
Favorite food exercise, 135–139
Fear, effects on breathing, 133
Fellowship of suffering, 20
Female gender
    and depression, 3
    as predictor of eating disorder risk, 3
    psychoeducation on, 44–45
Female therapists, body image issues, 180
Feminine qualities, devaluation of, 4
Femininity, cultural construction of, 8
Feminist frame, xi, 11–12
    for eating disorders, 3–4
    emergence of, 8
    as equalizer in therapeutic
        relationships, 14
    for group therapy, 116
    reservations about forgiveness
        interventions, 235–236
    therapist example, 12–14
Feminist-oriented group therapy
    for adolescents with eating disorders,
        111, 116–117
    assessment and preparation for, 112–113
    between-group contacts, 118–119
    core therapeutic factors, 114–116
    empowerment issues improvisations in,
        121–122
    feminist theory and therapy, 116
    group cohesion, 113–114
    group duration and graduation, 119
    group format and demographics, 117
    group in action, 120–124
    group process, 117–124
    improvisation examples, 120–124
    learning from others in, 115
    objectification improvisations in,
        123–124
    oppressive social contacts
        improvisation, 120–121
    as path to fulfillment, 124–125
    psychological work factors in, 115–116
    self-revelation factors in, 115
    supportive factors in, 114–115
    voice and self-in-relation
        improvisations, 122–123
Feminist research, marginalization of, 5
Feminist therapists, 12–14
Financial constraints, 83
Folate, 71